JUDICIAL CLERKSHIPS

JUDICIAL CLERKSHIPS

A Practical Guide

Mary L. Dunnewold
Beth A. Honetschlager
Brenda L. Tofte

CAROLINA ACADEMIC PRESS
Durham, North Carolina

Library of Congress Cataloging-in-Publication Data

Dunnewold, Mary L.
  Judicial clerkships : a practical guide / Mary L. Dunnewold, Beth
A. Honetschlager, Brenda L. Tofte.
    p. cm.
  ISBN 978-1-59460-641-0 (alk. paper)
  1. Law clerks--United States. I. Honetschlager, Beth A. II. Tofte,
Brenda L. III. Title.

  KF8807.D86 2010
  347.73'16--dc22

                                        2009050358

Carolina Academic Press
700 Kent Street
Durham, North Carolina 27701
Telephone (919) 489-7486
Fax (919) 493-5668
www.cap-press.com

Printed in the United States of America
2018 Printing

We dedicate this book to "our" judges:
Robert E. Bowen, Jack Davies, Michael J. Davis,
Harriet Lansing, and Jonathan Lebedoff

Contents

Acknowledgments

Many people have contributed to this book in many ways. We would like to thank the former and current judicial clerks and externs who contributed their time and expertise by filling out our survey and talking to us about their experiences: Megan Blazina, Corinna Venters, Stephanie Angolkar, Jennifer Rolfsrud, Chris Gangl, Shari Selander Frey, Jay Jerde, Colleen Daly, Erika Anderson, Dan Sagstetter, Ed Tillman, Austin Franklin, Joel Zylstra, Wes Abrahamson, Lauri Traub, Tricia Niebuhr, Rachel Bowe, Adam Maier, Adrienne Meyers, Katherine Manuel, Lara Nafziger, Amy Draeger, Brian Saame, Clare Priest, Emily Pelant, Greg Woodford, Jess Birken, Katie Dunn, Kevin Urbik, KrisAnn Kliebecker Lee, Natalie Runden, Nisha Taneja, Amy Busse, Anna Cheng, Christian Brandt, Jen Reise, Matt Resch, Megan Brennan, Megan Clinefelter, Andrea Specht, Alan Blair, and Marcia Miller.

We are also very grateful for the excellent research assistance we received from our student research assistants: Ashlee Bekish, Jessica Taralson, Ami C. Janda, Matt Thompson, and Tara James. We also thank the Hamline Law Library librarians, particularly Megan Jens and Regina Watson, for their first-rate assistance. Thank you, too, to Deb Halfman for her assistance in navigating Pacer and to Karen Westwood for her help completing the index to this book.

We owe special thanks to our wonderful legal research and writing colleagues, and many other colleagues at Hamline, who reviewed drafts and otherwise provided moral support, especially Mary Trevor, Kim Holst, Ken Swift, Kelly Mickelson, Nancy Lochner, Jeanne Eliou, Stachia Ullmann, and Jim Morrow. In particular, we thank Marcia Miller for her extensive proofreading and identification of "wonky" bits. And we would be lost without our amazing administrative assistants, Pam Buth and Gloria Strom.

For financial support for the project, we thank Hamline University School of Law and the Legal Writing Institute.

Finally, we would each like to thank our families for their support and forbearance: Jeff Ondich, Sam Dunnewold, and Elena Ondich; Donald, Nathan, and Mara Greenebaum; Scott Tofte, Noah Tofte, Luke Tofte, Emma Tofte, and Kristin Mickus.

Judicial Clerkships

Chapter 1

Judicial Clerkships: An Overview

Legal job experts highly recommend judicial clerkships as great post-law school jobs for new attorneys.

Former judicial clerks report that a judicial clerkship can be a career-defining experience.

Law school career offices regularly hold events to promote judicial clerkship opportunities and jobs with the courts.

So what's the big deal? A job as a judicial clerk, usually a one- or two-year commitment to work as an assistant to a trial or appellate court judge, does not pay as well as many private sector jobs. Most clerkships are not rewarded with the perks that big law firm jobs might offer, like an office with a good view, a year-end bonus, or occasional sporting or cultural event tickets. And, according to some critics, a judicial clerkship requires a new law graduate to delay the development of a "real" career for the duration of the clerkship.

Considering these downsides, you might wonder why judicial clerkships are so popular. But for most judicial clerks, the many benefits of clerking for a judge far outweigh any disadvantages.

1.1 Why Be a Judicial Clerk?

A judicial clerkship enhances an attorney's career in a number of important ways. Clerks develop professional and job skills that help them in later career pursuits; they develop personally and professionally rewarding relationships; and they advance their legal careers. In addition to these professional benefits, clerks take great personal satisfaction in their work.

Professional and Job-Skill Development

First, if you are a recent law school graduate, employment as a judicial clerk will provide both the opportunity to develop a "behind-the-scenes" understanding of how courts operate and the opportunity to develop practical legal skills. Working individually with one or more judges, a clerk gets first-hand exposure to how judges think and make decisions, invaluable information for a future law practice. Also, particularly when working for a trial court, a clerk learns the many practical details about how civil lawsuits and criminal proceedings wend their way through the courts, knowledge most students acquire only superficially during law school. In this sense, a clerkship is a tremendously useful extension of your legal education, *and* you get paid for your efforts.

A judicial clerkship also gives you time to practice and improve your legal skills before you enter the larger workforce, in effect "seasoning" you for legal work. Clerks spend much of their time researching, writing court documents, and acting as sounding boards for judges during the decision-making process, all opportunities to build on the basic writing and analysis skills learned in law school. In addition, during a clerkship year, a clerk will observe dozens of other attorneys in action. The clerk will read briefs and motion papers, observe oral arguments, and evaluate and cite check the work of other clerks. Through these experiences, a clerk can learn about more and less successful advocacy techniques, develop editing and critiquing skills, and learn to work collaboratively to turn out a good product. The clerk can also draw conclusions about the quality of work produced by certain law firms in the area—information that will be useful later when making career choices.

Finally, in most instances, a judicial clerkship will expose you to a broad range of legal issues and areas of the law. For instance, over the course of a clerkship, a clerk might research and write about criminal sentencing, a failed commercial contract, a constitutional challenge, a revocation of parental rights, and a complex product liability suit, among dozens of other issues. This broad exposure can help you identify areas of particular interest that you would like to pursue after your clerkship.

Relationship Development

The judicial clerkship experience also fosters relationships that will benefit you throughout your legal career. A clerk develops an important mentor-mentee relationship with the judge, a knowledgeable and usually well-connected member of the local legal community. Not only will you learn about sophisticated legal writing and analysis during your time with the judge, but assuming all goes well in your clerkship, the judge will also be a well-respected, valuable reference and resource for years after the clerkship.

Further, during a clerkship you will form relationships with other clerks, and these relationships will support you professionally for years to come. Clerks are thrown together for a year or two in a fairly small group—usually not more than a few dozen—and in fairly intimate conditions. Because of the confidentiality restrictions placed on judicial work, other clerks may be the only colleagues, other than the judge, with whom a clerk can discuss thorny legal issues or writing problems. They share offices, share a library, review each other's work, and eat in the same lunchroom. Consequently, clerks tend to form bonds that last beyond the temporal limits of the clerkship. These relationships may not only be useful in your future legal practice, but may enhance the quality of your experience as a practitioner in the local legal community.

Career Advancement

The prestigious judicial clerkship credential is essential to certain jobs and a significant boost for others. If you dream of pursuing a career in legal academia, a clerkship is almost a prerequisite. In other types of legal employment, as well, employers recognize that former judicial clerks bring with them certain skills and experiences that benefit their firms or organizations. Employers also enjoy enhanced prestige when they hire attorneys who bring judicial clerkship credentials to the job.

Some former judicial clerks report that once clerkship credentials appeared on their resumes, firms that previously expressed no interest in hiring them turned around and actively pursued them. So there is good evidence that a clerkship can help you land the job you want after law school. In fact, because they recognize the value of the experience to a future employee, some law firms who extend offers to 2L summer interns will willingly delay the job's start date to accommodate a judicial clerkship.

Personal Development and Satisfaction

Although personal development and satisfaction may be nebulous ideas, former judicial clerks identify these as important benefits of clerking. Many judicial clerks report that the clerkship experience helped them develop the self-confidence to go out into the legal world and become outstanding attorneys. Clerks also take great satisfaction in knowing that their work impacted the legal world in real and important ways: they participated in the resolution of legal disputes that shaped the law and significantly affected people's lives. And by all accounts, the judiciary, with its demanding and ever-increasing workload, could not operate without clerks.

In addition, a clerkship can act as a welcome transitional time between law school and the working life. During that time, clerks can recover from the often stressful pace of law school and consider what comes next. At the same time, they can collect valuable information about different areas of the law and make contacts that will enhance their career prospects. Also, the pace and workload of a clerkship is usually less demanding than the pace and workload of a new associate position in a law firm. Thus, clerks generally report that they enjoy a good quality of life that is a welcome change from law school.

Clerkships also provide both valuable life experience and experience developing the discipline and professionalism that legal jobs require. Through the cases they handle, clerks are exposed to a full range of human problems, and they can begin to evaluate the legal system's approach to those problems. In addition, clerks learn how to work hard without the reward of public credit and how to get along with a boss with high expectations, all while taking great satisfaction from the job. Both experiences will prepare you to work in the sometimes difficult law-firm culture.

Finally, judicial clerkships are fun. In a clerkship, you spend your time with other smart people, doing an exclusive job that will enhance the rest of your career. For a year or two after law school, this can be a welcome, enjoyable break before the advent of serious career building.

1.2 Types of Clerks and What They Do

Generally, judicial clerkships fall into two categories: clerkships with trial courts and clerkships with appellate courts. While trial and appellate court clerkship experiences are similar in many ways, some important differences are discussed below.[1]

---

1. Justice Paul Anderson of the Minnesota Supreme Court tells this joke to illustrate the difference between law professors, appellate judges, and trial court judges. He attributes the joke to Justice Douglas Amdahl, who served as the Chief Justice of the Minnesota Supreme Court from 1981 to 1989.

A law professor, an appellate judge and a district court judge went duck hunting together. When they arrived at the lake, they went to their respective blinds where they waited for a duck to fly by. All three of them knew that there were certain ducks that they could shoot and certain ducks that were off limits. The law professor was the first to see a duck and as he took aim, he said to himself, "I think I need to develop a test to determine whether I am allowed to shoot this duck." He then proceeded to develop a four-pronged test which included: webbed feet, a bill, head coloring, and wing coloring. By the time he had developed the test, the duck was long gone and he was unable to shoot the duck.

Trial Court Clerks

Trial court clerks are the judiciary's jacks-of-all trades. They do anything and everything related to the judicial decision-making process, from handling attorneys' calls to researching issues that come up during trials and require immediate resolution. More specifically, as a trial court clerk, you might research and prepare written materials to assist the judge with decisions; attend hearings, trials, and settlement conferences with the judge; draft orders; take phone calls; perform administrative tasks like scheduling; write letters for the judge; and do anything else the judge asks you to do. These positions are usually fast-paced and require excellent organizational skills.

Trial courts hear a wide variety of cases, so in a trial court clerkship, these tasks come up in many different substantive contexts. Federal trial courts are more likely to hear certain kinds of cases arising under federal law, like intellectual property issues and certain kinds

---

After a while, another duck flew by. This time it flew in front of the appellate judge. As the appellate judge took aim, he said, "I think I need to do a little research to see if there is any kind of test to determine whether I can shoot this duck." Sure enough, with a little research, he found a four-pronged test developed by some law professor. By the time he found the four-pronged test, the duck had flown so far away, he also did not get a shot at the duck.

Finally, a little bit later, another duck flew by the district court judge. The judge pulled his gun out, aimed, and shot. Feathers flew all over and the duck fell into the lake. As the duck was falling, the district court judge said to himself, "I sure hope I'm allowed to shoot that duck."

Justice Anderson notes, "The foregoing story illustrates how, in a time sequence, law professors, appellate judges, and district court judges can approach the issues in the law. Professors have much time to contemplate and review the standards and criticize. Appellate judges also have significant time to review. District judges have to make a call on the spot and do so. They depend upon their general knowledge and instincts to get it right."

of criminal prosecutions. State trial courts are more likely to hear family law, tort, contract, and criminal cases.

Appellate Court Clerks

Although appellate court clerkships are generally more prestigious, they involve less work variety than trial court clerkships. An appellate clerk's primary job is to review the record in a case assigned on appeal, research and prepare a bench memorandum for the panel of judges hearing the case, and draft an opinion after the panel makes a decision. Appellate clerks may also attend oral arguments, check the work of other clerks, and even fill water glasses for the attorneys and judges before the day's hearings.

But generally the job of the appellate clerk focuses almost exclusively on research and writing, with the larger goal of helping the judges decide each case. Thus, compared to a trial court clerkship, the pace of an appellate clerkship may be slower, and the work may be more narrowly focused and academic.

Elbow Clerks

Within each type of court, there are also different kinds of clerks. "Elbow" clerks are hired by and work for individual judges, usually for a period of one or two years. Elbow clerks are the most common type of judicial clerks. Depending on available funding, judges may have one or several elbow clerks with offices in their chambers. Some individual judges hire long-term elbow clerks to avoid the disruption of training a new clerk every year or two.

Staff Attorneys and Career Clerks

Many courts retain a staff of attorneys who are not assigned to individual judges, but who help prepare cases for hearings, just as elbow clerks do. These staff attorneys often handle more routine matters or may specialize in a particular area, like family law, insurance, or pro se criminal matters. Although these positions tend to be less prestigious than elbow clerk positions, and they lack the benefit of working closely with a particular judge, they do provide similar exposure to the workings of the court. They also offer the same opportunities to develop research and writing skills.

Staff attorney positions can be either long- or short-term. Many courts hire central staff clerks right out of law school for a defined period of one or two years, basically offering the same arrangements as for the court's elbow clerks, who are hired by individual judges. Like most elbow clerks, these short-term staff clerks expect the position to be a jumping-off point for future career development; they don't expect to be clerks for more than a year or two. Most courts also hire long-term staff attorneys who have chosen clerking as a career. Staff attorneys may work for the court for several years, a decade, or more. Some courts hire both short-term central staff clerks and longer-term career clerks or staff attorneys.

Given the variables of trial courts versus appellate courts, elbow clerks versus central staff clerks, and long-term versus short-term appointments, every combination can be found somewhere in the state and federal court systems.

Judicial Internships and Externships

A judicial internship or externship is a short-term position in a judge's chambers,[2] usually for a semester or a summer. The position is typically unpaid, but it may be offered for academic credit. In fact, most law schools offer some sort of for-credit judicial externship experience to upper-class students, often with a classroom

---

2. Traditionally, an externship was a practicum learning experience sponsored by a law school for which a student earned academic credit, while an internship was a non-credit, volunteer position. Currently, the terms are commonly used interchangeably.

component that explores judicial decision making, opinion writing, and other relevant topics. Also, individual judges occasionally will advertise non-credit, unpaid internship opportunities in their chambers. These positions may be filled on a competitive basis, especially if they are with a particularly prestigious court or judge. Finally, determined and enterprising law students can sometimes manage to arrange individual judicial internships if they are willing to approach a number of judges and volunteer their time.

Judicial interns and externs do the same kind of work that paid clerks do, but on a much more limited scale. An intern might be assigned to write a bench memo for a case, draft an order, or review jury instructions, but unlike a permanent clerk, may not see the case all the way through the system. Interns will also observe hearings and oral arguments, and generally observe how the court works and how judges decide cases. They may be primarily supervised by the judge's clerks rather than interacting directly with the judge on a regular basis.

A judicial intern or extern should not expect to land a permanent job with the judge who sponsored the internship. But the internship experience can be a good resume builder for students interested in paid clerkships after law school. Students who have worked in a judicial setting know more about judicial decision making and court procedures than students who haven't. They have also had an opportunity to adapt their research and writing skills to the judicial setting. Consequently, a hiring judge is more likely to look twice at your resume if it includes a judicial internship or externship experience.

1.3 Types of Courts

If you have attended law school, you know the basics (and probably more) about the American court system. But you may not have considered the court system from the perspective of a job seeker. In that light, here is a brief review.

State Courts

Most state court systems are three-tiered,[3] and include district or trial courts, an intermediate court of appeals, and a supreme court. The names of these courts vary depending on the state. For instance, in New York, the "supreme courts" are the trial courts, and the "court of appeals" is the highest court. In contrast, in most states the "supreme court" is the highest court of appellate review and the "court of appeals" is the intermediate appellate court.[4] If you are applying for a clerkship in a state court with which you are not already familiar, be sure to check the hierarchy of courts in that state and know which type of court you are applying to. You can usually find a description of a state court system's organization on that state's court web site.

The work of trial courts and appellate courts differs in some important ways that potential judicial clerks should take into account. Trial (or "district") court judges handle trials and all the litigation-related motions and decisions that trials entail. They work with juries, the fact-finding bodies, or find facts themselves in non-jury trials, and they apply established law to reach decisions. Trial courts tend to carry a heavy work load; accordingly, clerkships in these courts can be busy and demanding, particularly because issues that come up may need quick resolution so a trial or motion hearing can proceed. State trial courts are usually organized around counties, so they operate within a defined geographic region.[5]

On the other hand, state intermediate appellate courts are intended to be error-correcting courts. That is, their job is not to make new law or to change the existing law, but rather to make

---

3. Delaware, Maine, Montana, New Hampshire, South Dakota, and Vermont have two-tiered court systems.

4. Throughout this book, we will use "supreme court" to refer to the highest court in a jurisdiction.

5. You can also access information about state courts on the website of the National Center for State Courts, http://www.ncsc.org.

sure trial courts correctly apply existing law. Because hearing evidence and deciding facts falls within the province of the trial court, intermediate appellate courts rarely reverse factual findings. Further, in most state court systems, all litigants are entitled to review in an intermediate appellate court. Consequently, intermediate appellate courts often have large case loads and may be under statutory time pressures to issue decisions quickly. To facilitate these large case loads, intermediate appellate courts are usually staffed with many judges, who hear cases in three-judge panels.

In larger states, the intermediate appellate court may be divided into separate appellate districts. In states that have one unified intermediate appellate court, the court may travel periodically to hear cases in different areas of the state.

In contrast to intermediate appellate courts, which must hear every appeal from the trial courts, state supreme courts generally choose which cases they hear, and they review cases en banc.[6] They decide to grant review based on a variety of factors, including the need for clarification in the law because of inconsistent earlier cases; the importance of the legal issue; and the novelty of the legal issue. Like the intermediate appellate courts, supreme courts review trial court decisions, and they also review intermediate appellate court decisions. But unlike an intermediate appellate court, a supreme court goes beyond error correction. Rather, it is the judicial body charged with changing the law, filling gaps in the law, and establishing policy in various areas of the law. Given this role, supreme courts spend more time on each case and may incorporate a broader range of research and information into their decision-making processes. State supreme courts are made up of seven to nine judges, and each judge usually has two clerks.

When considering clerkship opportunities in state courts, you should take these differences into account. Trial courts are busy,

---

6. En banc means "in full court." When a court sits en banc, the entire membership of the court, rather than a partial panel, participates in the decision making for each case. *Black's Law Dictionary* 606 (9th ed. 2009).

more focused on resolving immediate problems, and likely to require quick decision making. Because state trial courts are organized around small geographic units like counties, judges in more remote locations may sometimes have trouble attracting clerks; this may make rural clerkships easier to land. Intermediate appellate courts are not as fast paced as trial courts, but require quicker case turn-around than supreme courts. They employ many judges who may each be entitled to two clerks. Supreme courts take more time over their decisions, and they are more likely to decide cases that make a significant impact on state law. Because state supreme courts are generally smaller than state intermediate appellate courts, they offer fewer clerkship opportunities.

Federal Courts

The federal court system is also a three-tiered system. The trial-level district courts are organized around state geography. Each state is home to at least one federal district court; the larger states are divided into multiple districts. There are ninety-four districts in all, and each district has at least two judges.[7] Larger districts have many more judges, may also have magistrate judges, and may have courthouses in several locations within the district.

The federal intermediate courts of appeals, called circuit courts, review decisions of the federal district courts. There are twelve regional circuits in the United States, organized geographically, plus one specialty circuit called the Federal Circuit.[8] The number of judges serving each district varies, but the largest circuit,

---

7. U.S. Courts, http://www.uscourts.gov/districtcourts.html.
8. U.S. Courts, http://www.uscourts.gov/courtsofappeals.html. The Federal Circuit has nationwide jurisdiction in a variety of subject areas, including international trade, government contracts, patents, trademarks, certain money claims against the United States government, federal personnel, and veterans' benefits. *See* United States Court of Appeals for the Federal Circuit, http://www.cafc.uscourts.gov/about.html.

the Ninth, is staffed by about thirty judges. Each circuit hears cases in three-judge panels, with an occasional en banc hearing by the entire court. The circuit courts carry a heavy case load and, like state intermediate courts of appeals, are primarily error-correcting courts.

The United States Supreme Court reviews decisions of the federal circuit courts, as well as decisions of the states' highest courts that involve federal law. Review is discretionary and is granted through petitions for certiorari. The Court considers several factors when deciding whether to grant review: whether the circuit courts have reached conflicting decisions on a point of law, whether a state court has reached a conclusion at odds with federal circuit court decisions, and whether the legal issue is new and should be decided by the Court.[9] At present, the Court decides about eighty cases per year.[10]

Clerkships with the federal circuit courts and with the United States Supreme Court are coveted positions that go primarily to top students from highly ranked law schools. Many circuit court clerks first clerk for other courts, particularly federal district courts or state appellate courts. And some circuit court clerkships are considered "feeder" positions for United States Supreme Court clerkships. If you are interested in clerking for one of these courts, you might want to discuss strategy with your career office staff and professors at your school who have clerked in these courts.

Within the three court levels, the nature of the work in federal and state courts is comparable. The federal district courts conduct trials and hearings, and thus clerks deal directly with litigants and their attorneys, and with the many details of litigation. Clerkships in circuit courts primarily involve research and writing that assists the court with deciding appeals and issuing opinions. Supreme

9. Margaret Z. Johns & Rex R. Perschbacher, *The United States Legal System: An Introduction* 91 (2d ed. 2007).
10. David R. Stras, *The Supreme Court's Gatekeepers: The Role of Law Clerks in the Certiorari Process*, 85 Tex. L. Rev. 947, 965–66 (2007).

Court clerks spend a large amount of time on individual cases. They also evaluate petitions for certiorari and make recommendations about which cases the Court should take.

Specialty Courts and Other Clerking Opportunities

Both the state and federal court systems also have specialty courts on the trial and appellate levels, and these courts also employ judicial clerks. For instance, the federal court system includes the Court of International Trade, the Federal Claims Court, and bankruptcy courts at the trial court level. At the appellate level, it includes a Military Appeals Court, a Veterans Appeals Court, and a Temporary Emergency Court of Appeals, which hears cases involving federal energy regulations. Some states have created similar specialty courts for cases involving particular issues like tax and worker's compensation. When deciding where to apply for a clerkship, you might consider these lesser-known courts, especially if you are interested in eventually working in a particular specialty area. Information about these courts can be found on state and federal court web sites.[11]

Some administrative law judges in federal agencies also hire clerks. Information about these clerkships can be found on federal agency web sites.[12] Again, this can be a great way to get your career

---

11. The National Center for State Courts maintains an excellent web site with links to web sites for state courts, federal courts, tribal courts, international courts, and other relevant institutions. The web site can be accessed at http://www.ncsconline.org. Look for the link to court web sites. The federal government's comprehensive web site, USA.gov, http://www.usa.gov, also provides links to federal, state, local, tribal, and territorial court web sites.

12. See USA.gov, http://www.usa.gov/Agencies/Federal/All_Agencies/index.shtml, for an index of all federal agencies and their web sites. Most agencies list their job postings on the general government employment web site USAJOBS, at http://www.usajobs.gov, or the federal judiciary employment web site on U.S. Courts, at http://www.uscourts.gov/careers.

started if you are interested in a specific area of the law handled by an agency.

Finally, courts other than state and federal courts also hire clerks. In addition to the state-specific United States district courts, Puerto Rico and the District of Columbia have federal district courts. The territorial courts in the U.S. Virgin Islands, Guam, and the Northern Mariana Islands employ clerks, as do American Indian tribal courts. Check the territorial court web sites and the National American Indian Court Judges' Association web site for information.[13]

Hundreds of clerkships are available every year in trial courts and appellate courts, and in every area of the country. Whether you are looking for a job that gives you broad exposure to many areas of the law or intensive training in one specialty area like bankruptcy, you can probably find a clerkship that is right for you. Chapter Three will explain how to apply for clerkships so you can maximize your chance of landing one of these great career-enhancing jobs.

1.4 Additional Resources

John G. Kester, *The Brighter Side of Clerkships*, 36 J. Legal Educ. 140 (1986)

Kermit Lipez, *Judges and Their Law Clerks: Some Reflections*, 22 Me. B.J. 112 (2007)

---

13. Territorial court web sites can be accessed from USA.gov, http://www.usa.gov/Agencies/State_and_Territories.shtml. See National American Indian Court Judges Association, http://www.naicja.org, for information about American Indian Tribal Courts. Comprehensive information about tribal courts and what it is like to clerk for a tribal court can also be found in April Schwartz & Mary Jo B. Hunter, *United States Tribal Courts Directory* (3d ed. 2008), and Massey Mayo Case and Jill E. Tompkins, *A Guide for Tribal Court Law Clerks and Judges* (2007), http://www.colorado.edu/iece/docs/Thompson/Final_version_Guide.pdf.

J. Daniel Mahoney, *Law Clerks: For Better or For Worse?*, 54 Brook. L. Rev. 321 (1988)

Anna E. McDowell & Pamela S. Mzembe, *Working in Chambers: The Rewards of a Pre-Graduation Judicial Clerkship*, J. Kan. B. Ass'n, Aug. 2005, at 7

Abner J. Mikva, *Judicial Clerkships: A Judge's View*, 36 J. Legal Educ. 150 (1986)

Alexander M. Sanders, *Everything You Always Wanted to Know About Judges But Were Afraid to Ask*, 49 S. Cal. L. Rev. 343 (1998)

William H. Simon, *Judicial Clerkships and Elite Professional Culture*, 36 J. Legal Educ. 129 (1986)

Chapter 2

The Judicial Clerk's Job

Judicial clerks have supported the judiciary for over one hundred years. Although judicial clerks have become indispensable participants in the judicial system over the years, they have no statutorily mandated or otherwise specified duties. They do whatever their employing judges assign them to do, which may be writing opinions and may be announcing cases in court. Essentially, judicial clerks are extensions of the judges they serve.

2.1 Historical Overview of the Judicial Clerkship

The first judicial clerk was hired in the 1870s by Justice Horace Gray of the Massachusetts Supreme Court, apparently in response to the pressure of an increasing workload. Justice Gray moved to the United States Supreme Court a few years later, and he took with him the idea of a personal assistant to the judge, called a law clerk. These early clerks were usually recent Harvard graduates recommended by Gray's Harvard-professor brother and were paid from the Justice's own pocket.[1]

The idea caught on in the Supreme Court, and in 1886 Congress authorized the hiring of a stenographic clerk for each justice. Usually graduates of local law schools, these clerks got their jobs

---

1. J. Oakley & R. Thompson, *Law Clerks and the Judicial Process* 10–11 (1980).

through personal connections with the hiring justices. Their duties included everything from routine clerical work to reviewing cases and drafting opinions. In 1919, Congress authorized the hiring of a "law clerk" for each Supreme Court justice in addition to the existing "stenographic clerk." The institution expanded further in the 1930s and 1940s when, in response to an increasing workload, it spread both vertically to lower federal courts and horizontally, so that Supreme Court justices employed multiple judicial clerks, secretaries, and other staff. During this period, judicial clerks also became increasingly common in state courts. Finally, in the 1960s, caseloads within both the state and federal judicial systems increased so significantly that most judges came to depend heavily on judicial clerks to help them complete their duties.[2]

2.2 The Role of the Clerk in Relation to the Judge

Judicial clerks collaborate with judges to ensure that judicial decisions are well thought-out, accurately take the law and facts into account, and are communicated clearly. A clerk plays an important screening role in this decision-making process, directing the judge's attention to the most important or difficult matters in a case. The clerk also acts as a "sounding board" to the judge, helping the judge test ideas and arguments, and letting the judge know if a decision is off-track. As one judge put it, "I'm their client. They're my lawyers."[3] This comment speaks not only to the confidentiality of the relationship, but also to what judges look for in clerks. Judges value clerks who will ask questions and engage in a

---

2. *See id.* at 12–22.
3. David Crump, *How Judges Use Their Law Clerks*, N. Y. St. B. J., May 1986, at 43, 48 (quoting Judge Norman Black, of the United States District Court for the Southern District of Texas).

dialogue about the correct outcome of a case. They value the input of recent law school graduates, whose academic experience often brings a fresh perspective to their thinking. In the words of a former United States Supreme Court clerk, the clerk's job is "to challenge, to analyze, to provide new ideas, and to keep the boss out of trouble."[4]

The judicial clerk's influence during the collaborative process does not mean, however, that the judge relinquishes any part of the decision-making role. While most judges say they must rely on the work product of their clerks to get their own work done, and estimate that they follow their clerks' recommendations the majority of the time,[5] they take their role as independent decision makers seriously. The clerk provides advice and technical assistance, but the judge decides.

2.3 What Clerks Do

In the role of assistant and advisor to the judge, a clerk performs a wide variety of tasks. The roster of tasks varies somewhat in every chambers, but there is a core of responsibilities that will fall to most clerks. The following section examines basic judicial clerk duties. Certain tasks, like writing particular documents, will be discussed in more detail in later chapters.

Legal Research

Judges must make decisions based on the appropriate, current law. But the huge workload of individual judges makes it difficult

---

4. John G. Kester, *The Brighter Side of Clerkships*, 36 J. Legal Educ. 140, 142 (1986) (author was law clerk to Justice Hugo Black from 1963 to 1965).

5. Arthur M. Boley, *Pretrial Motions in a U.S. District Court: The Role of the Law Clerk*, 74 Judicature 44, 46 (1990).

for them to perform their own research. Consequently, judicial clerks usually perform the legal research that informs each judicial decision.

In a trial court chambers, research tasks may arise at various times during the course of litigation. For instance, in one case, a clerk may initially research whether summary judgment is appropriate; then later, during the trial, may research an evidentiary motion; and finally, after the trial, may research whether attorney's fees are warranted. In an appellate court, early in the process the clerk researches the legal issues the parties raise to verify that the briefs accurately reflect the law.

Unlike the research tasks you performed in law school, the research tasks you will undertake as a judicial clerk have a pre-determined starting point — the parties' submissions, for which the parties' attorneys will already have conducted research. The clerk's job is to verify the parties' research, provide an objective evaluation of its accuracy and completeness, and alert the judge to any problems with the research.

As part of the research phase of a case, a clerk also reviews the record to verify that the evidence supports the factual contentions advanced in the parties' submissions. At the trial court level, this means a clerk reviews the relevant evidence submitted by the parties in the form of affidavits, depositions, testimony, and so forth. At the appellate court level, this means a clerk reviews the transcripts and other documents that constitute the trial court record to ensure that the parties accurately represented the facts in their briefs.

Oral Briefing

Judicial clerks also meet individually with their judges to discuss cases, legal theories, and case law. In many courts, before an oral argument or hearing, the clerk prepares a written bench memorandum that presents an objective evaluation of the facts, law, and arguments in the case. The judge and clerk then meet with the bench memo in hand to review any difficult issues, examine the arguments, and confer about what questions the judge might ask the attorneys during oral argument. In trial courts, judges may ask clerks to orally brief them about issues that require quick resolution, rather than write more time-consuming memoranda. After an oral argument or hearing, the judge and judicial clerk usually meet so the judge can explain the disposition of the issues and prepare the clerk to draft an opinion or order.

Writing

Research and writing are probably judicial clerks' most important tasks. As a clerk, you may be called upon to write many different kinds of documents, including bench memoranda, orders, opinions, letters, and even drafts of speeches or articles that the judge is working on. Briefly, a bench memorandum is an objective legal memorandum that evaluates the facts, the law, and the parties' legal arguments in a case. Clerks prepare bench memoranda to assist judges during the decision-making process. At the trial court level, an order communicates the official outcome of a case to the parties and may or may not be accompanied by a memorandum explaining the decision. At the appellate court level, an opinion sets out and explains the outcome of a case on appeal. Appellate opinions comprise the case law you have been reading for several years if you are a law student or recent graduate. While some judges handle the opinion-writing process entirely on their own, a clerk commonly provides an initial draft opinion, which then takes final shape in a collaborative writing process involving both the judge and the clerk.

Finally, as a clerk, you may be called upon to perform miscellaneous writing tasks for the judge. Judges sometimes send letters to attorneys or others involved in a case, make speeches at continuing legal education (CLE) events, write bar journal articles, and produce other written products they may ask you to assist with. Your job is to put your writing skills to work in any way the judge requests.

Proofreading and Citation Checking

Because the judiciary sets both legal precedent and the public standard for writing in the legal community, every document the judiciary publishes must be meticulously edited and checked for accuracy. This proofreading and cite-checking job falls to judicial clerks. In some courts, every document issued from a judge's chambers is not only edited and checked by the drafting clerk, but is reviewed again with fresh eyes by a clerk who was not involved in the earlier drafting. Thus, as a judicial clerk, a small but important portion of your time may be spent proofreading the work of other clerks and verifying the accuracy of every reference, citation, and quotation.

Courtroom Duties

Most judicial clerks spend some time observing in the courtroom, but they may also be assigned more active duties during hearings, trials, and oral arguments. For instance, a trial court clerk may be responsible for setting up the courtroom, announcing the judge, administering oaths, accepting exhibits, operating recording equipment, and shepherding the jury from place to place. More substantively, a trial court clerk may also sit in on discussions and negotiations with the attorneys, take notes on the proceedings, and remain available for quick research as issues arise during trials.

Appellate court clerks usually rotate marshalling duties among the pool of clerks. The clerk-marshal may first prepare the courtroom for oral arguments by placing judges' name plates on the bench; setting out materials needed for the argument, such as pens and paper; and filling water pitchers for the judges and attorneys. During the argument, the marshal may announce the judges and operate the timing and recording equipment. In addition to marshalling, appellate clerks usually attend the oral arguments for the cases assigned to them and take notes during the arguments.

Chambers Administration

Chambers administration responsibilities may also take up a small percentage of a clerk's time, depending on the size of the judicial staff. A trial court clerk in particular may perform scheduling tasks, organize records, assemble documents, and make phone calls for the judge. Clerks may be responsible for upkeep of the chambers' library, including shelving books and inserting pocket parts. And almost all clerks will answer phones as needed. Some judges will want to have someone present in chambers during all regular working hours, so clerks and other staff may need to stagger lunch breaks and other absences.

2.4 Who Clerks Work With

A courthouse is filled with all sorts of people doing all sorts of jobs, although the staffing and position names may vary somewhat from court to court. As you head into a clerkship, you should understand how each person contributes to the work of the court and what that person's role is in relation to you.

Judges

Although they all wear black robes, not all judges are created equal. Generally, the judicial staff of each court or district includes regular, full-time judges (called "active judges" in the federal court), a chief judge, and a number of senior or retired judges. The court's chief judge supervises the administration of the court and, in appellate courts, may handle special motions, like scheduling motions. In federal courts, a judge age sixty-five or older may elect "senior status" under the "rule of eighty": when the judge's age and number of years on the federal bench add up to eighty.[6] Senior

---

6. U.S. Courts, http://www.uscourts.gov/faq.html.

judges continue to hear cases, but may chose to hear reduced case loads. In state courts, retired judges often fill in for a few weeks or months when a court is short-staffed because of vacations or other absences.

Federal district courts and some state courts also employ magistrate judges. Magistrate judges handle certain kinds of hearings and decisions, particularly pre-trial and post-trial matters like discovery requests and attorney's fees disputes. In federal court, magistrate judges are entitled to their own judicial clerks, so if you are working in a federal district court, you will encounter both magistrates and their clerks.

Judicial Clerks

In most courts, you will work alongside several different kinds of clerks, as described in Chapter One. Most judges will have one or two elbow clerks, but the court may also be assisted by central staff clerks, staff attorneys, and specialty clerks, like those who handle only pro se matters. For courts with a large staff of clerks, a chief judicial clerk will usually supervise central staff clerks and staff attorneys, although elbow clerks answer only to their individual judges. The chief clerk may also assist the chief judge in handling special orders and other less common decisions. Chief clerks are generally permanent employees of the court, as opposed to "term" employees.

Administrative Staff

In chambers. A judge's chambers is usually staffed by an administrative assistant who performs all the administrative work of the chambers not assigned to judicial clerks. An administrative assistant answers phones; performs word processing and document production tasks for the judge; may manage the judge's personal calendar and correspondence; and generally keeps the chambers running smoothly. The administrative assistant may have worked for the judge for many years and will see many judicial clerks come and go. As a judicial clerk, you should be scrupulously respectful of administrative assistants. They know more than you do about the daily operation of the chambers and about the judge's habits and temperament, and they can be helpful allies. A judge may also have a separate calendar clerk who handles all scheduling matters within chambers.

In the larger court. The clerk of court's office manages the administration of the larger court. This office handles filing and records management, jury assembly in trial courts, and courtroom administration. A clerk of court, who reports to the chief judge, heads up the office and oversees the staff of filing clerks and other clerical workers. Deputy clerks of court manage schedules and courtrooms. They may also perform specific courtroom duties such as administering oaths, handling exhibits, and supervising juries.

Finally, depending on the size and location of the court, the courthouse may be staffed by a receptionist who directs visitors and controls access between the public and protected areas of the courthouse, and by security personnel. Federal courthouses maintain strict security and most screen all visitors with metal detectors.[7] State courthouse security varies depending on the size and location of the court.

Courtroom Personnel

The courtroom will usually be staffed by a security officer, often called a bailiff. In addition to the bailiff and any courtroom staff supervised by the clerk of courts' office, like the deputy clerk, most court proceedings will be attended by a court reporter. The court reporter produces an official transcript of all proceedings. In federal courts and many state courts, judges are assigned their own court reporters; but judges may share court reporters in smaller courts.

---

7. U.S. Marshals Service, http://www.usmarshals.gov/duties/courts.htm.

Library Personnel

Most courthouses also include a law library staffed by at least one law librarian and other library staff. As you probably learned in law school, law librarians are your friends and can be great resources, especially when you are faced with a short-deadline research project on an unfamiliar topic. The law library can also provide a welcome change of scene when you are looking for a workspace away from your desk.

Other Personnel

In the courthouse, you may also encounter human resources personnel, court information officers, dining room staff, maintenance staff, and others. Every one of these employees contributes to the smooth operation of the court and probably has an interesting story or two about the happenings in the courthouse. Treat them with respect.

2.5 A Day in the Life of a Clerk

Many judicial clerks report that there is no typical day, especially for clerks working in trial courts where the duties can be quite varied.[8] But the following examples illustrate generally what day-to-day life is like as a judicial clerk.

---

8. For instance, some clerks rarely go into court, while others spend much of their day in court. Survey of Current and Former State and Federal Judicial Clerks, conducted fall 2008. On file with authors.

A Day in the Life of a Trial Court Clerk

8:00 a.m.   Arrive in chambers. Greet co-clerk and administrative assistant. Sign circulating birthday card for clerk in chambers next door.

8:05 a.m.   Turn on computer. Check voicemail and email. Respond to attorney inquiry about scheduling of upcoming case.

8:15 a.m.   Assess upcoming cases and schedule for the day. Retrieve file of case whose summary judgment motion was heard yesterday. Open file of order begun yesterday afternoon and begin writing.

8:30 a.m.   Judge calls clerks into office to review the day's schedule. Discusses upcoming speaking engagement and assigns research on the topic. Make notes about the requested research.

9:00 a.m.   Judge goes into court. Return to desk and continue working on order.

9:30 a.m.   Participate in phone conference to determine scheduling for upcoming case. Work out deadlines with attorneys. Make notes for writing scheduling order and plan to write it later in the day.

9:50 a.m.   Return to writing summary judgment order.

10:30 a.m.   Judge comes back into chambers during recess and assigns orders from motions heard during morning calendar.

10:45 a.m.   Return to writing summary judgment order. Answer phone several times because administrative assistant is out of the office.

11:15 a.m.   Finish draft of order. Print for proofreading. Make changes. Print for Judge's review.

11:20 a.m.   Begin writing scheduling order resulting from phone conference earlier in the day.

12:00 p.m.   Scheduling order completed. Go to lunch with co-clerk and court reporter.

1:00 p.m.	Return to chambers. Gather materials relevant to complicated case on schedule next week. Begin research.
2:15 p.m.	Go to courtroom to take notes on omnibus hearing.
3:00 p.m.	Return to chambers. Briefly discuss issues raised in hearing with Judge and take notes about research that will be required.
3:10 p.m.	Break time. Walk down to cafeteria and get iced tea and a cookie.
3:30 p.m.	Begin writing bench memo for case researched earlier in the afternoon.
4:35 p.m.	Notice that Judge has left for the day. Decide to call it a day. Finish up current section of memo. Save file. Turn off computer.
4:45 p.m.	Retrieve coat, say good night to administrative assistant, and leave chambers.

A Day in the Life of an Appellate Court Clerk

8:00 a.m.	Hang coat in chambers' closet and exchange sneakers for office shoes. Chat with administrative assistant about last night's basketball game.
8:05 a.m.	Enter clerks' office and greet co-clerk. Sit down at desk, turn on computer, and check court email account. Through email, sign up for continuing legal education program offered at the court next week during a lunch hour.
8:15 a.m.	Open Word file of *State v. Jones* bench memo, which you wrote several weeks ago. Scroll through document, considering how to turn it into *State v. Jones* opinion, taking into account Judge's instructions after oral argument and conferencing yesterday. Decide to begin from scratch with new document. Open new document file, pull out case copies for review, and begin drafting opinion.
9:45 a.m.	File clerk delivers next month's case files to administrative assistant in main office.

9:55 a.m.   Judge calls you and co-clerk into her office to discuss next month's assignments and distribute files. Have pleasant chat with Judge about post-clerkship job opportunity you are considering.

10:15 a.m.   Return to desk with files and enter bench memo due dates and oral argument dates on personal calendar. Continue work on *State v. Jones* opinion.

11:30 a.m.   Decide you need to recheck exact language in several cases cited in *State v. Jones* opinion. Decide a change of scene would do you good. Leave chambers and walk down the hall to court library.

11:32 a.m.   Greet staff attorney who always works at northwest corner of first table in the library. Chat for several minutes, then retrieve reporters and set them down at empty table. Go to staff clerks' offices adjoining library and make lunch plan with several clerks.

11:45 a.m.   Return to library table and sit down to review cases.

12:30 p.m.   Go to lunch in court dining room with co-clerks. Discuss, among other things, funny incident that occurred during oral argument yesterday.

1:30 p.m.   Return to chambers. At desk, open newly assigned case file, remove parties' briefs, and begin to read, making notes for bench memo. Resist impulse to edit briefs with red pen as you read.

2:30 p.m.   Begin to feel the need for caffeine, so decide to switch tasks. Begin to cite check an opinion drafted in Judge Smith's chambers, due day after tomorrow. Pull cited cases up on computer to check citations and content.

3:00 p.m.   Still feeling the need for caffeine. Decide to go downstairs to state law library to finish cite check and proofread opinion copy. Gather up *Bluebook*, opinion copy, pens, colored index card you use as proofreading aid, and change for the vending machine outside the library. Head downstairs.

3:15 p.m.   Refreshed by candy bar eaten outside the library. Sit down in library to proofread opinion copy.

4:00 p.m.   Return to chambers. Sit down at desk and finish cite
              checking opinion on computer.
4:28 p.m.   Notice that co-clerk is packing up belongings and shut-
              ting down computer. You do the same.
4:30 p.m.   Say good night to Judge and administrative assistant.
              Somewhat nervously, ride down in elevator with Chief
              Judge, who engages in friendly conversation. Say good
              night to court receptionist in lobby and security offi-
              cer at door. Exit building.

2.6 Some Negative Aspects of Clerking

No job is perfect, and clerking is no exception. Although most
former clerks consistently describe their experiences as positive,
some parts of the job and some particular employment situations
may be difficult.

First, over the course of a clerkship, the job is not uniformly challenging. Many clerks report that at the beginning of their clerkships,
they were anxious because they felt unprepared for the significant
responsibility placed on them with very little specific training. It can
take anywhere from a few weeks to many months to feel competent
in the job. After several months, as clerks learn the job and master
the required skills, they tend to feel more comfortable. But then towards the end of a clerkship, the work may start to feel routine and
repetitive. Some clerks report that a two-year clerkship is too long
because the work is not variable enough to remain interesting.

Former clerks also note a few frustrations particular to the job.
For instance, clerks work extremely hard for the most part, but do
not get any public credit for the work they produce. Whether the
clerk drafted the opinion and the judge did not change a word or
the clerk simply provided the basic foundation for the opinion, in
the end, only the judge gets to sign it. Also, pro se defendants who
seem fully deserving of assistance may approach clerks for help.
But clerks generally cannot practice law, especially in a case before

the court, and must refuse to assist the parties no matter how sad their stories.

Moreover, clerks can feel quite isolated. They spend much of their time reading and writing, which can be difficult for more extroverted personalities. And the pool of work peers can be small if the court employs only a few clerks.

As a clerk, you must also be prepared to deal with the difficult and sometimes disturbing circumstances presented by some of the cases you will handle. You may encounter violent criminals, disfigured victims, and upsetting behavior. It can be hard to put these cases out of your mind when you head home at night.

Finally, because a judicial chambers can be like a small family— consisting of the judge, the administrative assistant, and a few clerks—if the individual personalities within it do not "click," the work situation can be difficult. For instance, not all judges are the wonderful mentors their clerks would like them to be. Some have thorny personalities, some don't provide enough constructive feedback to help their clerks feel secure about their work, and some don't assign their clerks enough work to make the job satisfying. Also, clerks sometimes have to share office space with other clerks, with whom they may disagree about furniture arrangement, music selections, and other personal issues.

While some of these problems are inherent in the job, you can research particular judges to find out what kind of employers and mentors they are. Chances are, you will find a judge you are happy to work for and learn from, so you'll have an overall great clerkship experience.

2.7 Additional Resources

Arthur M. Boley, *Pretrial Motions in a U.S. District Court: The Role of the Law Clerk*, 74 Judicature 44 (1990)
Christopher D. Bryan, *The Role of Law Clerks in Reducing Judicial Backlog*, Colo. Law., May 2007, at 91

LaDoris H. Cordell & Florence O. Keller, *Pay No Attention to the Woman Behind the Bench: Musings of a Trial Judge*, 68 Ind. L.J. 1199 (1993)

Pamela Coyle, *Bench Stress*, A.B.A. J., Dec. 1995, at 60

David Crump, *How Judges Use Their Law Clerks*, N.Y. St. B.J., May 1986, at 43

Jefferson Lankford, *Judicial Law Clerks: The Appellate Judge's "Write" Hand*, Ariz. Att'y, July 1995, at 19

Todd C. Peppers, Micheal W. Giles, & Bridget Tainer-Parkins, *Inside Judicial Chambers: How Federal District Court Judges Select and Use Their Law Clerks*, 71 Alb. L. Rev. 623 (2008)

Faye A. Silas, *Mum's the Word: The Law Clerk as Confidant*, A.B.A. J., Aug. 1985, at 36

Chapter 3

Applying for a Clerkship

Now that you've learned what it's like to be a judicial clerk, you may be interested in applying for one of these great jobs. This chapter provides basic information to get you started. You can find more information at your law school's career office and in the resources listed at the end of the chapter. You should also conduct your own research to get the most up-to-date information and to learn about specific clerkships, judges, and courts.

3.1 Qualifications — What Are Judges Looking For?

Because judges are individuals, they all look for slightly different qualifications in clerks. But if you are worried that you don't have the correct qualifications to clerk for *any* judge, talk to your career office and read on. You will probably be able to land a clerkship somewhere, and because clerkships are such great experiences, you will probably be satisfied, even if the court or judge is not your first choice.

That said, most judges look for law students and law graduates who have done well in law school, as demonstrated by their grades and class rank. In a 2006 survey of federal district court judges, sixty percent of the judges considered class rank as the first or second most important factor in choosing a clerk.[1] State court judges

---

1. Todd C. Peppers, Micheal W. Giles, & Bridget Tainer-Parkins, *Inside Judicial Chambers: How Federal District Court Judges Select and Use Their Law Clerks*, 71 Alb. L. Rev. 623, 633 (2008).

also seek clerks with strong academic credentials. But even students in the bottom half of their law school classes get judicial clerkships, often in clerkship positions that are less well known.

More specifically, judges look for clerks with excellent legal research and writing skills. This is particularly true for appellate court judges, because most of the work done by appellate court clerks is research and writing. Thus, many judges seek to hire clerks who have written articles for, or served as editors of, law reviews or other law school publications, because of their extensive research, writing, editing, and citation-checking experience. Many judges rate applicants with moot court experience almost as highly as those with law review experience, because an applicant who has written a moot court brief has also done a substantial amount of research and writing. If an applicant does not have law review or moot court credentials, but has taken a law school seminar or independent study course that required a major written project, the applicant may still be considered well qualified. Even an applicant with writing experience from outside of law school—writing reports for a job or articles for a publication, for example—will have a leg up on those with less writing experience on their resumes. In a similar vein, because correct and accurate citation is important to judges, particularly if their opinions are published, judges seek clerks with excellent citation skills.

Some judges prefer to hire clerks who have taken particular law school courses. Trial court judges like to see courses in evidence, criminal law, and trial advocacy on applicants' transcripts, and federal court judges look for courses in jurisdiction and federal courts. A judge on a specialty court may look for clerks who have taken courses in the court's subject area. Thus, a bankruptcy judge will hire clerks who have studied bankruptcy law, for example, and an administrative law judge will hire clerks who have taken administrative law.

Not all judges hire new law school graduates; some judges only hire clerks who have worked for several years after law school. While some of these judges simply prefer more mature clerks, others prefer clerks with specific experience, for example in litigation or in a particular practice area.

It may surprise you to learn that one of the most important factors a judge looks at when hiring a clerk is the applicant's personality. Judges and clerks work closely together in chambers with few other people, so judges look for clerks with whom they are compatible. In addition, judges look for people who are interesting—perhaps someone who has some life experience, who had an interesting job between college and law school, or who simply has a different background from the judge. A potential clerk's hobbies and interests—the stuff at the bottom of the resume—is of interest to a judge, because they give the judge a clue about the kind of person the applicant is.

Like other employers, judges look for applicants who are enthusiastic about working for them. Your interest in the judge, the court, and the subject matter the court deals with is important. In general, judges look for clerks who are curious and who are interested in the intellectual challenge of the law.

Some judges prefer to hire clerks from particular law schools—top-rated schools, local schools, or their alma maters, for example. While it is probably too late for you to change the school from which you will graduate (or have graduated), your career office can help you find judges who are likely to hire students from your school.

Your connection to a location may also be important to a judge, particularly a state court judge. Most clerkships only last a year or two, so a judge probably isn't worried that you will leave town just when you are trained. But some judges believe that because the publicly funded court system educates clerks, clerks have an obligation to give some benefit back to the local community. Thus, a judge may be more likely to hire an applicant if the applicant plans to stay in the area to practice law after the clerkship.

A potential clerk's "connections" may or may not be important to a judge. The higher the court level, the more important an applicant's academic and law review credentials are. Thus, even the best connections probably won't get you a job in some courts if your grades are poor. Nevertheless, your connections may at least get your application considered. A judge may receive hundreds of applications, and someone (probably one of the judge's current clerks or the administrative assistant) goes through them and chooses those for the judge to consider. If one of your references knows the judge and calls or sends a letter of recommendation to the judge, your application may be looked at more closely. In addition, judges take their fellow judges' opinions seriously. A recommendation from a judge for whom you interned, externed, or clerked can move your application to the top of the pile.

Most judges are not looking for clerks with a particular political ideology. In the survey of federal district court judges mentioned above, an applicant's political ideology ranked last on the list of ten factors the judges considered; only fifteen percent of the judges even considered this factor when hiring.[2] Political ideology may be unimportant because most cases decided by judges simply are not subject to ideology. And to the extent that judges do consider ideology when hiring clerks, they may actually prefer to hire clerks whose views differ from their own, so the clerks will challenge their thinking.

3.2 Preparing for a Clerkship

There is no single way to prepare for a clerkship, in part because judges differ in what they look for in clerks, and in part because there are many ways in which you can acquire valuable skills and experience. You can prepare by taking courses and getting writing experience as discussed in the previous section. Here are some additional ways you can prepare for a clerkship.

Because most clerks do a lot of legal research and writing, a great way to prepare for a clerkship is to work on beefing up these skills. Even if you were not chosen to be on the staff of your law school's

---

2. *Id.* at 639.

law review or other journals, you can nevertheless write and submit an article to them or to any law journal in the country. You can also enter legal writing competitions. Often these competitions attract only a few entries, so your chances of winning are good. Some competitions even award cash prizes. Your law school likely has information about writing competitions; talk to your first-year legal writing professor or career office staff. In addition, bar associations, particularly on the local and state level, produce journals and are often looking for articles. If you do any extra writing, you will gain experience, have another potential writing sample to submit with your application, and demonstrate your initiative and ability to work independently. Try to get writing experience during (or before) your second year of law school — preferably fall semester — so that you can add it to your resume before you apply for a clerkship, and so that you can use the product as a writing sample to submit with your application.[3]

A law school clinic can also help prepare you for a clerkship. If you are allowed into court as a student attorney or observer, you will gain insight into the court's functions and the judges' personalities, which can help you decide where to apply.

One of the best ways to prepare for a clerkship while in law school is to work as an intern or extern for a judge. One study showed that one third of judicial clerks had been interns or externs while in law school.[4] Although the terms are interchangeable, as discussed in Chapter One, externships are usually sponsored by law schools, often with a coursework component, for which students earn credit, and internships are usually volunteer positions arranged individually by students. Find out what your law school offers; if the program doesn't suit your needs, approach judges on your own.

---

3. Some judges hire students as early as the fall of their second year of law school for clerkships that begin after graduation.

4. National Association for Law Placement, *Courting the Clerkship: Perspectives on the Opportunities and Obstacles for Judicial Clerkships* 47 (2000).

In either kind of position you will learn how the court operates and may be able to do some writing for a judge, which will allow you to get up to speed more quickly as a clerk. Internships are a particularly good idea for summer, especially the summer after the first year of law school when many students struggle to find law-related jobs.

Other kinds of legal jobs can also help prepare you to clerk. The best jobs are those that require you to research and write or that allow you to get into the courtroom. It's possible to volunteer to work for a legal employer as well; consider this if you have just finished your first year of law school and can't find a paying legal job.

3.3 When to Clerk

While most judicial clerkships are filled by recent law school graduates, not all are. You can also clerk during law school (although the position will probably be called an internship or externship), after another clerkship, or even after another job.

Internships and Externships During Law School

As mentioned above, judicial internships and externships can be good stepping stones to judicial clerkships. If you have had one of these positions, you may be able to get your foot in a clerkship door that would not otherwise be open to you. Interns and externs don't have as much responsibility as clerks and may not have as much direct contact with judges. But an intern or extern will learn about the court, the judge, and local lawyers and law firms, and will be exposed to different areas of the law. If you're unsure about whether or where you want to clerk, working as an intern or extern can help you decide. However, as discussed previously, if you work as an intern or extern you may not be able to clerk for the same judge, because some judges will not accept clerkship applications from their present or former interns and externs.

Clerkships Immediately Following Law School

There are a number of reasons to clerk right out of law school. A clerkship's limited time span has advantages for new lawyers. Clerking can give you a year or two to observe different lawyers and law firms and research different areas of the law, which can help you make career decisions. A clerkship can also give you a chance to try out a new location to see if you would like to move there permanently. In addition, if you need a temporary job because of a family or work commitment, a clerkship might be perfect. And even if you accept a job with another employer before you are offered a clerkship, some employers will allow you to defer your start date to clerk for a year or two.

Clerking After Another Clerkship

As noted in Chapter One, some clerkships are considered "feeder" positions for other clerkships. But even if you are not in one of these positions, your first clerkship can help you get a subsequent clerkship. You may be preferred over other applicants because you have already been trained by your first judge.

Why move on to another clerkship? A second clerkship can give you the chance to learn from another judge, to experience working in a different level or kind of court, and to put off making a more permanent career decision. Some clerks like clerking so much that they move into long-term career clerk or staff attorney positions.

Clerking After Working in Another Job

Some clerkships are open only to applicants who have post-law school work experience. These are likely to be clerkships in specialized courts; the judges on these courts may only hire clerks with litigation or particular substantive-area experience. Even judges who don't require clerks to have post-law school experience may prefer clerks with experience. Also, it may simply be easier for a judge to hire a working candidate, especially if the judge needs a clerk immediately or at a time other than August or September when most clerkships begin. And federal judges who follow the federal clerkship hiring plan are not bound by the timelines in the plan for applicants who are no longer in law school.[5]

Clerking after you have worked in another job has advantages. The learning curve probably will not be as steep, even if you never clerked previously, because you understand the culture and expectations of legal-profession employers. Also, taking a clerkship after another job can help you break into the legal-employment scene in a new location or ease back into law practice after you have taken time off or worked in a nontraditional legal job. Finally, a clerkship after another job can be a "time out" if you want to make a career change, but are not sure where you'd like to work.

Law school career offices have reciprocity agreements. If you no longer live near your law school, the career office of a nearby law school may be able to help you find a clerkship in the area. Contact the career office of your law school for more information.

3.4 Application Process Overview

Once you've decided you want to work as a judicial clerk, you'll need to figure out how to apply. The following is an overview of the application process. You can find much more detailed information in resources dedicated to helping you get a legal or clerkship job.[6]

Your most important information sources and allies in applying for clerkships are the career services professionals at your law school. Plan on talking to them, going to their presentations, and using the resources in their office and on their web site.

---

5. *See* Federal Judges Law Clerk Hiring Plan, http://www.cadc.us courts.gov/internet/lawclerk.nsf/Home?OpenForm [hereinafter Law Clerk Hiring Plan].

6. In particular, see Debra M. Strauss, *Behind the Bench: The Guide To Judicial Clerkships* (2002), and Chapter 25 of Kimm Alayne Walton, *Guerilla Tactics For Getting the Legal Job of Your Dreams* (2d ed. 2008).

Keep in mind a few things as you apply for judicial clerkships. First, keep an open mind about where and for whom you are willing to clerk. Clerkships vary in competitiveness. If you only apply for the most competitive, you may not land a clerkship. But if you are willing to apply for a clerkship in a less sought-after location or court, you may have no trouble getting a clerkship. Second, view researching and applying for clerkships as a project that you need to manage. There are many courts, judges, and clerkships, and their application procedures and deadlines differ. Allow yourself plenty of time and develop a process to keep track of details. Third, you should not apply for a clerkship unless you are willing to take it. If you are offered a clerkship, you are expected to accept it, perhaps on the spot. So don't apply for a clerkship until you have done your research and are certain you want the job.

How to Find Clerkships, Judges, and Courts

An important part of your application process is investigating potential clerkships, judges, and courts to determine where you would like to clerk. Because some judges hire clerks up to two years before their clerkships begin — in the fall of the students' second year of law school — it's never too early to begin your research. While the summer after your first year of law school is a good time to start, don't be discouraged if it's nearing (or even after) graduation and you are just beginning. You will likely still find clerkships to apply for.

Factors to consider. As you research, keep these factors in mind: the location of the court, the type of court, the type and duration of clerkship, the characteristics of the judge, and the competitiveness of the clerkship.

First, consider the location of the court and whether you want to stay in the community where your law school is located, want to return to your home community or state, or are willing to move somewhere else. The most popular locations — cities like New York and San Francisco — attract the most applicants. But there are many other locations to choose from: federal district courts are located in every state, and state trial courts are located in every county of every state. Some judges are based in one location but travel within a circuit.

Second, consider the type of court for which you would like to clerk. Remember that clerkships can be found in specialty courts, as well as in federal and state trial and appellate courts. Chapter One describes the variety of courts that hire clerks.

Third, think about the type and duration of clerkship you would like. See Chapters One and Two for descriptions of clerks' roles in the different kinds of courts and clerkships. Most clerkships last only one or two years, but some judges allow their clerks to remain longer or prefer to hire career clerks. And, as previously discussed, some courts hire staff attorneys for long-term positions.

Fourth, you should also consider the particular judge. Judges have different personalities, hiring preferences, and ways in which they interact with and use their clerks. In addition, some judges have special status, which affects the work their clerks do. The chief judge of a district or circuit has more administrative duties than the other judges, so that judge's clerks probably also have more administrative duties. (The chief judge position rotates in most courts, though, so a judge's status can change.) If you are considering applying to a magistrate judge, investigate the type of hearings and cases the judge handles—some magistrates only handle pre-trial and post-trial matters or only hear civil cases. Senior judges may also hire clerks. A senior judge may have a lighter caseload, or a caseload that doesn't include criminal cases, for example, which will affect a clerk's job.

Finally, related to the above factors is the prestige or competitiveness of the clerkship. As noted, clerkships in some locations are more competitive than those in other locations. Also, the higher the court, the more competitive the clerkship. While you may aspire to a highly competitive clerkship, you may not have a realistic chance of getting it because of your academic credentials or because of the sheer number of applicants. So also consider some of the less-prestigious clerkships and locations, either as a first step towards getting a more competitive clerkship or as an end in itself.

Information sources. With these factors in mind, begin your research, preferably at your law school career office. Tell the career services professionals that you're interested in a judicial clerkship and ask them what resources they have. They, themselves, will be resources and will be able to tell you about clerkships. They will also likely have informative handouts, online materials, and books and binders you can borrow or read in the office.

The career office can also help you find your most important information source: people who know judges or who are judges. For example, the staff probably has contact information for students and alumni who have clerked, interned, or externed for judges. They probably also know which professors at your law school were judicial clerks and are willing to talk to students about particular judges or about clerking in general. And either the career office or alumni office likely keeps track of judges who have hired graduates of your law school in the past and alumni who are now judges. Look around the law school for other resources as well: for example, the clinical professors are probably familiar with local trial court judges and can give you information about them.

You can also learn about judges by observing or meeting them. Judges no doubt visit your law school during the year for various reasons — to teach classes, hear oral arguments, or give speeches or CLE seminars. Your career office may invite judges to the law school specifically to talk to students about clerking. Attend these events and talk to the judges if there is an opportunity to do so. Judges also appear at events in the community, such as CLE seminars and bar association functions, which you can attend. Of course, you can even visit judges' courtrooms to observe them in action.

Another way to learn about judges is to read their opinions. As you know, you can find appellate and some trial court opinions on Westlaw, LexisNexis, and free web sites such as court web sites.[7] To find decisions and opinions by specialty and state trial court judges,

---

7. See Chapter Four for web sites that publish court opinions.

which are not likely to be published or available on the commercial or free web sites, check out local legal publications such as bar association journals, which report local legal news.

If you are interested in clerking for a federal judge, you will need to become familiar with the Online System for Clerkship Application and Review, known as "OSCAR."[8] As the name implies, this web site allows you to apply for federal clerkships online. It lists many of the federal judges and includes information about when judges are hiring, when clerkships begin, how to apply, and what application materials are required. Register for a free account and start exploring the web site. Read the informational paragraphs and FAQs, find the list of judges, and familiarize yourself with the searches and filters. The site contains lots of information, so expect to spend some time learning how to use it; the career office staff can also help you navigate the site. When you're ready to apply, you can upload your application materials to the site, and then submit them electronically. Note that not all federal judges use OSCAR, though, and some listed judges do not accept applications through the site. To find information about these judges and their application procedures, start with the federal courts web site, which lists all federal courts and provides links to their web sites.[9]

Information about state court clerkships is collected by the Vermont Law School Career Services Office in its *Guide to State Court Judicial Clerkship Procedures*, which is available online.[10] The guide is continually updated and lists application procedures and deadlines for state court clerkships at all levels in all states and some U.S. territories. Information about individual judges is not included

---

8. Online System for Clerkship Application and Review, https://oscar.us courts.gov/.

9. U.S. Courts, http://www.uscourts.gov/.

10. Vermont Law School Career Services, http://www.vermontlaw.edu/ x1101.xml. The guide is password protected; your career office probably has a subscription, and the staff will allow you to view the guide in the office or give you the user ID and password.

in the guide, though; for this information, go to state and county court web sites.[11]

Newly appointed judges offer good opportunities for clerkships because they generally begin their duties soon after appointment and are in immediate need of clerks. Your career office probably keeps track of newly appointed local judges. You can search for newly nominated or confirmed federal judges in the Congressional Record database on Westlaw or LexisNexis. *United States Law Week* also lists federal judge nominations and confirmations. To find new state court judges, check the court web site, bar association web site, or general or legal news sources for the relevant state.

Because there are so many judges and clerkships, there is neither uniformity in application procedures, requirements, or deadlines, nor is there one source of information. Some, but not all, federal judges comply with a hiring plan that specifies the earliest dates clerkship applications will be accepted and interviews given.[12] Some, but not all, federal judges list their deadlines and requirements on OSCAR. The Vermont Law School Career Services *Guide to State Court Judicial Clerkship Procedures* contains information about state court application procedures and deadlines, but because many judges hire on their own schedules, the information is not complete. Remember that not all judges have clerkship openings every year because they may have clerks continuing from previous years. If the information you need is not available from these or other sources, call the judge's chambers.

Components of the Application

This section briefly discusses the components of a typical clerkship application, but you should follow the specific directions of

---

11. The guide includes court web site addresses. The National Center for State Courts also has links to all state court web sites: http://www.ncsc online.org/.

12. *See* Law Clerk Hiring Plan, *supra* note 5.

each individual judge to whom you are applying. Several of the resources listed at the end of the chapter go into much more detail about applying than there is space for here. Also, your career office staff can help you with applications; ask them if they will review your application.

It's a good idea to submit all parts of your application together. That's easy to do if you are applying to a federal judge who takes applications via OSCAR, because once your application is complete it will all be submitted to the judge electronically. If you are mailing an application, you may need to collect recommendation letters from your recommenders. Some career offices will help you assemble and mail applications.

As for the application timing, the earlier you can submit your application the better. Some judges receive hundreds of applications, particularly federal judges who accept applications via OSCAR. Going through all the applications can be an overwhelming task, and the judge (or the judge's clerk or other staff person who screens the applications) may stop reading applications after going through enough to produce a good selection of applicants. Thus, you should consider the first day the judge or court accepts applications as your deadline—get your application in on that day so it has a better chance of ending up on the judge's desk.

Here are a few more application tips: figure out some way to keep track of what you have submitted, to whom, and when (perhaps use a spreadsheet); and keep copies of everything you submit in case you need to refer to them later, and so that you can bring copies to your interviews. And needless to say, make sure your application materials are perfect, with no typos, grammatical errors, or punctuation errors. Proofread them yourself, and have someone else proofread them as well.

Cover letter. Your cover letter should be short. The judge knows that clerking will be a valuable experience for you, so you needn't say that. Simply state where you are a student, when you will graduate, and when you can begin or the court term for which you are applying; identify the items you have enclosed with the letter; and state your contact information. If you have not enclosed recommendation letters with your application, include the names, addresses, and phone numbers of your recommenders, either in the letter or on a separate page.

You may wish to include some additional information. If you took a course from the judge or have some other direct experience with the judge, mention that. In a cover letter to a judge on a specialized court, succinctly describe your relevant experience. Because judges are less inclined to interview applicants from out of state, if you're applying out of state, explain briefly why you want to work for that judge or court. If you plan to visit the area, include the date of your visit in case the judge would like to interview you then.

You can let your personality show in a cover letter, but should keep the information to a minimum. For example, if you can tie your experiences into the reasons you deserve the job, that's great. Just be careful not to come across as insincere or arrogant. It's hard to go wrong with a brief cover letter, and the more you add, the more that can go wrong.

Resume. Tailor your resume to emphasize the skills, courses, and experiences mentioned above that will be of interest to a judge. If you are applying in the fall of your second year of law school, so have only taken first-year courses, you can list the relevant courses you are presently taking.

Remember that because judges spend a great deal of time with their clerks, they look for clerks who are interesting people. So be sure to include an "interests" or "hobbies" section on your resume. If you discover that you and a judge share a particular interest, of course you should include it on your resume. Don't exaggerate, but "once you've done [potential hobbies] even once, you can list them as hobbies."[13]

Writing sample. Send your most recent and best writing sample. Even though your very first legal writing assignment may have gotten a high grade, your legal analysis skills have no doubt ad-

---

13. Walton, *supra* note 6, at 364.

vanced since you wrote it. This is one reason to take a course that requires writing early in your second year of law school.

The type of writing sample you send will depend on the kind of court you are applying to. For a trial court clerkship application, submit a practical and concrete document, like a brief or an office memo. For an appellate court clerkship application, submit a more academic and theoretical paper, such as a paper written for a seminar or independent study course. While law review articles may seem like good choices for writing samples, that's not necessarily the case. Judges value clerks' law review experience, but many do not believe law review articles truly represent applicants' writing abilities because they have been so heavily edited.

Remember that the judge (and the current clerk, who may be the first to read your writing sample) is a busy person. The judge will not take time to read numerous long papers, and will not want to waste taxpayer money and administrative time printing out long papers submitted electronically. So don't send your entire fifty-page moot court brief. Rather, send a short writing sample or an excerpt of a longer document, no more than ten to fifteen pages. Judges are most interested in your legal analysis skills, so include a discussion or argument section, rather than a facts section. Attach a cover sheet that states your name and contact information, briefly describes the document, and if necessary, explains the context and any omissions.

Make sure the writing sample represents your own work. If you submit a seminar paper, you can make the changes suggested by your professor as long as the writing is your own. Submit only the part of your moot court brief written by you, not by your partner. And if you do submit a law review article, it should be your own final draft, unedited by others.

If you plan to use a document you wrote for a job as a writing sample, get permission from your employer first. You must comply with client confidentiality rules, which means client names and identifying information should be redacted (replace the client name with "client," for example). A bench memo you wrote while working as a judicial intern or extern would be an excellent writing sample. But if you drafted opinions for the judge, you probably should not submit one as a writing sample. Even if the judge you worked for has no objection, the judge you are applying to may consider it poor judgment to use an opinion draft as a writing sample. You are being evaluated in part on your professionalism, so it's important to comply with confidentiality rules and exhibit discretion and common sense. See Chapter Twelve for additional ethical considerations regarding disclosure of information.

Transcript. Judges usually do not require official transcripts with applications, but some may. If you do need to submit an official transcript, be sure to order it on time.

Letters of recommendation. Even if recommendation letters are not required, it's a good idea to submit two or three. Judges are interested in your legal research and writing ability, so the best recommenders are people who are familiar with your legal research and writing skills.

Choose your recommenders carefully. They should be enthusiastic about you and should be able to point to your specific accomplishments, not just your skills in the abstract. Someone who has a connection with the judge is a good choice, as long as that person knows you and knows your legal abilities. You can get detailed information about choosing recommenders from your career office and from sources that discuss job searches in general.[14]

Law school professors are valuable recommenders, so part of your preparation for applying for clerkships is developing relationships with law school professors. Doing well in a professor's class is a start, but you'll need to make sure the professor knows something more about you than the grade you received on an exam. Speak up in class, talk to the professor outside of class about the course, work as a research assistant for the professor or, if all else fails, take the time to introduce yourself to the professor and explain

---

14. See, for example, Strauss, *supra* note 6, at 118–24, and Walton, *supra* note 6, at 346–52 and 1208–12.

why you want to be a clerk. If you are unsure of which professors to approach, ask the career office staff for advice.

Legal employers also are good recommenders. As with professors, though, make sure whomever you ask for a recommendation knows your work.

Be considerate of and helpful to your recommenders. Give them plenty of warning about deadlines. Remember that professors, and even employers, are often away from their offices and email during the summer, so you should allow extra time if you contact them during the summer. Make it easy for recommenders to write letters— supply each recommender with detailed names and addresses of the judges to whom you are applying (including the judges' correct titles), a copy of your resume, and perhaps your writing sample and transcript. If you are a student asking a professor for a recommendation, fill out the Family Educational Rights and Privacy Act (FERPA) paperwork so the professor can disclose information about your education record. Also, explain to recommenders why you want to clerk.

If you apply using OSCAR, your recommenders must upload their letters to the OSCAR site. The process may be unfamiliar to recommenders who are less tech-savvy than you are. But some career offices can help by collecting and uploading letters for professors. Again, allow plenty of time.

If you want to submit all of your application materials in one envelope, ask each recommender to enclose the letter in an envelope and sign across the sealed back flap. Ask your recommenders to get their completed letters to you a few days before the date you plan to send your materials.

Interview Process

If you are called for an interview—congratulations! The judge likes you on paper, and wants to see what you're like as a person and whether you will be a good fit in chambers.

Prepare for the interview by becoming more familiar with the judge and the judge's most recent and important decisions. Search on one of the commercial or free web sites for opinions and in legal and general news sources for articles about the judge and cases he or she presided over. Check with your career office, former clerks, and applicants who previously interviewed with the judge to find out what to expect during the interview.

You can practice interviewing as well. Your career office probably offers mock interviews with the staff or alumni. Or you can set up your own mock interview with a friend or family member. Have your "interviewer" ask you questions you're likely to get and critique your performance afterwards. Figure out ahead of time how you'll answer questions; you want to be as prepared as possible without sounding rehearsed.[15]

When you go to the interview, take copies of all of your application materials. If you have several versions of your resume, make sure you take the correct one. Turn off your cell phone before you walk into the judge's chambers.

Who can you expect to interview with? When you are called for an interview, ask who besides the judge will be interviewing you and how long the interview will last. While you will most likely interview with just one judge, in some jurisdictions the entire court interviews each applicant. Because a judge's chambers consists of a close-knit group of people, everyone on the staff is likely to be involved in hiring clerks. So you should expect to interview with the clerks and perhaps the administrator, secretary, or court reporter, as well as the judge. Even if the staff does not formally interview you, they *will* evaluate you. Treat everyone in chambers with respect — don't patronize or ignore anyone.

During the interview, the judge will try to determine if your personality is a fit in chambers. So be yourself and make sure you are interesting. Talk and ask questions — ask the judge about recent

---

15. See pages 143–45 of Strauss, *supra* note 6, and Chapter 9 and pages 1217–19 of Walton, *supra* note 6, for questions you can expect and tips on answering them.

cases or talk about shared interests.[16] Be aware that to get to know you, some judges ask personal questions that other employers will not (and, by law, should not) ask, such as questions about your family or your political persuasion.

If you need to travel for the interview, you do so at your own expense (which is one reason to be selective about where you apply). If you have an interview scheduled with an out-of-town judge, you may call other judges in the same location and ask whether they would like to interview you on the same day. Some judges may conduct virtual interviews so applicants don't need to travel.

Follow Up

After the interview, send the judge and anyone else you interviewed with a brief thank-you note. Remember that every communication with the chambers will be evaluated, though, so make each letter unique rather than sending boilerplate notes.

If you don't hear anything from the judge after interviewing, wait two or three weeks and then call the chambers and politely ask the clerk, assistant, or secretary about the status of your application. You can also reiterate your interest in clerking for the judge.

If the judge likes you, you may be offered a job on the spot at the end of the interview. Unlike job offers from other employers, clerkship offers should be accepted immediately. While the judge might allow you a day to decide—perhaps you need to talk to your spouse or you have another interview scheduled for the next day—some judges will withdraw an offer if you hesitate. Some applicants try to manage the timing of interviews and possible offers by applying to their first-choice judges first and waiting to apply to other judges. But if you do this, you run the risk of losing out on any clerkship. See the resources at the end of this chapter and talk to the career office staff for advice about timing applications.

---

16. See pages 147–50 of Strauss, *supra* note 6, and Chapter 9 and pages 1219–20 of Walton, *supra* note 6, for suggested questions to ask.

On the other hand, the judge may call to offer you a job. After accepting the job orally, send a letter to confirm your acceptance. Once you accept a clerkship, contact the other judges you have applied to and ask that they remove your name from consideration. Others to contact and thank (besides your family and friends) include your career office and your recommenders.

If you decide on the basis of your interview that you really do not want to work for the judge, call the judge's assistant or clerk as soon as possible and ask that your name be removed from consideration. Be polite and tactful, because, as mentioned above, you should not normally apply to a judge unless you would be willing to accept an offer.

3.5 What to Do If You Don't Get Hired

If, after all the work of researching clerkships and judges, applying, and perhaps interviewing, you don't land a clerkship, what should you do? First of all, understand that there is a degree of chance in any job search—maybe through no fault of your own, things just didn't work out this time.[17] So don't beat yourself up or engage in endless negative rumination. Take some time off and then take some positive steps.

Start by talking to the staff in your career office. They can help you figure out if something went wrong at a particular point in the process. Maybe your cover letter has a glaring typo, or something you said in interviews was perceived incorrectly. They can look over your application materials or do a mock interview with you.

Then consider sending out more applications. Clerkships open up all the time, because new judges are appointed and clerks leave in the middle of their terms, for example. So even if the normal

17. We are writing this book during a recession, and some courts have hiring freezes—that's the kind of situation over which you have no control and that you should not blame yourself for.

hiring cycle is over, you will probably find clerkships to apply for. Let your recommenders, friends, contacts, and the career office staff know that you're still looking, so if they hear of anything they can alert you. You could even take another job and apply for a clerkship again in a year or two. Also, if you are still interested in clerking for a judge to whom you previously applied you can write a letter to the judge expressing your continued interest.

Almost all judicial clerks enjoy their clerkships and find them extremely rewarding. So even if you get a clerkship with a judge who was not your first choice, you will probably have a wonderful experience. And if you didn't get a clerkship, we urge you to keep trying.

3.6 Additional Resources

Many print and internet information sources about judges, courts, and clerkships exist, only some of which are listed here. Check your career office's library, and local law, university, and public libraries for these and other sources. Remember that web sites can disappear, their addresses can change, and the information posted on them can change. The career office may have more up-to-date information. If you can't find the information you need elsewhere, call the judge's chambers.

Best print resources about clerkships

Debra M. Strauss, *Behind The Bench: The Guide To Judicial Clerkships* (2d ed. 2002)

Kimm Alayne Walton, *Guerilla Tactics For Getting the Legal Job of Your Dreams* (2008)

Print resources about judges, clerkships, and courts

Almanac of the Federal Judiciary (published twice annually)
The Directory of Minority Judges of the United States (4th ed. 2008)
Federal-State Court Directory (published annually)
Federal Regional Yellow Book (published twice annually)

Federal Yellow Book (published quarterly)
Judicial Yellow Book (published twice annually)
April Schwartz and Mary Jo B. Hunter, *United States Tribal Courts Directory* (4th ed. 2010)

Internet resources about judges, clerkships, and courts

Bar association web sites
Court web sites
Massey Mayo Case & Jill E. Tompkins, *A Guide for Tribal Court Law Clerks and Judges* (2007)
    http://www.colorado.edu/iece/docs/Thompson/Final_version_Guide.pdf
Federal Administrative Law Judges Conference
    www.faljc.org
Federal Judges Law Clerk Hiring Plan
    http://www.cadc.uscourts.gov/internet/lawclerk.nsf/Home? OpenForm
Federal Judicial Center—biographies of federal judges; publications about judges, courts, and clerking
    http://www.fjc.gov/public/home.nsf
LexisNexis—biographical information about judges in the Martindale-Hubbell database
National Center for State Courts—links to state court web sites
    http://www.ncsconline.org/
National Tribal Court Law Clerk Program
    http://lawweb.colorado.edu/ilc_clerkships/
National Tribal Justice Resource Center
    http://www.ntjrc.org/
    http://www.ntjrc.org/tribalcourts/tribalcourtdirectory.asp (Tribal Courts Directory)
OSCAR (Online System for Clerkship Application and Review)
    https://oscar.uscourts.gov/
Tribal Court Clearinghouse
    http://www.tribal-institute.org/index.htm
    http://www.tribal-institute.org/lists/justice.htm (links to tribal courts)

U.S. Courts web site, maintained by the Administrative Office of the U.S. Courts—federal court vacancies, locations of federal courts, links to federal court web sites
http://www.uscourts.gov/index.html

Vermont Law School Career Services, *Guide to State Court Judicial Clerkship Procedures* (password protected—get the password from your career office)
http://www.vermontlaw.edu/x1101.xml

Westlaw—biographical information about judges in several databases, including:
Almanac of the Federal Judiciary (AFJ)
Profiler-Profiles of Attorneys and Judges (PROFILER-WLD)
West Legal Directory-Judges (WLD-JUDGE)

Chapter 4

Legal Research Refresher

Conducting legal research is one of a judicial clerk's most important tasks. As a clerk, your role will be to verify the parties' research, evaluate its accuracy and completeness, and alert the judge to any problems with the research. In addition, you might be required to go beyond the parties' research to investigate an issue the judge has a concern about, or to research non-legal topics.

The legal research process judicial clerks follow differs from the process law students and law firm associates follow in a couple of ways. First, as a clerk you will rarely start from scratch because you will use the authorities cited in the parties' submissions as a starting point for your research.

Second, you will generally not need to define the issues or figure out all the potential arguments the parties could make. Rather, even if the facts of a case could give rise to additional claims or arguments, the parties are limited to those they pled or preserved for appeal. There are exceptions to this general rule, though, because judges can reframe the parties' issue statements and can raise issues sua sponte[1] in the interest of justice. Thus, in some cases you may be called upon to identify and research new issues.

In addition to requiring clerks to research issues for specific cases, some judges expect their clerks to keep abreast of developments in the law in general or in a particular area. For example, a trial court judge may assign a clerk to read all criminal case opinions by higher courts in the jurisdiction and to alert the judge of significant de-

---

1. "Without prompting or suggestion; on [their] own motion." *Black's Law Dictionary* 1560 (9th ed. 2009).

velopments that could affect how the judge handles criminal matters. This kind of research is fairly easy: the opinions may come to the court as slip opinions or advance sheets, or the clerk may simply need to scan the higher courts' web sites or legal newspapers for relevant opinions. A clerk can also set up an alert on LexisNexis, Westlaw, or another online legal research service, which will automatically send notifications of new cases in a particular area of law.

4.1 The Importance of Thorough Legal Research

If you have been hired as a judicial clerk, you are probably already a thorough and efficient legal researcher. It's important that you maintain high legal research standards during your clerkship for several reasons.

First, the accurate application and orderly development of the law may depend on your research. While the parties' attorneys will have identified authorities in their briefs, their research and analysis may not be complete or impartial because they are engaged in advocacy. Your job will be to check up on the attorneys' research and conduct additional research if necessary so that the authorities cited in the judge's final decision are the most relevant and up to date. The judge has a duty to dispense justice fairly, and the judge can't do that without knowing about all of the relevant law.

Second, the reputation of the judge depends in part on the thoroughness of your research. Judges, particularly those who face re-election, are constantly being scrutinized. If you fail to discover that a statute has been amended, which results in the judge's decision being reversed, it is the judge, not you, who will be criticized. Even if a case isn't reversed, if the analysis was based on incomplete research, the judge may be criticized by courts or commentators.

Finally, providing excellent research is its own reward. Preparing a thoroughly researched and analytically sound document will earn you the confidence of the judge. The reputation you earn in the courthouse as a respected legal mind will bolster your position in the legal community and improve your career options.

4.2 Getting Help with Research

At some point in the process of researching an issue you may discover you could use some assistance. Perhaps you don't know anything about the area of law and want to find the most informative secondary source. Or you can't find anything directly on point. Or you have the opposite problem: you have found too much, especially if you're doing electronic research. Maybe you can't locate an authority cited by one of the parties or need help using a particular source.

Before you waste too much time you should stop and ask for advice. Talk to or email other clerks; one of them may have faced the same issue in the past and can steer you in the right direction. Talk to the judge, who may remember having decided a similar case. The chambers or court probably maintains a database of the judge's decisions or opinions that you can search for similar issues.

Your best resource for getting help with research, though, is a law librarian. Like you, many law librarians have law degrees and have clerked for judges or practiced law. But unlike you, they have had extensive professional training in identifying, finding, and using legal research materials. Librarians can assist you by suggesting search terms, suggesting sources or particular authorities to consult, finding materials in a library or online, and finding research guides that list sources of information. Because a librarian's job includes staying up to date on research tools, a librarian can be especially helpful in assisting you to find and use ever-changing internet resources. And a librarian's assistance may be essential if you find yourself researching types of law that you had little or no exposure to in law school, such as administrative or international law.

You should begin your research in the law library most closely associated with the court, which may be the court, circuit, county,

or state law library. If the court law library isn't convenient or does-
n't have the resources you need, contact the law library at a local law
school or at your law school. The librarians at your alma mater
should be happy to help you. For more unusual research requests
consider contacting a librarian at the state law library, the law library
at a public university, the library associated with the state legislature, the Law Library of Congress, or the library at a state or federal agency that regulates the conduct of the parties in the case you
are working on. Many library web sites have live-chat features and,
of course, they list reference librarians' email addresses and phone
numbers.

If you need help conducting a search on LexisNexis or Westlaw,
contact the service's research attorneys or customer-support personnel.
They can help you construct queries and suggest databases in which
to run them.

It's a good idea to get acquainted with these resources and people before you need them. Find the library and introduce yourself
to the librarians and start developing rapport. Figure out how to
contact the Westlaw, LexisNexis, or other subscription service customer-support personnel. Familiarize yourself with library web sites.

4.3 The Legal Research Process

The most effective legal researchers are systematic, organized,
and thorough. But the legal research process varies by project. It varies
depending on the issues, the complexity of the case, the research
the parties have already done, and the research you have already
done. For example, if you previously researched and wrote a bench
memo for a case, and now are turning the memo into an opinion,
you may need to do little new research other than updating the authorities you cited in the memo. On the other hand, if the judge wants
you to research an issue not raised by the parties, you may need to
start from scratch. Here are some general observations about the
legal research process.

First, the research process often is not linear. You may start with statutes, go to regulations, go to agency decisions, and then go back to statutes, for example. You may begin to write, and then realize that you need to do more research.

Second, there is not one research path that works for every research project or for every researcher. You should develop the flexibility to begin at different places, use different tools, and take different steps, depending on the project. While it is often best to begin with secondary sources, that's not always true. And your research process may differ from that of your fellow clerks because there can be more than one way to get to the same point.

Finally, research almost always involves trial and error. You should expect this and not get frustrated if you go down blind alleys or run a search that turns up 2,000 hits. In addition, expect a certain amount of trial and error in your understanding of a legal problem. Before you begin, you may think that X is the most important issue, but after some research you may find that Y is actually more determinative.

Despite the potential for variation between research projects, you can expect to take the following steps in your research process.

Read the Record and the Parties' Submissions

Before you undertake any legal research, you need to understand the facts and procedural posture of the case. Read the relevant parts of the record, the parties' memos or briefs, and any decisions or opinions written by your court or lower courts on the case. These documents will identify the issues, the arguments, and relevant authorities, which will give you the lay of the land.

Read the Authorities Cited in the Court Documents and the Parties' Submissions

Next, read the authorities that the parties cited in their submissions and that the lower courts cited. Doing so should give you a general understanding of the law and will give you a start on your research. As you read the authorities keep track of the authorities cited in them that you plan to read.

Make a Research Plan

After you have read the authorities cited by the parties, you will need to do additional research to make sure the parties' research was complete and is up to date. Prepare a written research plan to follow as you research. Research plans vary by project, but a research plan generally should include a statement of the issues, a list of search terms, and a checklist of sources you will consult and the order in which you will consult them. A sample research plan is included at the end of this chapter. Follow these steps in creating a research plan:

Identify the issue(s). Identifying the issue will be easy if the parties (and the lower court, if there is one) framed the issue consistently. But if the parties framed the issue inconsistently, you will need to decide which, if any, version is correct. Consult with the judge if necessary. Write down a preliminary statement of the issue — the act of writing will help you understand it. You can change the issue later if your research indicates that you have not formulated it properly. Meanwhile, the written issue statement will be a reminder of what you *should* be researching, if you start to get off track.

Identify search terms. Identify search terms to look up in a case-law digest or statutory index or to use when running electronic searches. Find topics in the headnotes of the cases the parties cite; a legal thesaurus or law dictionary can suggest additional terms.

Create a checklist of sources to consult. List the kinds of sources you will consult, in the order you will consult them. Include the finding tools (discussed below) you will use to find authorities. Identify the searches you plan to run on legal research web sites and in the chambers or court database. If you are still unfamiliar with the law after reading the parties' memos or briefs and the authorities they cite, the first sources on your checklist should be secondary sources that can give you additional background information. Then the checklist should identify the kinds of primary authorities you will search for.

Follow the Research Plan

Once you have created your research plan, follow it. Go through the checklist of sources systematically and check them off as you consult them. Keep track of additional research leads that you come upon so you can check those out as well. Remember to stay focused on the issue—look back at the issue statement at the beginning of your plan from time to time. It won't do you any good to research side issues or issues that the parties could have raised but didn't (unless the judge wants you to research them). Don't forget the important step of updating your research using citators, pocket parts, or other tools.

Unless the issue is one of first impression in the jurisdiction or the judge requests that you research the law of other jurisdictions, stick to mandatory authority (of course, reading secondary authorities is acceptable to gain a general understanding of the law). Make sure that you understand whether the issue is governed by statute, regulation, case law, or another kind of authority. And determine whether the issue is governed by state or federal law and which courts' opinions are binding.

If you get stuck while researching, consider asking a law librarian or another clerk for help. Or you could go back to a secondary authority to gain a broader or different perspective about the issue. Effective legal researchers use a variety of sources and methods to make sure they cover the area: they research using both print and electronic materials, both primary and secondary authorities, and sources from different publishers. Sometimes taking a break from research to do some other task can be the best way to get unstuck.

Remain flexible, though. Even though you have created a research plan, you can alter it as you go along. Don't let the plan keep you from doing additional research or from investigating new search terms suggested by your research, for example.

Keep Track of Research and Take Notes

Keeping track of research is key to research efficiency. You should check off the sources on your checklist as you consult them and keep a record of the terms you search and the online queries you run. Keeping a record like this will save you time because you won't have to repeat research steps you've already taken. You can look at the searches you've already run and come up with new searches. And you can show your research trail to a librarian and ask where to go next. Finally, if the judge has questions about your research, you'll have a record of it to show the judge.

Besides taking notes about your research trail, you should take notes about the authorities themselves. At the very least, keep a record of each authority's full citation, the method you used to locate it, and whether and how you updated it.

Once you have determined that an authority is relevant, read the entire authority. When reading a case, never simply read the summary or headnotes (which are not part of the court's opinion) or jump to the most relevant-sounding language. Read the entire case to make sure you understand the factual context and the court's holding and reasoning. Read any dissent or concurrence as well— doing so may help you understand the majority opinion. Likewise, read an entire statutory or administrative code section and look for related sections that affect how that section applies to your situation, including definitions of relevant terms.

As you know, reading like an attorney is different from reading like a lay person. You should use active reading techniques. For example, when reading a case, critically evaluate the court's analysis and think about how the case can be synthesized with what you've already read. In addition, make sure you understand everything you read. Look up unfamiliar words in a legal or general-purpose dictionary and re-read text if you didn't understand it the first time. Be careful to distinguish dictum from the holding of a case.[2]

---

2. "Dictum," short for "obiter dictum," is "[a] judicial comment made while delivering a judicial opinion, but one that is unnecessary to the de-

One way to take notes about the cases you read is to brief them. You probably briefed cases for your first-year courses in law school, but you may not have done so since then. Briefing is a useful process because it forces you to read carefully and restate information in your own words, which helps you better understand a case. Because you are briefing for your own use, you can use whatever format you choose, but case briefs generally contain at least these parts: facts (both operative and procedural), issue(s), holding(s), and reasoning. Some attorneys include additional parts, such as the rule, a synthesis of the case with other cases read, and notes about any dissent or concurrence. After you have briefed the important cases you will have a uniform set of concise notes that will be easier to work with than the narrative notes you took while reading the cases.

Make sure that your notes are accurate. There's nothing quite as frustrating as trying to check a quote and discovering you wrote down the wrong page number, or worse, the wrong case citation. It's also extremely important to reproduce quotations accurately. Missing just one small word (like "not") can make a huge difference. Make sure as well that your descriptions of cases are accurate.

Once you have accumulated a stack of authorities you'll need to sort them in some way to keep track of which issue or sub issue they are relevant to. You can create electronic or physical files in which to place authorities. Another simple way to take notes about and sort cases is to create a cover sheet for each one that summarizes the important information and that allows you to quickly identify each case's relevance. Use visual organization techniques, like spreadsheets, to organize your thoughts about and synthesize a group of authorities.

---

cision in the case and therefore not precedential (although it may be considered persuasive)." *Black's Law Dictionary* 1177 (9th ed. 2009).

Know When to Stop Researching

Knowing when to stop researching can be the most challenging part of the research process. Law students and new attorneys often lack confidence in their legal research skills so keep researching when their time would be better spent outlining or writing. Procrastinators use research as a way to put off beginning to write. Judicial clerks often have tight deadlines and must be efficient legal researchers and writers, so knowing when to stop researching is important.

You know you are done with your research if the same authorities keep turning up. If you have conducted research in a number of different ways, using different finding tools, different searches, and different sources, but keep running across the same authorities, you have probably found all there is to find.

In addition, if you are continuing to find new cases but the facts and law seem less and less relevant, you may have found the most relevant cases. Remember that there often is not a perfect case. Especially in courts of last resort, in most situations if the answer was obvious the case wouldn't be in front of the court. If, on the other hand, you are still finding precedential cases similar to your case, don't stop researching. Rather, concentrate on narrowing your research to identify the most relevant cases.

Finally, if you have taken all the steps in your research plan, then you may be at a logical stopping point.

Remember that research and writing need not be separate activities. You can begin writing even if you think you may have more research to do. And even if you believe you have completed your research, you may find during the writing process that you need to go back and do more research.

4.4 Legal Research Materials

Legal research materials come in a variety of categories and are available in different formats. You are certainly familiar with many legal research materials; this section will remind you of those and may identify some materials you are unfamiliar with. This information is merely a summary; see the resources at the end of the chapter or ask a law librarian for more information.

Not every source of legal research materials is equally useful or reliable. Government publications and official publications of primary authorities can be assumed to be reputable. But the reliability of other sources of information, especially information published on the internet, is not as clear.[3] You should evaluate sources in terms of whether the publisher of the information is reputable and knowledgeable, whether the information is authentic and objective, whether the information is current, and whether the information is easily searched for and retrieved.[4] Again, when in doubt, ask a law librarian to help you make these determinations.

Categories of Legal Research Materials

Legal research materials can be divided into a number of categories: (1) sources that contain primary authorities, (2) sources that contain secondary authorities, (3) finding tools, and (4) citators.[5] Good legal researchers make use of all of these materials.

Sources that contain primary authorities. Primary authorities consist of case law and enacted law. While you are familiar with case law and statutes, you should not forget administrative law when researching primary authorities. Sources that contain these authorities include case reporters, statutory and administrative regulation codes, and online databases.

Sources that contain secondary authorities. Secondary authorities are commentary on the law. Table 1 lists the most commonly used sources of secondary authorities.

---

3. For example, Wikipedia entries are written by a wide range of authors, and the information may not be accurate or comprehensive.

4. Lisa Smith-Butler, *Cost Effective Legal Research Redux: How to Avoid Becoming the Accidental Tourist, Lost in Cyberspace*, 9 Fla. Coastal L. Rev. 293, 298 (2008).

5. Laurel Currie Oates & Anne Enquist, *Just Research* 17 (2d ed. 2009).

Table 1. Sources of Secondary Authorities

Treatises, hornbooks, and nutshells
Encyclopedias — both comprehensive and state-specific
Volumes of ALR annotations
Publications containing restatements of the law
Publications containing model and uniform codes
Jury instruction guides
Legal periodicals, including law reviews and practice-related periodicals such as bar association journals
Practice materials, including deskbooks, practice manuals, form books, CLE materials, and specialized electronic databases
Current awareness materials, including newsletters, looseleaf services, and listservs
Legal newspapers
Legal dictionaries
Legal thesauruses
Self-help law books and web sites

Finding tools. Finding tools are materials and web sites that are used to find primary and secondary authorities. Major types of finding tools are statute subject indexes, case-law digests, citators, periodical indexes, internet legal research searches, internet search engines, and portal web sites.[6] In addition, references to other authorities in cases, secondary authorities, and statute annotations can be thought of as finding tools.

Another kind of finding tool is a research guide (also referred to as a bibliography, pathfinder, resource guide, or subject guide). A research guide lists the most important primary and secondary authorities for a particular topic and may also present an overview of the topic. Research guides are usually prepared by law librarians. Some research guides are books; others are documents posted on web sites.

---

6. Portal web sites are web sites that collect links to other sites; they are described more fully below.

Citators. Citators are used to check the currency of primary and secondary authorities and as finding tools. KeyCite on Westlaw and Shepards in print and on LexisNexis are citators.

Locations of Legal Research Materials

Legal research materials are published in print and electronic formats. Judicial clerks should "aim to be ambidextrous"[7] and be able to use both print and electronic resources because some sources are only available in one medium, the clerk's preferred medium may not be available, the judge may prefer one medium over the other, and some sources are easier to use in one medium than in the other.

Print materials. Almost all primary authorities, with the exception of unpublished opinions and trial court decisions, are available in print format. Most secondary authorities also are available in print, but in recent years some secondary authorities such as law review and legal news articles have been published only on the internet.

Many clerks prefer to research electronically, but researching in print resources is a better choice in a number of circumstances. If you are unfamiliar with the law or are researching broad concepts, it's often best to begin your research in print materials because it may be easier and more efficient to browse a table of contents, index, or the authority itself in print format than online. Once you have acquired some knowledge or narrowed your inquiry, you can more easily construct a focused online query. And of course if the authority is not available online, or the court does not have a subscription to the online database containing the authority, you must use the print version.

Electronic materials. More legal research materials are becoming available in electronic format all the time. Some authorities are available only online, such as many unpublished opinions.[8] And

---

7. Christina L. Kunz et al., *The Process of Legal Research* 23 (7th ed. 2008).

8. Many unpublished federal court opinions appear in the *Federal Appendix*, though, which appears in print.

some clerks must rely on electronic versions of sources because they work in courts or locations with small or nonexistent law libraries and don't have access to many books.[9]

Even if materials are available in print format, they may be easier to use or retrieve in electronic format. Citators, for example, are much easier to use online than in print. Some information is more effectively searched for online, including very specific information, like a proper name or a unique word or phrase; cases with specific fact patterns; legislative history; the latest authorities, news, or trends; and information in a particular field of a document (like the title of an article or a case name). And many authorities are simply easier to retrieve electronically than in print.

Nevertheless, there are drawbacks to conducting research electronically. If you run into any of the following problems and cannot quickly find a solution, contact a law librarian or a research attorney for the legal research service you are using.

The biggest drawback of doing electronic research is the potential to waste time. You can easily waste time if you jump online without first becoming familiar with the topic or planning your research. Another way to waste time is to allow yourself to get sidetracked because of the ease of linking from one authority to another. If this happens, look back at the issue in your research plan and refocus.

Electronic research also can produce too many results, which can cause you to become overwhelmed. To narrow your results, reconsider your search terms, use the "locate" or "focus" feature, or go back to a secondary authority or the parties' submissions to get a better understanding of the law before running another search.

You also run the risk of encountering the opposite result: coming up with too few results and missing relevant materials because

---

9. *See* Massey Mayo Case & Jill E. Tompkins, *A Guide for Tribal Court Law Clerks and Judges* 38 (2007), http://www.colorado.edu/iece/docs/Thompson/Final_version_Guide.pdf (noting that clerks who work remotely from their tribal courts may need to use internet resources).

your search is too narrow. Beware of stopping your research after you have found one great case. Don't become "overly charmed by the apparent suitability of a retrieved case,"[10] and think that you are done with your research. Remember that your research must be thorough and you should use a number of different search strategies and sources to find relevant authorities.

If you are having trouble finding the authorities you expect to find, it may be that you are not using the research service effectively or efficiently. For example, you may be using search terms, fields, or connectors incorrectly; searching in the wrong database; not starting broadly enough; or not using narrowing techniques. Always check the scope of the database—it's possible that the authority or information you're searching for simply isn't available in the database. Your approach to a database may be outdated. Electronic database services make improvements frequently; thus, even if you are familiar with a service you should arrange to get additional training regularly. The account manager for the court's subscription service can likely set up training for you and your co-clerks. LexisNexis and Westlaw also have online tutorials that you can use.

It's a good idea to be familiar with several database services and to know their strengths and weaknesses. Free sites tend to have less advanced search capabilities than commercial sites, and less-expensive commercial sites have less advanced capabilities than the more expensive and comprehensive sites.

Finally, you should remember that not all information on the internet is good information. Web sites published by educational institutions, government entities, and bar associations are generally reputable. For other sites, you should evaluate the reliability of the publisher and the information. And you should not assume that online information is current; if the publisher of the material does not update the material, the mere fact that it is online doesn't make it up to date.

10. J.D.S. Armstrong & Christopher A. Knott, *Where the Law Is: An Introduction to Advanced Legal Research* 108 (3d ed. 2009).

Categories of electronic materials. The variety and number of legal research materials on the internet increase continually, as do the features and search capabilities of the web sites. Some categories of internet sites are described below. The categories are not mutually exclusive because some web sites fit into more than one category. The list should provide you with an idea of the available resources and the kind of site to look for or ask a librarian about.

Many authorities, especially primary authorities, are available on numerous web sites. You need not rely exclusively on Westlaw and LexisNexis—other sites are reliable and can meet different needs. Table 2 lists a selection of specific sites; the additional resources at the end of the chapter identify even more sites.

Search engines like Google and Yahoo can be used to search for sources of substantive law or for research guides, for example. Sometimes a quick search in a search engine is a good way to begin research.

Portals are web sites that collect links to other sites. Many law libraries maintain portals on their web sites. They are often particularly useful starting points for researching the law of the state the library is located in.

Metasites, like portals, provide links to other web sites but also link to their own documents that contain substantive information about the law. Metasites are maintained by law libraries, individuals, and companies that distribute legal research and technology information.

Comprehensive legal research sites contain primary and secondary authorities and come in both fee-based and free varieties. Lexis-Nexis and Westlaw are the most familiar fee-based services and have the best coverage, search capabilities, and added editorial content. Cheaper fee-based sites include Casemaker and Fastcase, which are available at very low cost or free to members of state bar associations that offer them as member benefits.

Government sites, maintained by government entities of all types and levels, contain a wealth of information. Courts, legislatures, agencies, and other government entities post opinions, court rules, constitutions, statutes, and regulations on their web sites. In addition, legislative and rulemaking materials, including legislative history, session laws, and rulemaking records are available on government web sites.

Law library sites often act as portals and provide links to legal resources elsewhere on the internet. Many also post online research guides. In addition, it's possible to chat with a reference librarian from many law library sites.

Research guide sites primarily contain links to research guides. As mentioned above, research guides can be useful starting points for legal research.

Working paper sites are repositories for working papers, which are articles written by attorneys and law professors, and which have been published or may be published in the future. Working papers are a good source of the latest scholarship about legal topics.

Online legal dictionaries are useful for immediate look-up of unfamiliar words.

Bar association sites provide links to state and federal law and government sites, report legal news, and include useful information like judge biographies. Many bar associations post their publications on their web sites (although the publications may only be accessible to members). Bar associations that subscribe to Casemaker or Fastcase for their members' use provide links to these sites on their web sites.

Law firm sites often post articles written by attorneys who specialize in particular areas of the law.

Legal blogs are maintained by attorneys and law professors. Some focus on particular substantive areas of the law and collect or link to news about the latest developments in the area of interest to the blog author.

Table 2. Categories and Examples of Online Legal Research Sites

Search engines

Dogpile	http://www.dogpile.com/
Google	http://www.google.com/
Yahoo	http://www.yahoo.com/
Or use your favorite search engine	

Portals

GovEngine.com (portal to federal, state, and local government sites)	http://www.govengine.com/
USA.gov (United States government portal)	http://www.usa.gov/
State and Local Government on the Net	http://www.statelocalgov.net/

Metasites

Cornell University Law School's Legal Information Institute	http://www.law.cornell.edu/
Findlaw	http://www.findlaw.com/
Justia	http://www.justia.com/
LLRX	http://www.llrx.com/

Comprehensive legal research sites

Fee-based

HeinOnline	http://heinonline.org/
LexisNexis	http://www.lexisnexis.com/
Loislaw	http://www.loislaw.com/
VersusLaw	http://www.versuslaw.com/
Westlaw	http://web2.westlaw.com/

Free

Casemaker (free with some state bar memberships)	http://www.casemaker.us/
Fastcase (free with some state bar memberships)	https://www.fastcase.com/
LexisONE	http://law.lexisnexis.com/ webcenters/lexisone/
Also see metasites	

Government sites

Federal government

GPO Access (Government Printing Office)	http://www.gpoaccess.gov/
Thomas (Library of Congress)	http://thomas.loc.gov/
U.S. Courts	http://www.uscourts.gov/

State governments

The National Center for State Courts (links to state court web sites)	http://www.ncsconline.org/

Law library sites

Georgetown Law Library (links to research tutorials and numerous research guides)	http://www.ll.georgetown.edu/
Law Library of Congress	http://www.loc.gov/law/
Marion Gould Gallagher Law Library, University of Washington School of Law (links to numerous research guides)	http://lib.law.washington.edu/
See also the web site of your law school's law library or a law school in the court's jurisdiction	

Research guide sites

Zimmerman's Research Guide	http://www.lexisnexis.com/ infopro/zimmerman/
See also law library sites and metasites	

Working paper sites

Bepress Legal Repository	http://law.bepress.com/repository/
Social Science Resource Network	http://ssrn.com/

Online legal dictionaries

Law.com	http://dictionary.law.com/

Bar association sites

American Bar Association	http://www.abanet.org/
See also state or local bar association web sites	

Law firm sites	
See metasites and comprehensive legal research sites for directories of, and links to, law firm sites	
Legal blogs	
Blawg (legal blog directory)	http://www.blawg.com/
Blawgsearch (legal blog directory)	http://blawgsearch.justia.com/

4.5 Additional Resources

These books and articles give research guidance, contain detailed information about legal research sources, and list electronic resources. Some have associated web sites that keep the URLs up to date.

J.D.S. Armstrong & Christopher A. Knott, *Where the Law Is: An Introduction to Advanced Legal Research* (3d ed. 2009)

Carolina Academic Press Legal Research Series (state-specific research guides; currently available for about half the states)

Timothy L. Coggins, *Legal, Factual and Other Internet Sites for Attorneys and Legal Professionals*, 15 Rich. J.L. & Tech. 13 (2009), *available at* http://law.richmond.edu/jolt/v15i4/article13.pdf

Morris L. Cohen & Kent C. Olson, *Legal Research in a Nutshell* (9th ed. 2007)

Laurel Currie Oates & Anne Enquist, *Just Research* (2d ed. 2009)

Kent C. Olson, *Principles of Legal Research* (2009)

Lisa Smith-Butler, *Cost Effective Legal Research Redux: How to Avoid Becoming the Accidental Tourist, Lost in Cyberspace*, 9 Fla. Coastal L. Rev. 293 (2008)

Jackie Woodside, *Introducing Students to Online Research Guides*, 17 Perspectives 171 (2009)

4.6 Sample Research Plan

Preliminary Steps
1. Identify issue(s):

2. Identify search terms:

Secondary Authority Research
3. Identify any online searches run and the database(s) in which you ran them. Indicate whether these searches were helpful or unhelpful. Did they find too many authorities? Too few?

4. Legal Encyclopedias (list names, volumes, subjects, section numbers):

                                        Updated? _____

5. Treatises (list names, subjects, section numbers):

                                        Updated? _____

6. Law Review Articles

    A. List search terms used in the Index to Legal Periodicals or LegalTrac:

    B. List article names and citations:

7. A.L.R.s (list volumes, titles, section numbers):

                                        Updated? _____

8. Restatements (list subjects, section numbers):

                                        Updated? _____

9. Other Secondary Authorities (such as practice materials, jury instructions, CLE materials) (list names, section numbers):

                                        Updated? _____

Primary Authority Research

10. Statutes

    A. Identify useful search terms located through the index, table of contents, or other sources:

    B. Identify any online searches run and the database(s) in which you ran them. Indicate whether these searches were helpful or unhelpful. Did they find too many authorities? Too few?

    C. Identify statute(s) found (list volume names or numbers, if applicable, and section numbers):

    D. Was there helpful information in the annotations to the statute? If yes, what?

                                  Updated? _____

11. Regulations

    A. Identify useful search terms located through the index, table of contents, or other sources:

    B. Identify any online searches run and the database(s) in which you ran them. Indicate whether these searches were helpful or unhelpful. Did they find too many authorities? Too few?

    C. Identify regulation(s) found (list volume names or numbers, if applicable, and section numbers):

                                  Updated? _____

12. Cases

    A. Identify useful search terms located through a print digest's index, table of contents, or other sources:

    B. Identify any digests used and topics and key numbers from the digests:

        <u>Digest Name</u>   <u>Topic</u>   <u>Key Numbers</u>   <u>Updated?</u>

    C. Identify any online searches run and the database(s) in which you ran them. Indicate whether these searches were helpful or unhelpful. Did they find too many authorities? Too few?

D. Provide case names and citations and a brief description of each case for relevant cases found:

Case name & citation	Relevant to which issue?	Brief description	Shepardized or KeyCited?

Next Steps

13. Identify what, if any, additional research steps you plan to take:

Chapter 5

Legal Writing Refresher

Most law clerks have a record of producing strong legal writing. In fact, the judge probably hired you partly because of your excellent writing skills. As you begin your clerkship, you may want to review some writing basics so your work product is as polished and professional as possible.

5.1 The Importance of Writing Excellence

Judicial clerks should maintain high writing standards during a clerkship for several reasons. First, judges, the law clerk's primary audience, are extremely busy people. A typical judge will read thousands of pages in a month, tens of thousands of pages in a year, including submissions from parties, supporting bench memoranda from their clerks, and case law. Given this workload, judges depend on their clerks to make their jobs manageable by producing clear, concise, immediately understandable writing and analysis. Further, if the clerk has drafted a document that will be issued under the judge's signature, like an order or opinion, an excellent first draft from a law clerk will make the judge's revising and rewriting task significantly easier. Given a strong first draft, the judge can focus on revising the substantive content of the document rather than on sentence structure and punctuation.

Second, some of the law clerk's writing will end up in the final product issued from the court to the public, communicating decisions in legal disputes that significantly affect people's lives. Not only must those decisions be clearly and accurately conveyed for the sake of the parties to the immediate lawsuit, they must also make sense as precedent for the legal community as a whole. Most law clerks can probably remember reading certain cases in law school and wishing they were better written. Well-written decisions and opinions make everyone's job easier.

Further, writing generated by the courts sets the standard for the legal profession as a whole, and that standard must be high. Judges can hardly fault attorneys who appear before them for poor writing and communication skills if their own work product is not professional and error free. Because clerks are usually both the original drafters of judicial documents and the final proofreaders and citation checkers, they play an important role in establishing those high standards.

Finally, during a clerkship, judicial clerks' main work product—the work that will serve as the primary basis for evaluation of their skills—is writing. As a clerk, you will demonstrate your competence in legal research and analysis and your commitment to professionalism through your writing. You should seek to instill utmost confidence in your work overall through excellent writing.

5.2 How Writing for the Court Differs from Writing in Law School

The basic writing and legal writing skills learned during law school will serve you well as you strive for excellence in the judge's chambers. A well-written sentence and a cogent analysis are essentially the same in any context. But writing for a court is not like writing for a law review. While a law review article may examine an issue's every angle in depth, most documents written for a court should be focused and concise, providing only the information required to decide the issue.

To produce excellent writing in any context, a writer must first understand the audience and purpose of the document, and then must take them into account when choosing words, designing structure, and providing details. The following sections examine the audiences and purposes that judicial clerks commonly encounter.

Audience

Judicial clerks write primarily for four audiences: the judges they work for, attorneys (including judges and law clerks in future cases), the parties in cases before the court, and the public. Each group of readers has different characteristics and needs that must be taken into account.

As discussed above, judges carry a heavy workload, so one of their main needs is efficiency. In the interest of efficiency, judges require thorough, accurate, and easy-to-read documents that support their decision-making process. Only the information relevant to the decision-making process should be included. As noted above, law review-style writing, which generally aims for a scholarly tone and seeks to show the depth and breadth of the writer's knowledge, should be avoided.

To further promote efficiency, judges also need their clerks to adapt individual documents to the particular situation at hand. Consequently, clerks must evaluate each writing situation and respond accordingly, with some amount of flexibility. For instance, a judge may be well-versed on a particular legal issue because it arises over and over again in certain types of trials. While a written document — a bench memo — analyzing that issue in a particular case may be called for, the judge may not need a complete explanation of all the case law on the subject. Rather, a shorter, less comprehensive analysis that just sets out the parties' arguments and the suggested resolution may suffice and will avoid wasting the judge's time. As a clerk, if you have a question about the depth of analysis required for any particular assignment, you should always ask the judge.

Individual judges may also differ in the amount of formality they expect in their clerks' written work, especially work that will only be used in chambers. While some judges will expect a formal tone at all times, others will accept a more relaxed tone in the clerks' writing. (If you work for a judge who falls into the latter category, however, be careful not to confuse informality with sloppiness.) You can develop a feel for the appropriate tone in documents for use only in chambers by reviewing the work of more experienced clerks.

Attorneys, another audience, also value efficiency in writing. But their more critical needs are for clarity, consistency, and legitimacy in judicial writing. An attorney reading judicial writing — whether an order issued in a current case or a published opinion from past years — wants to readily understand the effect of the writing and what action, if any, it requires of the reader. Decisions must be explained in enough detail that readers can grasp and evaluate the rationale, whether they agree with it or not. Finally, the tone of the writing must be in keeping with the importance of the enterprise: decision making in a fair and impartial justice system. Thus, it should be formal and authoritative.

Finally, if a clerk is writing for the non-legally trained public, including, usually, the parties to a case, the writing must be as uncomplicated and straightforward as possible. Clerks write for this audience when they produce jury instructions, letters to jurors, or other kinds of correspondence. Because the education and sophistication level of this audience can vary greatly, clerks should take care when writing in this context to explain all legal terms and use simple, concrete language. If the audience for a particular document is exclusively the parties to a case, and the clerk is familiar with the parties, the tone and complexity may be adjusted to those particular readers. Generally, the tone should be formal, but accessible.

Purpose

Just as the audience affects a document's tone and need for detail, so does the purpose. Unlike the writing most students learn to do in a legal writing class, whose purpose is primarily to predict or overtly persuade, most writing done by judicial clerks is intended to inform, educate, or subtly persuade. Sometimes these purposes overlap in one document. When writing, the clerk should think about the purpose of each document and adapt the writing accordingly.

Trial court orders and findings of fact and conclusions of law are examples of documents intended to inform. These documents must be thorough and accurate, especially because they document what happened in the trial court and create the record from which an appeal may be taken. The tone should be authoritative and formal.

Bench memos aim to educate judges about the law and arguments in particular cases. This educative purpose, combined with audience considerations, allows for a more flexible, individual approach to tone and style. In fact, in bench memos, unlike many other kinds of judicial writing, clerks can feel freer to let their own voices come through. But bench memos should not sound professorial, despite this educative purpose.

Ostensibly, opinions and decisions are also informative documents. They communicate decisions in the course of a law suit and explain the supporting rationale. But published opinions also establish the precedent that guides the legal community in future decision making and, as such, must convince readers that cases are correctly decided. This presents a sometimes difficult tension. As a society, we require our judges to be objective, fair, and impartial, and we expect their writing to reflect corresponding values. But at the same time, an opinion must be sufficiently persuasive that it will be accepted as legitimate precedent.

These dual purposes dictate that the utmost care and attention must be paid to opinion drafting. The tone must be authoritative, but persuasive writing techniques may be used to support the outcome. Unpublished opinions require less detail than published opinions because they usually do not set precedent, but they must maintain that authoritative tone. Of course, an opinion drafted by a clerk will be revised and edited by the judge, who will shape the final tone and content. But the better the clerk's initial draft, the easier the judge's job.

5.3 Structuring Legal Analysis

In any legal writing context, the same general principles apply to structuring legal analysis. In general, readers need to be educated about the law before they can consider how it applies to the facts. Conclusions should be stated up front, not hidden in the depths of an argument or revealed only at the end. Roadmaps, headings, and executive summaries facilitate easy navigation within a document. Following these general principles will help you produce well-organized, readable writing.

IRAC

The IRAC paradigm, or some variation on it, that you probably learned in your legal writing class during law school applies in any judicial writing that includes legal analysis, such as a bench memo or opinion. The IRAC paradigm directs a writer to order the analysis of a single legal issue in a particular sequence, broken down into the following steps:

Issue. The thesis sentence should identify the issue to be addressed in this entire section of analysis. Some legal writers prefer to use a "CRAC" format instead of IRAC. Under the CRAC format, the thesis sentence states the writer's conclusion about the particular issue rather than just identifying the issue. A writer may decide to add a sentence or two explaining the issue or conclusion if the discussion that follows is complicated or lengthy.

Rule and rule explanation section. The rule that governs the legal issue, synthesized from the relevant authority, should be explained immediately following the initial issue statement. The general principles that apply to the analysis should be set out first, including the language of any statutory sections that govern. This discussion of relevant general principles should be followed by discussion of specific reported cases that show how the rule has been applied by past courts. This section, often called a rule explanation section, should also bring out any policy considerations the authorities raise that may enter into the analysis.

Analysis. The analysis section discusses how the law set out in the rule section applies to the facts of the particular case. In objective documents, like bench memos, this section should also explore counterarguments that might be raised. In documents with a more persuasive purpose, counterarguments should be anticipated and addressed, although this can be done less explicitly than in an objective document.

Conclusion. The final conclusion section should briefly restate and summarize the prevailing argument and explain how the issue should be resolved.

While the basic IRAC paradigm applies to judicial writing, as a clerk you may encounter many reasons to vary the paradigm. The judicial writing context may be more sophisticated than the writing contexts you encountered in your legal writing classes. For instance, to maximize efficiency for a judicial reader, a clerk may elect to integrate the discussion of reported cases into the analysis. Thus, rather than discuss each case separately, you can bring cases into the discussion as they affect the analysis on a particular aspect of the issue.

Further, a clerk may vary the depth of discussion in the rule, case, or analysis sections, according to the judge's familiarity with an issue or particular stated requirements. For instance, sometimes the judge may require only a very broad summary of the law, or may want a thorough discussion of the law, but only a very conclusory analysis. Thus, the basic parts of the IRAC organizational paradigm may be altered to suit a particular document's purpose.

Other Organizing Principles

The more sophisticated legal documents become, the more important visual rhetoric becomes. Visual rhetoric includes headings, thesis sections, explicit transitions, and other "readers' road markers." These organizing devices accomplish the important purpose of helping readers understand where they are in the document at all times and what to expect next. But use of these devices also reflects on the writer's competence, instilling confidence in the writer's intelligence and analytical skill. The more easily readers can follow your written product, the more they will trust you. Thus, you should make liberal use of visual signals that help readers actually use the document.

5.4 The Writing Process

In essence, law clerks are professional writers. A significant portion of the law clerk's work involves writing, and much of that writing is done without immediate supervision. No one looks over the clerk's shoulder to make sure a particular process is followed. No one will require outlines, first drafts, or rewrites after critique. A judge will not be particular about how a document comes about, as long as it lands on the judicial desk on time. Thus, as a clerk, you must be independently certain that your individual writing process allows you to fulfill your responsibilities.

Every writer's process is different. There is no one way or best way to begin writing. Outlines or flow-chart diagrams work for some writers. Doing a "brain dump"—typing everything that comes to mind on the topic and saving the organization for later—works for other writers. You should use whatever process works best for you.

You probably developed a successful writing process for assignments you wrote during law school. But a judicial clerkship is a demanding job, and it requires a workable, reliable writing process. Several points are worth keeping in mind as you refine your writing process and adapt it to clerking.

First, the writing process should be recursive, not linear. Specifically, to successfully produce the sophisticated writing required of a judicial clerk, you cannot expect to pound out a draft from beginning to end, make a few editorial changes, and turn it in. Instead, you should expect to circle back to different portions of the document numerous times, revising not only typing and spelling errors, but also content, structure, and style. The writing need not start at the beginning of the document, and each part of a document need not be completed in linear order. For instance, you may start by drafting the first section of analysis, go back to the beginning to write a conclusion, return to the analysis for revisions, move on to write another section of analysis, and then go back to the thesis for polishing, continuing in that fashion until the document is complete. No particular order is dictated, and sometimes moving on to a new section to allow more time to contemplate a difficult section is the best choice.

Second — a closely related point — writing is "thinking in ink."[1] The actual process of writing helps the writer analyze the subject at hand and draw conclusions. Thus, as you write, new ideas will bubble up that you should incorporate into the analysis or implement in the structure of the document during the revising stage. In fact, it is not unusual for writers to change their initial conclusions after drafting documents because their writing processes have opened up new perspectives and allowed the pieces to come together in a different way. So, as a clerk, you should *use* the writing process as an analytical tool to help you refine the analysis; it is not necessary to wait for absolute certainty about a conclusion before you begin to write.

Finally, know yourself as a writer, and plan your writing process accordingly. For instance, if you are full of energy in the morning, but tend to fall asleep at your desk in the afternoon, plan to edit and proofread first thing in the morning, but research in the library (which is more likely to involve standing up and moving around) in the afternoon. If you do not like to make outlines, but usually end up with messy, disorganized drafts, try a new organizing approach. Get a white board and draw a flow chart in different colors. Write notes about different issues or elements of your analysis on different colored sticky notes or index cards, and then organize them by color.

---

1. *See* William Zinsser, *Writing to Learn* 11 (1988) (discussing idea that "writing is thinking on paper").

You may need to work deliberately to identify the weak points in your writing process—where you waste time, where you get off track. But once you have identified your weaknesses, devise and implement a plan to address them. Talking to other clerks about their writing processes may give you ideas about improving your own.

Prewriting

The prewriting stage of the writing process can be broken down into two primary tasks: evaluating the purpose of the document and preparing the substance of the document. The evaluative task should be fairly straightforward. First, identify your audience and any constraints or particular expectations the audience will bring to the document. Plan the tone and scope of the document accordingly. Second, identify the purpose of the document and determine how much information must be included to accomplish that purpose.

Some judicial clerks will write the same kinds of documents over and over again. For instance, appellate clerks write primarily bench memos and opinions. For these writers, establishing the appropriate scope and tone will become habitual, so these issues need not be re-evaluated for every project. But other kinds of clerks, especially trial court clerks, may jump from one kind of document to another and should routinely think about scope and tone during the prewriting stage.

Preparing the substance of the document, so that you are ready to write a draft, is more complicated. First, you must identify the issues. As a judicial clerk, you will usually start by evaluating the parties' presentation of the issues. As you review the material in the file, such as briefs, transcripts, and supporting exhibits, and conduct research, you will need to decide whether the parties' characterization of the issues is correct and whether they have missed any issues that should be brought to the reader's attention.

Once you have identified the issues, formulate and implement a research plan around those issues. Even when the parties have done the research and submitted documents that discuss the relevant authority, the clerk must independently research the issues to make certain that the parties did not miss or ignore any relevant authority. Chapter Four reviews the research process in more detail.

The third prewriting step involves reading the authorities and analyzing the issues. While the parties' submissions provide a starting point for the analysis, you should evaluate whether the authorities have been fairly interpreted and adequately explained, and you should independently decide which outcome they support and why.

Finally, you should devise a plan for the document. This may mean writing a traditional outline, organizing your note cards in order of usefulness, or creating a flow chart of the issues. Although, as discussed below, a first draft does not have to be a good draft, both the drafting process and the revising process will go more smoothly if you take time to plan the document before you begin to write.

Writing the First Draft

Writing the first draft should be part of the writer's thought process, and as such, it should not be aimed at producing a product ready for submission. Accordingly, expectations about first draft quality should be low; bad first drafts are part of the process.[2] Generally, legal writers who spend more of their time revising and editing produce better work than writers who spend more of their time writing a first draft.[3] Jump-starting the process by turning off the "inner editor" and just writing is more efficient, and produces better work, than agonizing over every sentence.

Writing bad first drafts means, of course, that you must plan to spend plenty of time revising and editing. In fact, in the words of

---

2. *See* Anne Lamott, *Bird by Bird* 21 (1994).
3. Anne M. Enquist, *Unlocking the Secrets of Highly Successful Legal Writing Students* (March 8, 2007), http://ssrn.com/abstract=969526.

Supreme Court Justice Antonin Scalia and legal writing expert Bryan Garner, the writing process should go something like this: "Sit down and write. Then revise. Then revise again. Finally, revise."[4] As professionals, law clerks have the responsibility to produce readable, correct writing that judges or other audiences can quickly and easily understand. A bad first draft moves in that direction, but revising, and revising again, must be a central part of the process.

Revising

During the revising stage, your purpose is to make sure you have provided the information your readers expect to receive in the document and that it can be easily accessed. Accordingly, during this stage, you should not only revise the analysis and organization to address problems that emerged during the drafting stage, you should also revise for accuracy, readability, and usability. During this stage, apply the following principles.

Spend more time revising and editing than writing. Cicero, the great Roman orator, once wrote, "If I had had more time, I would have written a shorter letter."[5] Excellent writing is not about getting the words on the page to begin with. It's about revising what is already on the page, so that the writing is more concise, more accurate, and easier to read. Few writers can artfully marshal structure, style, ideas to be expressed, and clarity all at once or give birth to the perfect sentence or paragraph on the first try. Write the first draft quickly, and plan to spend significantly more time revising and editing.

Check large-scale organization. During the revising process, consider whether the large-scale organization, the order in which different legal issues are addressed within a discussion section, makes sense given the issues and applicable law raised in the case. Large-

---

4. Antonin Scalia & Bryan A. Garner, *Making Your Case: The Art of Persuading Judges* 80 (2008).
5. Dangerous Intersection, http://dangerousintersection.org/?p=84.

scale organization is often determined by the structure of the applicable law. For instance, if a cause of action involves proving specific elements, the large-scale organization should revolve around the elements that are at issue. In other situations, the structure may instead be determined by the relationship between the issues raised in a case. Thus, if the case presents two issues, one of which is procedural and could nullify the need to address the substantive issue, the procedural issue should be addressed first. The discussion should start with a thesis section that explains the "umbrella rule"[6]—the overarching legal principles or issues and how they relate to each other— and identifies the order in which the issues will be addressed. The document should also make liberal use of headings that identify where the discussion of different issues begins and ends.

Check small-scale organization. Each discrete "chunk" of legal analysis should be structured using the basic IRAC paradigm. Check to make sure that each section includes an initial identification of the issue or the conclusion you will reach about that issue, a rule, rule explanation, application of the rule to the facts, and a final conclusion. If one section of the IRAC is missing, be sure you can explain why it is missing. Otherwise, consider revising.

Check use of key language. Every legal issue centers on a key word or phrase, and some issues involve a main phrase and several sub-phrases. When working on a writing project, you should identify key language for every issue and use that same language frequently and consistently throughout the relevant section to help readers easily follow the analysis.[7]

For instance, suppose a document addresses whether under the criminal statutes, a defendant used a dog as a "dangerous instrument" during a robbery. The writing task is to define the main legal idea,

---

6. *See* Linda H. Edwards, *Legal Writing* 134 (4th ed. 2006).
7. The legal writing community is indebted to Professor Mary Beth Beazley of the Ohio State University Michael E. Moritz College of Law for the invention of the handy moniker for key language: "phrase that pays." See her book, *A Practical Guide to Appellate Advocacy* 50 (2d ed. 2006), for more discussion of the "phrase that pays" idea.

"dangerous instrument," and to analyze whether in this case the facts satisfy the definition. Your key language is "dangerous instrument"; consequently, that phrase should be used in all major sentences and statements, such as topic sentences, holdings, and conclusions.

For example, the main rule that applies should be built around the key language: "A dog may be used as a dangerous instrument when...." Similarly, stated holdings of past decisions should include the key language: "The court held that the dog was used as a dangerous instrument because...." And finally, the specific analysis for the case should be structured around the same language: "Here, the Defendant used the dog as a dangerous instrument because...." The entire analysis should be built around and focused on that key language, and the phrase should appear at least once per paragraph. If it does not, readers may lose track of what exactly is at issue.

Once the key language for the current writing issue has been identified, you may want to print it in big letters at the top of the page or post it on sticky notes around your desk or computer as a reminder while you write. During one read-through in the revising process highlight the key language every time it appears. If it does not appear at least once per paragraph, more revisions are required.

Make sure every paragraph starts with a topic sentence or connector. When readers know why they are reading the information presented to them, they process and remember the information better. A topic sentence should tell readers exactly that: why they are reading this particular paragraph. Additionally, topic sentences should help readers see how information in a new paragraph connects to information in the previous paragraph, which also helps them process information more quickly and easily.

For instance, to return to the previous example, suppose a paragraph will discuss three recent cases illustrating when a dog has been used as a dangerous instrument under a statutory definition (the writer has explained the statutory definition in the immediately preceding rule paragraph). In the topic sentence of the new paragraph, the writer should convey that idea in the topic sentence: "In three recent cases interpreting the statutory definition, the court has determined that a dog is used as a dangerous instrument if its owner explicitly or implicitly encourages it to attack or fails to control an attack."

The topic sentence should also move the analysis forward rather than acting merely as a placeholder. The above topic sentence sets out the principle the writer wants readers to understand from the cases, thus it moves the analysis forward. In contrast, consider this topic sentence: "Another case that discusses dogs used as dangerous instruments is *State v. Bodoh.*" This sentence does not provide any useful new information to readers. During the revising process, it should be replaced with a more substantive topic sentence.

Sometimes, however, a new substantive topic sentence is not required. For instance, if a new paragraph continues to support or explain the point set out in the topic sentence of the previous paragraph, a short connector phrase will suffice. Thus, if the paragraph started with, "In three recent cases interpreting the statutory definition...," but a discussion of all three cases did not fit in that paragraph, the next paragraph could continue the analysis and could be introduced only by a short connector. That connector could be something as simple as, "Similarly, in the second case...."

A final note about revising topic sentences: when the first sentence from every paragraph is copied and pasted in order on a blank page, the sentences read as a whole should provide a rough outline of the document. If they do not, chances are readers will have difficulty following the flow of information, and more revision of topic sentences is required.

Check paragraph unity and coherence. In addition to checking that each paragraph starts with a topic sentence, you should make sure that the content of each paragraph relates to its topic sentence. The paragraph should develop the point set out in the topic sentence. Also, make sure each paragraph includes a beginning, a middle, and an end. The flow of the paragraph should follow an identifiable pattern, like cause and effect, problem and solution, or chronological development.

Finally, make sure that all sentences within a paragraph are connected, one to the next, so that the readers can easily follow the development of ideas. This may involve using connector words that explicitly describe the relationship—words like "further," "consequently," "similarly," and "likewise." Or it may involve overlapping or "dovetailing" ideas in sentences so that the ideas are implicitly interlocked: "In January 2006, *Ms. Martin applied to law school. When Ms. Martin applied*, she explained in writing that she had been arrested for arson in 1986." This repetition of language helps readers understand immediately how the idea in one sentence leads to the idea in the next sentence, so the ideas fits together like jigsaw puzzle pieces.

    Evaluate paragraph length. If circumstances required it, most of us could hold our breath for at least one minute. But we would rather not; we would rather breathe every ten seconds or so. Similarly, readers *can* read a two-page paragraph if circumstances require it; but they would rather not. Readers need to take "mental breaths," just like they need to take actual breaths. Long paragraphs require too much concentration and are difficult to follow. Few circumstances justify them.

    As a general rule, if a paragraph is longer than two-thirds of a page, you should revise. This may be a matter of identifying separate thoughts in the paragraph and addressing them in separate paragraphs. If the paragraph contains only one thought, but the thought is so complex that explaining it takes up more than two-thirds of a page, it probably involves sub-parts that can be addressed in separate paragraphs, resulting in multiple paragraphs (a "paragraph block") that address one topic. Sometimes, of course, simply editing the sentences within the paragraph so they convey the information more concisely will transform an overly long paragraph into a readable paragraph.

Editing

    During the editing process, your attention should turn from big-picture issues like overall structural coherence to the minutiae of writing. The editing process should focus on word choice, precision, conciseness, punctuation, and citation placement. Following a few general principles will help ensure that your writing is concise and easy to understand.

Check sentence length. Long sentences, like long paragraphs, can be hard to follow. A busy reader can more efficiently process information if it is presented in shorter sentences and fewer words. Although some long sentences can be eloquent and appropriate, especially when they help vary the rhythm of the text, long sentences can sometimes be a symptom of other writing problems, like lack of clarity and imprecision.

In general, you should consider revising any sentence over twenty words long. If the sentence contains more than one idea, it may need to be turned into multiple sentences, each expressing one idea. If it contains only one basic idea but is too wordy, you should consider whether every word in the sentence is necessary, following the principles listed below.

Edit for wordiness. Wordiness results when writing includes unnecessary words and phrases, like throat-clearing expressions, redundancies, qualifiers, and clutter words. Eliminating these types of words and phrases from your writing can dramatically improve the clarity and readability.

Throat-clearing expressions are those initial phrases that get the writer "revved up" before the main idea, but do not add to the meaning of the sentence (not to be confused with connector phrases, which are important for clarity). For instance, consider the following sentence: "It should also be noted that courts currently apply a no-fault rule in this area." The sentence should be revised to read, "Courts currently apply a no-fault rule in this area." If the idea is not noteworthy, it should not be on the page.

Many throat-clearing expressions start with an "it is" phrase ("it is important that," "it is obvious that," "it is expected that"). When editing, circle all sentences that begin with "it is" or "it was" and consider revising them to eliminate these phrases.

Redundancies, phrases that use two or more words to express an idea when one will do, should also be eliminated. For instance, the phrases "suddenly exploded," "local residents," and "specific example" can all be edited to omit the first word while maintaining meaning. After all, are there any explosions that are not sudden, residents that are not local, or examples that are not specific? Carefully scrutinize your writing for the many different ways in which these unexpected surprises have become an integral part of your writing. (That sentence was a test.)

Qualifiers, words that usually end in "ly," should be eliminated from your writing. "Clearly," "obviously," and "basically" are good examples. If you write a good sentence, the idea it contains will be clear. If an idea is basic or obvious, the reader should understand that from the context. Saying an idea is clear does not make it so. Good writing makes it so.

Excessive preposition use, resulting in a "prepositional-phrase train wreck," also signals wordiness. In a prepositional-phrase train wreck, prepositional phrase after prepositional phrase pile up next to each other in a sentence until the pressure causes the sentence to jump the track. In the resulting wreck, both the meaning of the sentence and the readers' attention may be lost.

Prepositions are those little words that convey the relationships between other words in the sentence — "of," "in," "at," "before," "after," "for," and so on.[8] While prepositions do serve a grammatical purpose and must be used in many sentences, most writers could probably eliminate half the prepositional phrases in their writing, considerably shortening many sentences. The presence of more than two or three prepositions signals that a sentence probably needs editing. Consider this sentence: "At this point in time, the burden is on the plaintiff to support the motion for summary judgment before the court." The sentence contains five prepositional phrases (phrases beginning with "at," "in," "on," "for," and "before") and, at twenty-one words, is probably twice as long as it needs to be. Revised to eliminate prepositional phrases, the sentence, now at nine words, could read, "Now, the plaintiff must support the summary judgment motion."

---

8. For a complete list of prepositions, see Guide to Grammar and Writing, http://grammar.ccc.commnet.edu/grammar/preposition_list.htm.

The preposition "of" is a particular offender. "Of" phrases often show possession, which can be shown more simply with a possessive noun. For instance, "the ruling of the court" should become "the court's ruling," and "the testimony of the defendant" should become "the defendant's testimony."

Nominalizations also signal wordiness. Nominalization are verbs turned into nouns, and they can usually be recognized by their "-ion," "-ment," "-ance," and "-ity" endings. For instance, "determine" is a verb, but "determination" is a noun; "assess" is a verb, but "assessment" is a noun. So compare the following sentences: "The court made a determination that the evidence was admissible," and "The court determined that the evidence was admissible." The first sentence contains ten words, while the second sentence contains only eight. In fact, the sentence could probably be further revised down to five words: "The court admitted the evidence." If legal writers cut every sentence by twenty to fifty percent, and thus reduced the total word count in their documents by that percentage, their readers could probably go home an hour early.

Eliminate unnecessary passive voice. Unnecessary passive verb use also results in wordy, less effective sentences. A passive verb shows a state of being rather than an action, for instance "the car is red." Sometimes, a writer needs to show a state of being, in which case a passive verb is appropriate. In other cases, however, writers use passive verb when a more effective, direct, and usually less wordy active verb would be the better choice.

Forms of the verb "to be" — "is," "was," "were," "are," "be," and "being" — signal passive voice. For instance, notice the passive verbs in this sentence: "The no-fault rule **is** the more recent rule **being applied** by most jurisdictions in divorce actions." Both "is" and "being applied" are passive. The main subject, "most jurisdictions," does not appear until about half way through the sentence, so the reader cannot immediately identify the actor. And the passive verb phrase "is … being applied by" requires four words. The sentence can be shortened and revised for easier mental processing if the actor appears early in the sentence, followed immediately by an active verb:

"Currently, most jurisdictions [actor] apply [active verb] the no-fault rule in divorce actions."

Sometimes the actor in a sentence may be unknown, making passive voice appropriate, e.g., "The money was stolen." Also, sometimes good advocacy requires the writer to avoid pointing out the actor in a particular sentence. For instance, if you're writing as an advocate for the defendant, you may want to avoid saying "Defendant stole the money," so instead you can say, "The money was stolen." In the end, however, during the editing process you should make sure that any passive verb use is deliberate.

Check sentences for basic grammar and usage errors. During the editing process, you should also read for grammar and usage errors. Although a multitude of such errors are possible, here are some common problems that you should specifically look for.

First, make sure the subject, verb, and object in every sentence make sense together and are not "mismatched." For instance, this sentence contains a subject-verb-object mismatch: "The mature minor doctrine, which was adopted by the court to allow minors to refuse or consent to medical treatment without their parents' consent, held that Ms. Morrissey could refuse treatment for scoliosis." This sentence is not technically correct because a "doctrine" cannot "hold" anything. The subject, verb, and object are not compatible. A revised sentence would read, "The court of appeals, which adopted the mature minor doctrine to allow minors to refuse or consent to medical treatment without their parents' consent, held that Ms. Morrissey could refuse treatment for scoliosis."

Second, make sure modifiers are properly placed and modify the right word or phrase. For instance, "The judge reminded defendant he was under oath at the October 21 hearing," contains a misplaced modifier. Readers cannot tell whether the judge did the reminding at the October 21 hearing, or if the defendant was under oath at the October 21 hearing. Depending on which is true, the sentence could be revised in either of the following ways: "At the October 21 hearing, the judge reminded defendant that he was under oath," or "The judge reminded the defendant that, at the October 21 hearing, he was under oath."

Third, because legal analysis often involves analogical argument, sentences that make comparisons appear frequently in legal writing. When editing a comparison sentence, be sure the sentence compares like things: person to person; court to court; case to case. For instance, the following sentence makes an inapt comparison: "Like *Garfield*, Smith threw the ball after the play was over." Because "*Garfield*" is italicized, it necessarily refers to a case, not a person. But logically, a case cannot be compared to a person. The sentence could be revised in either of the following ways: "Like the defendant in *Garfield*, Smith threw the ball after the play was over," or "Like Garfield, Smith threw the ball after the play was over."

Fourth, check parallelism in all sentences that include phrases in a series, and make sure each phrase employs the same subject-verb-object construction. For instance, the phrases in this sentence are not parallel: "Ms. Lee acted as an attorney because she counseled Ms. Smith on her rights, spoke with the landlord about those rights, and her work was not merely preparatory in nature." The last clause in the series should be edited to start with an active, past tense verb, like the first two: "Ms. Lee acted as an attorney because she **counseled** Ms. Smith her on her rights, **spoke** with the landlord about those rights, and **performed** work that was not merely preparatory in nature."

Fifth, avoid simplifiable jargon. First, look for legal jargon: Latin words and phrases like "arguendo" and "inter alia"; bad usage habitual to the legal profession, like "said" used as a substitute for the article "the"; and unnecessarily stuffy words like "hereinafter" and "heretofore." Then look for regular English jargon: multi-syllable words and multi-word phrases that can be replaced with simpler language. For instance, the following sentence can be simplified considerably: "Assuming, arguendo, that the aforementioned plaintiff was aware of the attendant risks of being a patron at a sporting event...." The better sentence is, "Even if the plaintiff knew the risks of going to a baseball game...."

Move citations out of textual sentences. Sentences that begin with citations are hard to read because so much information must be processed before readers have any idea what the sentence is about. For instance, in the following sentence readers must wade half-way through before the main point begins to emerge: "In *Manson v. Braithwaite*, 432 U.S. 98, 113 (1977), the Supreme Court stated that the standard for evaluating eyewitness identification evidence is fairness as required by the Due Process Clause." Revised, the sentence (and corresponding citation sentence) would look like this: "The standard for evaluating eyewitness identification evidence is fairness as required by the Due Process Clause. *Manson v. Braithwaite*, 432 U.S. 98, 113 (1977)." This sentence is easier to read and understand because it focuses immediately on the main substantive idea rather than on the citation.

Use a desk reference to answer questions. A desk reference can provide comprehensive information on writing issues relevant to legal writing, from writing mechanics to document design. A good desk reference will include a thorough index, which can be used to access information on particular issues. Several excellent legal writing desk references are currently on the market and are listed in the additional resources section at the end of this chapter.

But remember that the desk reference is only as good as its user. That is, you need to know yourself as a writer, and thus know when to consult the desk reference. If the correct usage of "affect" and "effect" always confounds you, take the time to look these words up before you use them. If the correct forms of the verbs "lie" and "lay" have always eluded you, consult a reference if you encounter these verbs during the editing process. It's a good idea to keep a running list of your own personal grammar and usage demons, and then review the list and the relevant rules before you begin the final editing process.

If a writing question arises but you have not yet acquired a desk reference, try finding an answer on a legal writing or general writing web site. For instance, you can access the Government Printing Office *Style Manual*, which is a widely used English usage manual, on the GPO website.[9] Purdue University and the Univer-

---

9. *See* U.S. Government Printing Office Style Manual, http://www.gpo access.gov/stylemanual/index.html.

sity of North Carolina offer comprehensive general writing advice in online writing labs, as do many other universities.[10] Other sites can be located through a Google search, but be careful to choose reputable sites—like those connected to a school or university—so you can confidently depend on the advice.

Proofreading

Spell checking programs do not catch all errors, and in fact miss many embarrassing ones.[11] The computer cannot tell the difference between "from" and "form," "trial" and "trail," or "statute" and "statue," for example. Grammar checking programs can also steer you in the wrong direction. For instance, a grammar checker suggested to one writer that the sentence "The search function **has been** done for a couple of days" should be revised to read "The search function **has not been** done for a couple of days." It will indeed be quite a day when a computer can catch us in the act of lying, but those days are not upon us yet. In the meantime, while you should certainly run a spell checking program on every document you write, and may also want to run a grammar checking program, do not depend on these tools alone to catch your errors.

---

10. *See e.g.,* The Purdue Online Writing Lab, http://owl.cnglish.purduc. edu/; The Writing Center, University of North Carolina at Chapel Hill, http://www.unc.edu/depts/wcweb/.

11. Word has it that a few years ago, an attorney at a noted law firm prepared a congratulatory letter to send to the recently elected president of a prestigious legal organization. The letter was written, printed, and signed before someone noticed that in the first line of the letter, the writer congratulated the recipient on his "recent erection."

Figure 1. Example of Faulty Grammar Checker Results

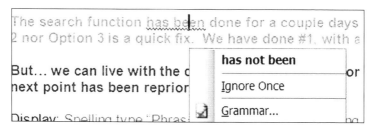

If you are not a skilled proofreader, applying some of the following techniques may help you improve your proofreading results.

1. Use a ruler or piece of colored paper to help you go line by line through the document.
2. Read the document aloud.
3. Proofread after you have put the document aside for a day or two so you have a fresh perspective.
4. Read it both on the computer screen and on a printed copy.
5. Proof for different types of errors with each pass (e.g., spelling, citations, line spaces, headings).
6. Keep a list of your most common errors (like typing "form" instead of "from") and run a "search and replace" just for those words.
7. Read the document backwards.
8. Read once to check only proper names.
9. Read once to check all two letter words for correctness (they are often interchanged, e.g. "of" and "or").
10. Take a short walking break to revive your attention.

Proofreading skills can be learned. As a judicial clerk, you will proofread documents that will set the writing standard for the legal community. Thus, it is worth putting time into developing excellent proofreading skills.

5.5 Editing Tables

Problem Words and Phrases

Nominalizations	Instead:
Enter into an agreement	Agree
Contains a provision	Provides
Have a collision	Collide
File a motion	Move
Give consideration to	Consider
Had knowledge that	Knew
Make an assumption	Assume
Make a decision	Decide
Places emphasis on	Emphasizes
It is a requirement of the statute that	The statute requires

Throatclearing:	Instead: Eliminate
It is interesting to note that	
It is important to remember that	
It seems that	
It is clear/obvious that	
It is widely understood that	
As noted above	
As to	
With respect to	

Wordy phrases:	Instead:
At the time that	When
At the point in time when	When
As a result of	Because
By reason of the fact that	Because
Due to the fact that	Because
For a period of one week	For one week
For the purpose of	To
Inasmuch as	Since
In many cases	Often
In order to	To
It was formerly the case that	Formerly
Previous to	Before
That was a case where	There

Intensifiers	Instead: Eliminate
Clearly	
Extremely	
Obviously	
Quite	
Very	

Suggested Connector Words and Phrases

To Show Additional Information on Same Topic:	To Show Analogy/Comparison:
Further	In comparison
In addition	In contrast
Additionally	Analogously
Also	Likewise
In fact	Nevertheless
Moreover	Although
First, second, third ...	However
Besides	On the other hand
Next	Similarly
Finally	Whereas
And	
To Show Causation:	**To Introduce an Example:**
Because	For example
Due to	For instance
Since	Specifically
Therefore	In particular
Thus	To illustrate
So	Namely
Accordingly	
Consequently	
Hence	
To Introduce an Alternative Point:	**To Emphasize:**
But	Indeed
Contrary to	In fact
Although	Of course
Conversely	Actually
Alternatively	
On the other hand	
However	
On the contrary	
To Signal a Concession:	
Although	
Even though	
No doubt	
Granted that	

To Signal a Conclusion:	To Show a Time relationship:
Therefore	After
In conclusion	Afterward
Hence	Before
Thus	At last
To conclude	Currently
In the end	During
In sum	Now
In short	Recently
As a result	Subsequently
	Then
	Later
	Meanwhile
	Previously
	Next
	Formerly
	Eventually
	Initially
	Earlier
	Until
	Since
	Thereafter

5.6 Additional Resources

Suggested Legal Writing Desk References, Usage Guides, and Style Books

Deborah C. Bouchoux, *Aspen Handbook for Legal Writers: A Practical Reference* (2d ed. 2009)

Anne Enquist and Laurel Currie Oates, *Just Writing: Grammar, Punctuation, and Style for the Legal Writer* (3d ed. 2009)

Bryan A. Garner, *The Redbook: A Manual on Legal Style* (2d ed. 2006)

Bryan A. Garner, *A Dictionary of Modern Legal Usage* (2d ed. 1995)

Margaret Shertzer, *The Elements of Grammar* (1996)

Richard C. Wydick, *Plain English for Lawyers* (5th ed. 2005)

Other Reading

Thomas Gibbs Gee, *A Few of Wisdom's Idiosyncrasies and a Few of Ignorance's: A Judicial Style Sheet*, 1 Scribes J. of Legal Writing 55 (1990)

Abner J. Mikva, *For Whom Judges Write*, 61 S. Cal. L. Rev. 1357 (1988)

Richard A. Posner, *Judges' Writing Styles (And Do They Matter?)*, 62 U. Chi. L. Rev. 1421 (1995)

Abby F. Rudzin & Lisa Greenfield Pearl, *Ten Brief-Writing Don'ts—The Judicial Clerk's Perspective*, 85 Ill. B.J. 285 (1997)

Patricia M. Wald, *"How I Write" Essays*, 4 Scribes J. Legal Writing 55 (1993)

Patricia M. Wald, *The Rhetoric of Results and the Results of Rhetoric: Judicial Writings*, 62 U. Chi. L. Rev. 1371 (1995)

Chapter 6

Citation Refresher

Citation—the very word can strike fear in the hearts of law students and practitioners alike. Or, it can bore law students and practitioners to death. Perhaps it is this combination of fear and loathing that results in a certain lack of citation mastery among practicing attorneys.[1] While less-than-perfect citation might be commonplace among attorneys, it is not an option for a judge. Now that you are a judicial clerk, it is not an option for you, either.

A judge will not likely edit citation format when reading documents you draft. Judges do not have time to comb through citation manuals looking for scintillating reading about comma placement—that is why you were hired. The judge trusts you to ensure that the content and format of all citations coming out of chambers is perfect.

In addition, it is your duty to ensure that citation does its "job." Citation lets readers know what sources support the judge's legal decisions and makes it possible for readers to find the sources. Legal readers are accustomed to having sources cited in specific ways, and this familiarity helps readers find sources with ease. If your ci-

---

1. *See, e.g., Gooch v. Tudor,* 674 S.E.2d 331, 338 (Ga. Ct. App. 2009) (holding that claim was abandoned when party's brief did not contain citations to legal authority or the record); *Chicagoland Chamber of Commerce v. Pappas,* 880 N.E.2d 1105, 1132–33 (Ill. App. Ct. 2007) (same); *Espitia v. Fouche,* 758 N.W.2d 224 at *3 n.5 (Wis. Ct. App. 2008) (unpublished table decision) (sanctioning attorney $100 for citing a case using the docket number as the reporter citation, the wrong party names, and the wrong district court).

tation is not where it is expected or is not in a format that is expected, readers will be confused and the citation will not have served its purpose.[2]

6.1 Judges' Preferences and Common Citation Systems

No matter what court you work in, one of the first things you need to learn is what citation system your judge wants you to use. In addition, you will need to know the judge's personal citation preferences, which may differ from the conventional citation rules. While judges typically tell their clerks they want citations to comply with certain citation systems, an assessment of a particular judge's decisions might reveal the judge's own stylistic preferences that do not strictly comport with those rules. For example, a judge might not want dates in statute citations or may never abbreviate the word "Commonwealth," even though the chosen citation system contains an abbreviation for the word. Since all writing that comes out of chambers must be in the judge's voice, you should adopt the judge's idiosyncrasies when drafting documents for the judge.[3] In most instances, these slight variations will not change the effectiveness of the citation. However, if a variation makes a citation hard to understand or, worse yet, incorrect, you must change the citation because your job is

---

2. Examples of specific citation formats are beyond the scope of this book. The additional resources listed at the end of this chapter include citation manuals and books that explain citation format and placement and help legal writers effectively use citation manuals.

3. *See* Massey Mayo Case & Jill E. Tompkins, *A Guide for Tribal Court Law Clerks and Judges* 45 (2007), www.colorado.edu/iece/docs/Thompson/Final_version_Guide.pdf (explaining that it is important for judges to communicate any unique abbreviations they use to their new clerks).

to clearly communicate the judge's decisions, and a citation's job is to let readers easily find sources. An incorrect or confusing citation could muddle the judge's message or result in negative attention from a panel of appellate judges. If you find yourself in this situation, explain to the judge why you are forsaking chambers' citation style.

The Bluebook and the *ALWD Citation Manual*

The two most well-known national citation systems are *The Bluebook* citation system and the Association of Legal Writing Directors citation system. Each system has its own manual: *The Bluebook: A Uniform System of Citation*, and the *ALWD Citation Manual: A Professional System of Citation*.[4] *The Bluebook* was first published in 1926 by Erwin Griswold, a Harvard law student.[5] *The Bluebook* is currently in its eighteenth edition and is published by the Harvard Law Review Association. *The ALWD Manual* was first published in 2000, and is published by Aspen Publishers.[6] The *ALWD Manual* is now in its third edition. Both manuals are scheduled to release new editions in early 2010. In the following discussion, references to *The Bluebook* are to the Eighteenth Edition and references to the *ALWD Manual* are to the Third Edition.

The Bluebook was the first legal citation system and, although many jurisdictions have not officially adopted it, *The Bluebook* is still the default for most courts. However, an increasing number of jurisdictions are adopting the *ALWD Manual*. The Association of Legal Writing Directors maintains a web site that lists jurisdictions

---

4. *The Bluebook: A Uniform System of Citation* (Columbia Law Review Ass'n et al. eds., 18th ed. 2005) [hereinafter "*The Bluebook*" or "*Bluebook*"]; ALWD & Darby Dickerson, *ALWD Citation Manual* (3d ed. 2006) [hereinafter "*ALWD Manual*"].

5. Carol M. Bast & Susan Harrell, *Has The Bluebook Met Its Match? The ALWD Citation Manual*, 92 Law Lib. J. 337, 339 (2000).

6. *ALWD Manual, supra* note 4.

that have adopted the *ALWD Manual*.[7] If your court is not listed
on the Association's web site, you are likely working in either a
"*Bluebook* jurisdiction" or a "local rules jurisdiction." In jurisdictions that have adopted local citation rules, the local rules trump
both national systems' rules. *The Bluebook* and the *ALWD Manual*
include information about local rules,[8] and the judge or another
clerk should have information about any unique citation systems
used in your jurisdiction.

Neutral Citation Format

Some states require the use of *public domain citations* or *neutral
citations* for citing cases. The terms are interchangeable, but *neutral citation* is the more common term and is used in this discussion. Neutral citation format is designed to provide broad access
to court decisions without the need for access to printed reporters
or commercial electronic research databases. In neutral citation jurisdictions, the courts assign citation numbers to cases and typically number all the paragraphs in orders or opinions. This allows
readers to access orders and opinions free of charge through the
court's web site and to pinpoint cite to selected paragraphs. States
that have adopted neutral citation systems post new court decisions
online so that they are accessible for free. Many of these states are
building up their electronic archives of older cases so that more
and more cases are accessible with neutral citations.

If a state entry in *Bluebook* Table T.1 begins with the following
language, that state has adopted a neutral citation format: "Public
Domain Citation Format: [State name] has adopted a public domain
citation format for cases after [date]. The format is: [example]." If
a state entry in the *ALWD Manual* Appendix 1 answers the ques-

---

7. Association of Legal Writing Directors, ALWD Publications: Adop-
tions (2009), http://www.alwd.org/publications/adoptions.html#A.
8. *The Bluebook, supra* note 4, at 27 tbl.BT.2, 193 tbl.T.1; *ALWD Manual, supra* note 4, at 359 app. 1, 409 app. 2.

tion "Neutral citation rules?" with "Yes," that state has adopted a neutral citation format. Most states that have adopted neutral citation rules still require parallel citation to a published reporter. Thus, reporters and electronic case law databases continue to be important to legal writers.

Be aware that just because a jurisdiction has adopted neutral citation format for cases, that does not mean you can toss out your citation manuals. The manuals include rules for citing more than just cases, and you will need to rely on whatever manual the court or judge has adopted for the rest of your citations.

The Bluebook and the *ALWD Manual* are not updated on predictable schedules, so it is important to look at your state court web site or ask the judge if your jurisdiction has recently adopted neutral citation rules. All state court web addresses are located on the National Center for State Courts web site[9] and at the beginning of individual state entries in *The Bluebook* (Table T.1).

6.2 Using *The Bluebook*, the *ALWD Manual*, and Other Resources

The Bluebook and the *ALWD Manual* do not vary greatly in their citation rules for court documents, the type of documents you will be drafting for the judge. If you are familiar with *The Bluebook*, you may not notice any difference in most of your citations if you must switch to the *ALWD Manual*, or vice versa. The key is to double-check. Although the general format of many citations is fairly consistent between the two systems, there are variations in abbreviations for case names, court parenthetical details, and book and treatise citations, among other things. No matter what national ci-

9. National Center for State Courts, Court Web Sites (2009), http://www.ncsconline.org/D_KIS/info_court_web_sites.html.

tation system you are familiar with, it should not be difficult to become familiar with the other one, if you must. The Association of Legal Writing Directors web site contains helpful charts that compare *The Bluebook* and *ALWD Manual* rules.[10] If you must learn a new citation system, you should bookmark the links to these useful charts.

Citing Non-Legal Materials

You may be called upon to cite non-legal materials and, although both *The Bluebook* and the *ALWD Manual* contain rules for citing non-legal materials like books and web sites, if you cannot find a citation rule that applies to your source, check *The Chicago Manual of Style.*[11] *The Chicago Manual of Style* is often the back-up resource that law journals and other legal publications refer to for citing unusual sources and is mentioned as a reliable style manual in *Law Clerk Handbook: A Handbook for Law Clerks to Federal Judges.*[12] Thus, the citation style will not be completely unknown to legal readers.

Citing International Materials

In our global economy, disputes increasingly involve international documents and materials that you may have never had to

---

10. ALWD-Bluebook Comparison Charts, http://www.alwd.org/PDF/ CitationManual_3rd/ALWD-Bluebook%20Comparison%20Charts.pdf; ALWD-Bluebook and Bluebook-ALWD Rule Conversion Charts, http://www.alwd.org/PDF/CitationManual_3rd/ALWDBluebook%20andBlue bookALWD%20RuleConversion%20ChartsALWDBLUEBOOKRUL.pdf.

11. *The Chicago Manual of Style* (15th ed. 2003).

12. Federal Judicial Center, *Law Clerk Handbook: A Handbook for Law Clerks to Federal Judges,* 2 (Sylvan A. Sobel, ed., 2d ed. 2007), *available at* http://www.fjc.gov/public/pdf.nsf/lookup/lawclhbk.pdf/$file/law clhbk.pdf.

cite before. *Bluebook* Rules 20 and 21, *Bluebook* Table T.2, and
ALWD Manual Rule 21 address citing international sources.[13]

Citing Tribal Materials

If you are a tribal judicial clerk, you may be called upon to cite
sources of Indian law for which there are no rules in either *The
Bluebook* or the *ALWD Manual*.[14] If you must cite a source and cannot find a rule in any of the usual places you would look, the following suggestions may help you decide how to cite the source.

First, ask the judge or look at the judge's previous writings to
see if there are established chambers' rules for citing the source. As
long as the judge's citations are consistent and helpful to readers,
they should be used in all documents coming out of chambers. Second, look at published tribal court opinions to see if previous courts
have cited the same or similar sources and then use those citations
as templates for your citation.[15] Third, many federal courts decide
issues of Indian law, and those decisions can be found in the West
Reporter system that you are undoubtedly familiar with. You can
model your citation on citations to the same or similar sources
found in those cases. Fourth, if you cannot find a good example,
pick the most analogous rule from the citation system the judge
generally uses and adapt the rule as needed for your materials, keeping in mind that the primary goal of citation is to help readers find
the cited source. Once you have adopted a citation format for a
source, use that format consistently.

---

13. You might also want to consult *The Inter-American Citator: A Guide
to Uniform Citation of Inter-American Sources for Writers and Practitioners*,
39 U. Miami Inter-Am. L. Rev. 275 (2008).

14. Although you might be called upon to find the best ways to cite
most Indian law, some relevant citation rules do exist. *See The Bluebook,
supra* note 4, at 241–42 tbl.T.1 (citation rules for the Navajo Nation and
the Oklahoma Native Americans); *ALWD Manual, supra* note 4, at 401
app. 1 (citation rules for the Navajo Nation).

15. *See* Case & Tompkins, *supra* note 3, at 36–41.

6.3 How Judicial Citation Differs from Law Review Citation

Most judicial clerks have had law review or law journal experience. The attention to detail and citation expertise learned while working on journals are important qualities judges look for when hiring clerks. However, there are differences between law review citation and judicial citation.

Scholarly writing is all about the footnotes. The more footnotes, the better. The longer the footnotes, the better. The more string cites in the footnotes, the better. This is not so with judicial writing. As discussed in subsequent chapters, you will rarely use footnotes in orders and opinions. String cites are also uncommon in judicial writing.

The primary audience for law review articles is law professors. The value of an article is often assessed by the quality and quantity of the sources cited in the footnotes. Academic authors provide comprehensive research that allows readers to build on the ideas expressed in articles and to take the next steps in scholarly, and often esoteric, discussions.

As discussed in Chapter Five, the audiences for judicial documents are more varied than the audience for law review articles. Attorneys involved in the case; attorneys reading the decision in the future; judges reviewing the decision for error; and members of the public, including the parties and law students, want to know what the judge decided and why. And they don't want to wade through fourteen string-cited cases and synthesize all the holdings to figure out what authority the judge relied on. A judicial clerk's responsibility is to find the most recent binding case or the seminal case on the subject and cite that case for the legal proposition at issue. String-citing three cases that all say the same thing is both unhelpful and confusing. Good judicial writing is never confusing.

Three major exceptions exist to the "no string cite rule." The first applies when you want to demonstrate the evolution of the law.

Imagine that you work for a state trial judge who is issuing an order on a motion for summary judgment. You want to cite *Celotex Corp. v. Catrett*,[16] a United States Supreme Court case establishing that the party seeking summary judgment bears the burden of showing that there is no disputed issue of material fact. Then you want to cite the case from your state supreme court that adopted this standard for cases arising under state law. This would result in a short and helpful two-case string cite.[17]

The second exception applies when a judge decides a case of first impression in your jurisdiction. The judge will need to explain the arguments on both sides of the issue and will likely want to show readers how many courts have adopted each of the competing views. In this situation, string cites will be necessary to show the weight of support for each view.

The final exception applies when a judge is deciding a case based, at least in part, on public policy. When judges decide cases based on public policy, they often cite several different types of sources for support. Judges may rely not only on legal precedent, but also on law review articles, amicus briefs, and non-legal sources such as psychological studies.[18]

Thus, while law review and journal experience might have been beneficial as you sought your job as a judicial clerk, you will need to selectively rely on what you learned in that position when you write for the judge. Rely on your expectation of perfection in citation and the eye for detail you developed cite checking hun-

---

16. 477 U.S. 317, 322–23 (1986).

17. If your judge is opposed to string cites, you can instead cite the state case and use a parenthetical explaining that when the state court made its decision it relied on Supreme Court precedent (assuming, of course, the state court opinion actually cites *Celotex*).

18. *See Brown v. Bd. of Educ.*, 347 U.S. 483, 493–95 (1954) (using evidence of the devastating psychological effects of public school segregation on African American children to support the holding that "in the field of public education the doctrine of 'separate but equal' has no place").

dreds of footnotes. Do not, however, use the documents you draft for the judge as a platform to show off your research skills. A single citation to the binding authority that the judge must follow is more beneficial to readers than a four-case string citation that shows your ability to research outside of the jurisdiction. Such a citation will only confuse busy practitioners and make them feel obligated to read four cases instead of one, something they do not have time for.

Be aware that the "no string cite rule" is merely a rule of thumb. The judge you work for might embrace string cites and might want you to use them when you draft orders and opinions. Obviously, do what the judge wants you to do.

6.4 Citation Basics and Reminders

We assume that readers are familiar with *The Bluebook*, the *ALWD Manual*, or both. As mentioned above, the differences between the two citation systems are not great, but they are important. Thus, as discussed above, the first thing you need to do when hired as a judicial clerk is learn which citation system the judge wants you to use, and become familiar with that system.

As a quick reminder, although *The Bluebook* is called a "uniform" system of citation, it actually contains two different citation systems: one for practitioners (the blue pages) and one for academics (the white pages). The blue pages cross reference the white pages and the white pages make up the majority of the book. If you were on a law review or journal in law school that used *Bluebook* citation format, you are likely very familiar with the white pages, but you must now re-acquaint yourself with the blue pages since judicial documents are considered practitioners' documents. If you worked on a law review or journal that used *ALWD Manual* citation format, and you are working for a judge who wants you to use that manual, you are lucky because the *ALWD Manual* does not differentiate between academic and practitioners' citation format. In that respect, the *ALWD Manual* contains the truly uniform citation system.[19]

As discussed above, the conversion charts on the Association of Legal Writing Directors' web site will be helpful if you must learn a new citation system. Obviously, if you are in a jurisdiction that has its own citation system, you must become familiar with that system.

Citation Placement

Besides citation form and the number of citations you use to support a proposition, you must consider citation placement and citation weight. You should cite the proper legal authority after every sentence in which you state a rule. In addition, at the trial level, you should cite the record for support for every fact that the judge finds, adopts, or discusses. Failure to tell readers where the relevant facts can be found in the record makes appellate review difficult and leaves the decision vulnerable to criticism that the judge did not fully consider all parties' arguments, adopted one party's version of the facts wholesale, or failed to support a decision.[20]

Since appellate courts have definite records before them, they typically do not cite as often as trial level courts. The parties know where they can find the relevant information in the record. Ask your judge how often you should cite in an appellate decision.

---

19. Suzanne E. Rowe, *Linking Citations to Text: Signaling Support,* Or. St. B. Bull., Nov. 2008, at 11, 11.

20. *See Allstate Ins. Co. v. Fisher,* 974 A.2d 1102, 1107–08 (N.J. Super. Ct. App. Div. 2009) (reversing trial court grant of summary judgment because the trial judge failed to cite the record when concluding that there were no genuine issues of material fact in the case, and reasoning that "[n]either the parties nor the appellate court is 'well-served by an opinion devoid of analysis or citation to even a single case'") (citation omitted).

Signals

When citing legal authority, you must let readers know the significance of the authority. Does it directly say what you are telling readers it says? Or, do readers need to make a connection or think about the relationship between the cited material and the subject matter of the sentence to understand how the authority relates to your case? Signals help you communicate this. Signals are those little words that introduce a citation: *see, but see, accord,* etc. They are valuable clues about the weight that should be afforded cited authorities and about the relationships between cited authorities.[21] *Bluebook* Rules B.4 and 1.2–1.4 and *ALWD Manual* Rule 44 address the use of signals. You should become familiar with these rules and use signals liberally.

Quotations

If you quote any material or make changes to quoted material, you must comply with *Bluebook* Rules B.12 and 5 or *ALWD Manual* Rules 47, 48, and 49. Although judicial plagiarism is not something we often think about, judges have a heightened responsibility to properly attribute materials that they quote, whether the quoted language comes from a case, a statute, an exhibit, or a brief. Accurate attribution to party briefs is especially important so that readers know where a recitation of party advocacy ends and the judge's analysis begins. Clerks can ensure that judges avoid controversy if they scrupulously follow the quotation rules.[22]

---

21. *See* Rowe, *supra* note 19, at 11–12 (explaining how to use the most common signals under both *Bluebook* and *ALWD Manual* rules); Charles R. Calleros, *Legal Method and Writing* 294–301 (5th ed. 2006) (same); Bryan A. Garner, *The Redbook: A Manual on Legal Style* § 8.16 (2d ed. 2002) (same).

22. *See* Joyce J. George, *Judicial Opinion Writing Handbook* 707–27 (5th ed. 2007) (discussing the prospect of judicial plagiarism and the need

6.5 Additional Resources

ALWD & Darby Dickerson, *ALWD Citation Manual* (3d ed. 2006)

Linda J. Barris, *Understanding and Mastering the Bluebook: A Guide for Students and Practitioners* (2007)

The Bluebook: A Uniform System of Citation (Columbia Law Review Ass'n et al. eds., 18th ed. 2005)

Peter W. Martin, *Neutral Citation, Court Web Sites, and Access to Authoritative Case Law*, 99 Law Libr. J. 329 (2007), *available at* http://www.aallnet.org/products/pub_llj_v99n02/2007-19.pdf

Tracy L. McGaugh & Christine Hurt, *Interactive Citation Workbook for ALWD Citation Manual, 2009 Edition* (2009)

Tracy L. McGaugh & Christine Hurt, *Interactive Citation Workbook for The Bluebook: A Uniform System of Citation, 2009 Edition* (2009)

Larry L. Teply, *Legal Writing Citation in a Nutshell* (2008)

---

for proper attribution, and concluding that since judges are not creating literary works, legal plagiarism is not a real possibility). *But see* Gerald Lebovits, Alifya V. Curtin, & Lisa Solomon, *Ethical Judicial Opinion Writing*, 21 Geo. J. Legal Ethics 237, 264–65 (2008) (opining that failure to cite copyrighted sources is judicial plagarism, but noting that "the line becomes blurred" when judges incorporate language from legal briefs into their orders and opinions).

Chapter 7

Drafting Bench Memoranda

Writing bench memos is a primary responsibility of most judicial clerks, particularly appellate court clerks. A bench memo supports the work of a judge by providing objective written analysis of a case or issue, presented in a prescribed format.

Not all judges at the trial court level require their clerks to write bench memos. Many will ask for an oral briefing, followed by a working draft of an opinion or order. But most trial-level judges will at least occasionally require a written work product that will assist them with decision making during the litigation process. In contrast, at the appellate level, clerks will research and write bench memos for almost every case they are assigned.

7.1 How Judges Use Bench Memos

A bench memorandum, like the objective office memorandum taught in most first-year legal writing classes, communicates an objective analysis of the facts and law in a case and recommends a course of action. The audience for a bench memo is either a trial court judge or a panel of appellate-level judges.

Appellate judges use bench memos to help them prepare for oral arguments, and trial judges use bench memos to help them decide motions from the parties. The format and tone of a bench memo are similar to the format and tone of an objective office memorandum. But the purpose of a bench memo goes beyond the purpose of an objective office memo. An office memo aims to help an attorney understand the law in a case and decide how to proceed

given that law. While bench memos similarly help judges understand the law in particular cases and make decisions about those
cases, bench memos must also help judges get past the advocacy
of the parties' briefs so they can reach independent decisions.

To be a useful tool in the decision-making process, the bench
memo must clearly and accurately describe the facts of the case,
the procedural posture, the applicable law, the parties' arguments,
and the clerk's independent analysis of the issues. The memo must
be objective and fair to the parties, but at the same time it must
help the judge test the analysis on both sides of the dispute. Although the clerk will usually be asked to recommend a final resolution in the memo, the memo's purpose is *not* to shift the decision
making to the clerk. Rather, the purpose is to enhance the judge's
own analysis.

Bench memos also help judges reconstruct their thinking about
a case if the case has been set aside for a few days or weeks because
of other work. In this sense, the memo serves as an "information
bank" for which the clerk is the scribe, and that information must
be accurate and complete. Finally, the bench memo will usually be
the template for the court's written order or opinion after a decision has been made. Thus, a well-researched and well-written bench
memo will save the clerk, who will subsequently draft the order or
opinion, significant time later in the process.

Trial and appellate court judges may use bench memos differently.
For instance, a trial court judge with a busy case docket may try to
rule from the bench on as many motions as possible. That judge may
want a fairly simple bench memo that provides a quick picture of
the relevant facts and law. Other trial judges may want more extensive bench memos that will help them evaluate the parties' written submissions on more complicated issues, like those presented
in a summary judgment or JNOV motion.

An appellate judge, on the other hand, usually decides fewer but
more complex cases, and thus devotes more time and attention to
each. That judge almost always needs a complete bench memo that
thoroughly analyzes each issue. Further, in appellate courts, the
bench memo will be read by every member of the panel, usually three

judges in intermediate appellate courts and the full court in state supreme courts, not just the clerk's own judge.

Individual judges may rely on bench memos at different times during the decision-making process. Some judges use the bench memo early in the process to help them develop an overall objective picture of the case. They will then follow up by reading the submissions from the parties, and, if applicable, any lower courts' decisions. If the judge starts the decision-making process by reading the bench memo, thorough and accurate analysis from the clerk is particularly important since the judge's first exposure to the case will leave a lasting impression. An appellate judge may start by reading the lower court's decision, relying on that decision to provide the foundation to the case, and then move on to the parties' submissions to get a picture of each side's argument. The judge will then read the bench memo last, once the facts and arguments are clear in the judge's mind, because it summarizes and evaluates the other materials.

You should check with the judge early in your clerkship about bench memo due date expectations. Meet these expectations meticulously so that all the materials needed to decide a case are available at the appropriate point in the process. In an appellate court, the bench memo should usually be completed at least one week before the panel is scheduled to hear the case. In a trial court, where the pace is generally quicker, the timeline may be shorter.

7.2 Bench Memo Preliminaries

While the process of preparing a bench memo will be fairly uniform from court to court, as a general rule, you should clarify the expectations of the judge you work for and follow the procedures and guidelines established by your particular court. As with most legal writing projects, when writing a bench memo you should expect to spend about half your time pre-writing and half your time drafting, revising, and editing.

Even seasoned judicial clerks sometimes need assistance and advice when preparing a bench memo. When you have questions about bench memo form or procedures, don't hesitate to make use of the human resources available to you, including other clerks, staff attorneys, librarians, and administrative support. Many courts provide guidelines or other resources that explain how to write a bench memo and review other issues like burden of proof and standard of review.

In the pre-writing stage of preparing a bench memo, a clerk must (1) review the procedure that brought the case before the court and determine the burden of proof at the trial level or the standard of review at the appellate level; (2) review the record; (3) formulate the issues for review; (4) review the research performed by the parties and perform independent research; and (5) evaluate the parties' arguments and positions. Some of these steps may involve different considerations in trial courts than in appellate courts. In the following discussion, if the processes for trial and appellate courts differ, they are addressed separately.

Procedure — Trial Court

The trial court clerk should first check that the court has jurisdiction over the case. Most of the time the parties have done this, but you should always make sure. The issue of original jurisdiction will come up most often if you are clerking for a federal judge since the federal courts are courts of limited jurisdiction. The clerk should also note which party has the burden of proof on each issue.

Procedure — Appellate Court

The appellate clerk should check the record to make sure that the issues raised by the parties are appealable. To be appealable, most issues must have been presented to and considered by the trial court and thus preserved for appeal. Generally, with a few exceptions, no new issues may be raised on appeal, and good attorneys will make sure the opposing party complies with this rule. But the clerk should double-check the trial court record and verify that the issues raised and briefed by the parties were raised at the trial court level and preserved for appeal.

The clerk should also check that the controlling jurisdiction's rules of appellate procedure authorize the appeal. Usually, an appeal must be taken from a final judgment entered in the lower court, although most court rules list several other types of actions in the lower court from which an appeal may be taken.[1] A judgment is "entered" either when it is signed by the trial judge or entered on the docket, depending on the jurisdiction. The appeal must be taken within the time period specified by the court rules.[2]

While most questions about the propriety of an appeal will be handled when the case is processed through the clerk of court's office, if you have any doubt about whether an issue was properly preserved below or properly appealed, you should consult a more experienced clerk or a staff attorney.

Standard of Review — Appellate Court

Early in the pre-writing process, an appellate clerk must identify which standard of review applies to the issues raised. Court rules usually require the parties to state the standard of review in their briefs.[3] But you should independently research and identify the applicable standard of review for each issue the parties raise, and you should note whether the parties disagree about the applicable standards. If there is any disagreement, the issue may require further research.

The standard of review dictates how the judge can approach particular kinds of issues. Because cases are often resolved based on the standard of review, you need to understand what standard applies in the case under review and then must use that standard to frame the analysis.

---

1. *See* Fed. R. App. P. 4.
2. *See* Fed. R. App. P. 3.
3. *See* Fed. R. App. P. 28.

In general, three standards of review apply to issues raised in an appellate court. First, upon review of factual determinations, an appellate court applies the *clearly erroneous* standard.[4] This standard applies to questions about who did what, where, and when; questions of intent and motive; and questions of ultimate fact, such as negligence.

Under this standard, which establishes an extremely narrow framework within which a court must work, the reviewing court must give substantial deference to the lower court decision maker. After reviewing the evidence, the court cannot reverse unless it is "left with the definite and firm conviction that a mistake has been committed."[5] The reviewing court cannot "reverse a lower court's finding of fact simply because [it] 'would have decided the case differently.' "[6] Consequently, appellate courts rarely reverse factual findings. Because this standard of review is very difficult to overcome, questions of this type are infrequently raised on appeal.

Second, legal issues, particularly constitutional and statutory interpretation issues, and issues about whether summary judgment was appropriately granted, are reviewed *de novo*.[7] Under the de novo standard, the reviewing court can independently decide the issue and need not defer to the trial court at all. These types of issues are usually described as being "a matter of law," but the standard often applies to mixed questions of fact and law, such as whether the facts as determined at trial meet a certain legal standard.

Finally, the *abuse of discretion* standard applies to discovery issues and to most courtroom management issues, such as motions for attorney's fees and scheduling motions.[8] This is an intermedi-

---

4. *See* Fed. R. Civ. P. 52.
5. *Anderson v. Bessemer City*, 470 U.S. 564, 573 (1985).
6. *Easley v. Cromartie*, 532 U.S. 234, 242 (2001) (quoting *Anderson*, *supra* note 5, at 573).
7. *See Salve Regina Coll. v. Russell*, 499 U.S. 225, 232 (1991); *Celotex Corp. v. Catrett*, 477 U.S. 317, 327 (1986).
8. *See Pierce v. Underwood*, 487 U.S. 552, 559 (1988).

ate standard, under which the trial court has significant latitude to make decisions. Appellate courts infrequently reverse these discretionary decisions. To reverse a trial judge's decision, the reviewing court must be firmly convinced that the trial judge acted arbitrarily or made a clear error.

Once you have established the proper standard of review for each issue in the case, you should consistently view the analysis of the issues through the appropriate lens. For instance, if the legal issue is whether attorney's fees were properly awarded in a case, you should frame the issue and conduct the analysis in terms of whether the trial court abused its discretion in awarding attorney's fees. If a factual issue is raised on appeal, you must review the record to evaluate whether there is any evidence to support the factual conclusion reached in the trial court. If there is, under the clearly erroneous standard of review, you should not recommend reversal.

Facts — Trial and Appellate Courts

Once you confirm that the case is properly before the court, you must review the relevant sections of the record or transcript and all supporting documents, like affidavits, to develop a complete and accurate picture of the facts. In the trial court, sources of facts will include the documents in the trial court file, any trial exhibits, transcripts from previous hearings, and your own notes from hearings. In the appellate court, the facts must originate in the record from the trial court, including transcripts. Relevant excerpts from the record may be reproduced in the appendices filed with the parties' briefs.

The judge usually does not have time to review the entire record independently to check the parties' characterizations of the facts, but will instead rely on the clerk to do this important task. Thus, you should devote plenty of time and care to reviewing the facts before putting them into written form in the bench memo.

To get a factual overview, read the parties' briefs or motion papers, including appendices, and any findings of fact made by the trial court. Next, check the facts cited in the parties' submissions against the record. Any factual inconsistencies should be noted and raised later in the bench memo. Factual disputes or inconsistencies may be raised in footnotes, although footnotes should be used sparingly in general.

Issue Formulation — Trial Court

Trial court clerks should read the parties' briefs and other submissions to get an idea of what is actually at issue in the case. At the trial court level, the issues can be messy. Parties often try to get a "big bang for their buck" out of a motion hearing, so you may need to address several different motions in one bench memo.

Additionally, the parties may frame the issues differently. If the parties disagree on how the issues are framed, you will need to frame the issues for the judge. You may have to do independent research to decide which version of the issues is correct. And, even after doing the research, you may decide that neither party formulated the issues properly and that a different formulation is appropriate. If you reframe the issues or adopt one version of the issues over another, make sure to tell the judge what you did and why you did it.

Trial-level law clerks must also be on the lookout for issues that the parties missed or peripheral issues that are implicated by the parties' briefs. If you think the parties completely failed to address an issue that is actually raised in their briefs, it is your job to research the issue and alert the judge to it.

Issue Formulation — Appellate Court

To formulate the issue statements, an appellate clerk should first review the trial court decision and the briefs to evaluate whether the court and the parties framed the issues consistently. The issues stated in the parties' preliminary statements should be consistent with the issues actually argued in the briefs. If there is any disagreement about the issues raised, you should evaluate the record to determine the actual issues raised by the appeal.

While new issues may not be raised by clerks, you may modify the issues for the bench memo if you disagree with the parties' formulation of the issues or if the trial court and the parties disagree on the issues. But if this happens, somewhere in the bench memo you should alert the judge or judges hearing the case to the discrepancy.

Research and Evaluation — Trial and Appellate Courts

Because a bench memo is *not* a mere summary of the parties' arguments, the clerk's next job is to independently research and analyze the issues in the case. Only rarely will the parties' submissions fully and accurately explain the governing law. And in fact, often the hardest part of writing a bench memo is getting past the advocacy of the briefs and deciding what the case is really about.

As discussed in Chapter Four, if you are not already familiar with the particular area of law relevant to the case, you should first get an overview by reading a hornbook, encyclopedia, or other secondary authority. While law school courses provided you with a broad foundation in all areas of the law, most issues addressed in bench memos will require you to review the specific law that applies to the particular case. Once you have gained a general understanding of the law, review the cases cited by the parties and, if applicable, the trial court. Finally, you must independently research the issues.

As you read cases during the research process, you should identify "big picture" patterns in the law that may be relevant to the decision, and you should evaluate whether the law in the specific area is changing, whether the language or reasoning seems to change from case to case, and whether identifiable policies underlie decisions in this area. It's your job to add an objective viewpoint to the case; accordingly, the judge will expect you to exercise independent judgment when evaluating case law.

7.3 Bench Memo Structure

The format of a bench memo is similar to the objective memo format taught in most first-year legal writing courses. While the particulars will vary from court to court, most bench memos will include six key sections: (1) caption, (2) procedural statement and history, (3) facts, (4) issues, (5) analysis, and (6) recommendations. The specific names of these sections and the general format may vary from court to court. A bench memo may be anywhere from a few pages to several dozen pages in length, depending on the particular issues raised in the case. Remember that the judge is a busy person, so the bench memo should only be as long as necessary to convey the relevant information.

Most courts keep a repository of bench memos that new clerks can rely on as samples. Before writing a bench memo for a particular judge, review some sample memos written by other clerks in the judge's chambers and model the memo on the samples.

Caption

The caption sets out all the identifying information about the case, including the usual "To, From" memo heading, the case title, the court in which the case will be heard, and the attorneys on the case. The caption may also include any scheduled hearing dates and a brief statement identifying the type of case, e.g., "no-fault insurance" or "criminal." Generally, courts will have standard case captions and, as a clerk, you need only follow a pre-set form.

Procedural Statement and History

The procedural statement and history should describe what procedural steps have led to this particular issue (in a trial court) or what happened in the court below (in an appellate court). It should include specific dates so the judge can understand how the procedural steps relate to each other chronologically.

Facts

The facts section should be objective and absolutely supported by the record. Only the facts relevant to the issues before the court and the facts necessary to understanding the context should be included. Further, all facts included in this section must be checked against the record, and if any facts are disputed, misstated by the parties, or contradicted by conflicting testimony, the clerk should point this out.

You will need to comb through the exhibits and other supporting materials to check that the parties' submissions actually support the propositions for which they are cited. For example, a party may cite one line of a deposition as support for a proposition. However, a thorough review of the entire section of the deposition may reveal that, when taken in context, the line does not actually support the party's argument. It is a judicial clerk's job to find these discrepancies and flag them for the judge. (Opposing counsel should have already done this for you, but that may not always be the case.)

If the parties agree on the facts, the facts section may be quite brief. Sometimes, it works best to draft the facts section of the bench memo last, after it's clear what facts were important to the analysis.

Issues

When drafting the issues, frame the questions objectively and specifically. In an appellate bench memo, the issue statements should incorporate the standard of review. For example, "Was Mr. Smith negligent?" should become "Was the jury's verdict that Mr. Smith was negligent clearly erroneous when he ...?"

Analysis

The heart of the bench memo is the analysis section. It should explain the applicable law and the parties' arguments, and provide an independent analysis of the issues. A bench memo written for an appellate judge should also explain the trial court's analysis and should take the standard of review into account. The analysis should be specific and focused, and it should apply the law to the facts of the case to be decided. It should not read like a law review article or historical treatise. Rather, it should be tailored to help the judge solve a problem.

As a starting point, you should use IRAC to organize the discussion of individual issues. Like other legal readers, the judge needs to know first what the issue is, second which law applies, next how that law applies to the facts of the case, and finally, what the writer concludes. In a bench memo, as opposed to an office memo, the "A" section, or analysis section, should explain both the arguments the parties make and your independent analysis of the issue. Multiple-issue bench memos will contain multiple IRACs. In more complex discussions that contain multiple IRACs, use subheadings or other visual rhetoric to help readers follow the organization. See Chapter Five for more discussion of organization.

Recommendations

The recommendations section comprises a few sentences that set out your conclusions about how the case should be decided. Most importantly, this recommendation should be based on your own thinking about the case. A judge truly appreciates a clerk who will take charge of a case and offer an honest, thoughtful, and thorough analysis. If the case is too close to call, the recommendations section should say so. Ultimately, your job is not to decide the case, but instead to give the judge the information needed to make a considered decision.

All clerks occasionally make mistakes and off-base recommendations in bench memos. In the end, remember that your value as a clerk is gauged not by your "batting record" for making the "right" recommendation, but by the thought, care, and professionalism you bring to the decision-making process.

7.4 Revising and Polishing the Bench Memo

As discussed in Chapter Five, writing excellence should be a top priority for judicial clerks, and writing excellence is achieved through editing. A clearly written, well-organized bench memo considerably advances the decision-making process because it quickly enhances the judge's understanding of the case. On the other hand, unclear writing may inadvertently send the judge in the wrong direction, which is a disservice to the clerk, the judge, the parties in the case, and ultimately the public.

Finally, to ensure a fresh perspective for editing and proofreading before submission, make a practice of completing bench memo drafts in advance of their due dates so you can then set them aside for at least a day before the final proofreading.

7.5 Bench Memo Checklist

Preliminary Matters
- Issues properly before the court?
- Standard of review or burden of proof established?

Caption
- Follows the standard format?
- All required parts included?

Procedural Statement and History
- All procedural steps set out chronologically?
- Specific dates provided?

Statement of Facts
- All facts relied on verified in the record?
- Stated objectively?
- Includes only essential facts?
- Accurate?

- Complete?
- Organized logically?
- Discrepancies in parties' versions of the facts explained?

Statement of Issues

- Stated clearly, concisely, and specifically?
- Organized in same order as issues addressed in analysis?
- Stated fairly and objectively?

Analysis

- Organized around the issues?
- Each issue introduced by a section heading?
- IRAC organization used for each issue?
- Only rule applicable to essential facts stated?
- Rule explained in sufficient but not too much detail?
- Mandatory authority relied upon unless the issue is one of first impression?
- Depth of application is appropriate to the complexity of the issue?
- Analysis specific and focused on solving the particular problem presented?
- Avoids including historical or other information not directly relevant to the analysis?
- Each party's arguments addressed in appropriate detail?
- Each issue ends with mini conclusion?

Recommendations

- Sets out a conclusion about deciding the case?
- Notes a close case?

Writing, Revising, Editing, Proofing, Citation

- Topic sentences used throughout to help guide the readers through the analysis?
- Grammar, usage, and style revised to make the document as clear and concise as possible?
- Proofread for spelling and other typographical errors?
- Citations double-checked for form, content, and placement?

7.6 Sample Appellate Court Bench Memorandum

BENCH MEMORANDUM

TO: Panel Judges
FROM: Judicial Clerk
DATE: February 28, 2008
CASE #: D1-08-1334
ORAL ARGUMENT DATE: March 6, 2008
LOCATION: Courtroom 100

NAME OF CASE:	TRIAL JUDGE: James Anders

State of Alaska,
    Respondent,
v.
Robert Robinson,
    Appellant.
	COUNTY: Juneau

ATTORNEYS:

Arthur A. Venters	Stuart T. Johnson
Juneau County Attorney	State Public Defender
221 Southwest Second Avenue	100 Law Center
Juneau, Alaska 95008	Juneau, Alaska 95007

NATURE OF THE ACTION:

Appellant Robert Robinson challenges the trial court's decision to require him to wear a leg restraint during his burglary trial, arguing that the restraint interfered with his right to a fair trial.

PROCEDURAL STATEMENT AND HISTORY:

7/24/07	Arrest for first-degree burglary.
11/28/07	Motion granted to restrain during trial.
11/29/07	Conviction for first-degree burglary entered and sentence imposed.
12/3/07	New trial motion entered.
12/4/07	New trial motion denied.
12/15/07	Notice of appeal filed.

FACTS

On July 24, 2007, in Juneau, Alaska, Robert Robinson was arrested for first-degree burglary. On the morning of the second day of his trial, the State moved to have Mr. Robinson restrained during the remainder of the trial. The judge held an in-chambers hearing to decide the issue. The State based its motion on a threatening note the sheriff had received the previous day which indicated that someone was going to help Mr. Robinson escape during the trial. The State also supported the motion with Mr. Robinson's criminal history, which includes convictions for two third-degree assaults, two burglaries, and one theft. The sheriff indicated to the court that no additional deputies were available to guard the courtroom. Over Mr. Robinson's objections, the court granted the motion to place him in a restraint.

Mr. Robinson was then restrained in a leg brace designed to look like a medical device. If the wearer of the brace tries to run while wearing it, the brace locks and the wearer is unable to bend his leg. Although the device was fitted under Mr. Robinson's pants leg, it did not fit him well, and he spent considerable time during the trial adjusting it and trying to get comfortable. Mr. Robinson's attorney renewed his objection to the device later in the day, arguing that the device was obvious to the jury because Mr. Robinson needed to adjust it constantly. The court overruled the objection and ordered that the trial proceed, although it did order that curtains be placed around the counsel tables so Mr. Robinson's legs would not be visible to the jury.

Mr. Robinson now appeals, arguing that he was denied his right to a fair trial, guaranteed by the federal constitution, because of the restraint placed on him during the second day of trial. He argues that the restraint was not necessary and the court did not use the least restrictive alternative when restraining him. Mr. Robinson requests that this Court reverse his conviction and remand his case for a new trial.

ISSUE

Under the Sixth Amendment, did the trial court abuse its discretion and violate Mr. Robinson's right to a fair trial when, after the sheriff received a note indicating that someone would help Mr. Robinson escape from custody, it required him to wear a leg restraint during trial?

ANALYSIS

The Court must decide whether Mr. Robinson was denied his right to a fair trial, guaranteed by the federal constitution, because of the restraint placed on him during the second day of his burglary trial. United States constitutional amendments six and fourteen guarantee the fundamental right to a fair trial. *Holbrook v. Flynn*, 475 U.S. 560, 567 (1986). Use of bodily restraints visible to a jury risks denying the defendant a fair trial because restraints may influence the jury to determine guilt on the basis of external factors rather than probative evidence. *Id.*

Because of the risk of jury influence, the United States Supreme Court has discouraged the use of restraints. *Illinois v. Allen*, 397 U.S. 337, 344 (1970). In *Allen*, the Court reasoned that the "sight of shackles and gags might have a significant effect on the jury's feelings about the defendant," is "an affront to the very dignity and decorum of judicial proceedings," and should thus be avoided. *Id.* But the Court also stated that under some circumstances, binding and gagging would be acceptable as the fairest and most reasonable way to handle a difficult situation. *Id.*

Under federal constitutional law, the presence of any external factor with the potential to impermissibly influence the jury is subject to close scrutiny. *Estelle v. Williams*, 425 U.S. 501, 504 (1976). To survive close scrutiny, the external factor must be related to accomplishing an essential state interest, such as courtroom security, and must be the least restrictive and least visible means available to accomplish that interest. *See Holbrook*, 475 U.S. at 568–71.

Discussion of fair trial issues in Alaska case law reflects the close scrutiny standard. To justify restraining a defendant, a trial court must find that there is an "extreme need" for the restraint and that there is no less intrusive alternative. *Contreras v. State*, 767 P.2d 1169, 1172 (Alaska Ct. App. 1989). Essentially, the trial court must ensure that courtroom security does not interfere with the presumption of innocence. *Thomae v. State*, 632 P.2d 236, 241 (Alaska Ct. App. 1981). Any additional security must be as unobtrusive as possible, and restraints are to be avoided if possible. *Id.* at 241–42. But the decision to restrain is within the trial court's discretion and may only be overturned if the court abused that discretion. *Stern v. State*, 827 P.2d 442, 448 (Alaska Ct. App. 1992).

The issues in this case, then, are first, whether the trial court abused its discretion in finding that there was a need to restrain Mr. Robinson under the circumstances, and second, whether there was a less restrictive alternative for addressing the security threat in the courtroom.

Need for Restraint

Generally, the Alaska courts have found restraints justified "to forestall the defendant's escape, to protect the safety of participants and spectators, or to insure the orderly process of the court." *Id.* Some cases also indicate that restraints are acceptable to "protect the safety and decorum of the court" or "to respond to some other manifest necessity." *Anthony v. State*, 521 P.2d 486, 496 (Alaska 1974); *see also Thomae*, 632 P.2d at 236.

In specific cases, the courts have found an "extreme need" when (1) the defendant is particularly dangerous and unpredictable; (2) the defendant has caused trouble while in jail; (3) the defendant has threatened to escape; (4) the defendant has previously committed violent crimes; or (5) the defendant has previously attempted to escape. For instance, in *Stern*, the defendant was restrained because he advocated killing police officers, was on trial for first-degree murder, and had a violent criminal history. 827 P.2d at 448–49. In *Contreras*, the defendant was restrained because he had a violent criminal history, was on trial for kidnapping and sexual assault, and had been convicted of four escapes from custody. 767 P.2d at 1172; *see also Newcomb v. State*, 800 P.2d 935, 941–42 (Alaska Ct.

App. 1990) (upholding restraint where defendant had criminal history including serious crimes of violence and was on trial for attempted murder and escape from a correctional facility).

Mr. Robinson argues that the trial court abused its discretion in ordering restraints in this case. He relies first on the fact that his criminal history is less violent than the criminal histories of the restrained defendants in the reported cases. Specifically, he has never been tried for murder or escape, as had all of the defendants in the cases. Further, Mr. Robinson contends that during the burglary addressed in this trial, he never threatened or harmed anyone. Finally, there is no indication he is dangerous now, he has no history of escape, and there is no proof that he knew anything about the threatening note sent to the sheriff.

The State counters, however, that the trial court had to take some action in response to the threatening note, and that the court's action was prudent given the circumstances. Further, the State argues that trial courts must be permitted considerable latitude when making decisions about the safety of the courtroom, and they should not be second-guessed by appellate courts.

The trial court probably did not abuse its discretion in ordering restraints in this instance. A court must have the discretion to protect the courtroom from threatened assault, and the case law provides fairly broad parameters for exercise of this discretion. United States Supreme Court cases recognize the legitimate state interest in protecting courtroom security when necessary, provided the court takes care to protect the presumption of innocence. While the facts in this case are somewhat less egregious than the facts in many of the reported cases, the definition of "need" in the case law is fairly broad, including even protection of the "decorum" of the court.

Mr. Robinson's history of assault also justifies the restraints. The case law allows a court to base its decision to restrain a defendant on the defendant's criminal record, especially if other factors augment the need for the restraint, such as a threat of escape. While Mr. Robinson was not on trial for murder, burglary is considered a serious crime of violence. Given the broad definition of "need" in the case law, and the considerable deference given to the trial court under the abuse of discretion standard, those facts are probably not sufficient to warrant reversal. As a matter of policy, a court should not be required to wait until action is taken on a threat or until a defendant acts out before ordering additional security measures if they are otherwise indicated. Rather, the court must have the discretion to act quickly to protect the security and decorum of the courtroom.

Least Restrictive Alternative

Generally, this Court has sanctioned restraints as the least restrictive alternative provided the trial court has taken some measures to conceal them from the jury. *See Stern*, 827 P.2d at 449. For instance, in *Stern*, paper was attached to the defense counsel table to conceal the defendant's leg irons from the jury. *Id.* Although the defense complained that the paper fell down, actually attracting attention to the defendant's legs rather than concealing the restraint, the court upheld the use of the restraint, apparently concluding that it was sufficiently concealed from the jury. *Id.* at 450; *see also Thomae*, 632 P.2d at 241–42 (holding presence of armed and uniformed trooper in the courtroom to guard defendant did not result in unfair trial where trooper took no action in jury's presence that would prejudice defendant).

Mr. Robinson argues that the use of this particular restraint actually called attention to the fact that he was restrained, and thus it cannot have been the least restrictive alternative. Specifically, Mr. Robinson argues that, although the State claims that the brace looked like a medical device if it was visible to the jury at all, the jury would not have been fooled into thinking the brace was in fact for medical purposes. He did not appear in the brace until the second day of trial, and there was no other information that would lead the jury to believe he had injured his leg between the first and second day. Further, Mr. Robinson argues that the brace was so ill-fitted and uncomfortable, it was impossible for him to sit still during the trial, thus he could not help but call attention to it.

The State counters that the brace was much less intrusive than traditional leg irons because the jury could view it as merely a medical device. The State also argues that Mr. Robinsons' fidgeting would not necessarily have been attributed to, or called attention to, the brace. Defendants are understandably nervous, and jurors could have viewed any discomfort exhibited by Mr. Robinson as completely natural.

The trial court probably did not abuse its discretion in concluding that the brace was an appropriate means of maintaining the security of the courtroom. The brace was designed to be hidden under a defendant's clothing and was in fact hidden for most of Mr. Robinson's trial. Also, the fact that the brace was designed to look like a medical device, not a security restraint, made it a reasonable choice for restraint. The jurors could have concluded that the brace was either an actual restraint or that it was medically necessary. In contrast, leg irons would have meant only that Mr. Robinson was in fact restrained. Further, no evidence suggests that the jury even noticed the device, much less concluded it was a restraint, not a medical brace. Even though Mr. Robinson may have been uncomfortable and fidgety, the jury would not necessarily attribute that discomfort to the brace.

Further, there was no less intrusive means available because there were no additional deputies available on the day of trial to provide extra security. Even if there had been deputies available, posting them in the courtroom may well have drawn more attention to Mr. Robinson than did this unobtrusive device. *See Thomae*, 632 P.2d at 241–42.

Finally, the trial court did all it could to ensure that the device would be unobtrusive when it ordered the defense table curtained when Mr. Robinson complained that he could not sit still. While Mr. Robinson argues that curtaining the table drew more attention to the fact that he was restrained, the curtains went up in response to his counsel's request that the brace be hidden. He can hardly complain when the judge acted in response to his own counsel's request. Further, the curtaining in this case was not more obtrusive than the falling paper approved by this Court in *Stern*.

Mr. Robinson also argues that the use of this restraint was not the most effective way to guard against an outside threat to courtroom security. Instead, the trial court should have used additional guards and posted them outside the courtroom if necessary. But since guards were not available, the court did what it could to guard against the threat. Because the trial court had a reasonable basis for its decision, the abuse of discretion standard has not been met.

Recommendation

I respectfully recommend that the Court affirm Mr. Robinson's conviction for first-degree burglary because there was a need for the restraint and the leg restraint was the least restrictive alternative under the circumstances. Therefore, the use of a leg restraint during Mr. Robinson's trial did not violate his right to a fair trial.

Chapter 8

Drafting Trial Court Documents

The trial court clerk's most important job is to make the clerk's judge "reversal proof." The documents a trial court produces are different from the documents an appellate court produces and, for the most part, may be new to judicial clerks who are just out of law school. American legal education focuses on the study of appellate court decisions. Unless you took a trial practice class, a legal clinic, or a judicial externship class, you may not have seen trial court documents before working for your judge.

Trial court clerks usually draft four major types of legal documents: (1) orders; (2) findings of fact and conclusions of law; (3) jury instructions and verdict forms; and (4) statements of reasons for imposing sentence. Within each of these document types, the possibilities for format and content are as limitless as the imaginations of the judge and the parties and attorneys appearing before the judge.

The following sections describe the purposes of these documents and explain how to draft them. Examples of an order and memorandum of law, findings of fact and conclusions of law, and criminal jury instructions and verdict form are included in this chapter.

Judges have their own preferences and writing styles. The following are, therefore, only guidelines. As with all documents that the judge will sign, make sure you are creating a document that meets the judge's criteria and comports with the judge's stylistic requirements.

8.1 Orders

Every motion filed in a case must be ruled on by the judge assigned to the case. Since the kinds and numbers of motions are almost unlimited, it should come as no surprise that much of a trial court clerk's time is spent drafting orders on motions. If you work for a trial court judge, you will likely be called upon to draft several different kinds of orders, some of which are cursory and some of which are more complex.

Orders do not have to be formal written documents. As long as the decision makes a difference in the case and represents the judge's ruling, it is an order. Oral rulings from the bench, decisions made in group telephonic conversations, and decisions made in letters are all orders and are all potentially appealable.[1]

Trial court judges at both the state and federal level have crowded dockets. Unlike an intermediate appellate court that only decides fully briefed and vetted issues, or the highest appellate court in a jurisdiction that usually gets to choose the cases it will decide, a trial court must decide all issues in all filed cases, whether the issues have merit or not. Even if a judge thinks an issue is "a no-brainer," or is an irrelevant distraction, the judge must render a decision. A judge does this by filing an order.[2] Although a judge can issue a cursory order stating that a motion is denied because it is merely

---

1. Most issues are not ripe for appeal until the trial judge has issued a final judgment in the case. However, sometimes a ruling can be appealed before final judgment is rendered. This is called an *interlocutory appeal* and usually "involve[s] legal points necessary to the determination of the case ... [or] collateral orders that are wholly separate from the merits of the action." *Black's Law Dictionary* 113 (9th ed. 2009); *see also* 28 U.S.C. § 1292 (2006) (explaining when interlocutory appeals are allowed).

2. Some judges call orders that contain all the judge's reasons for deciding a certain way "opinions." To differentiate between trial court decisions and appellate court decisions, we use *order* to refer to trial court decisions and *opinion* to refer to appellate court decisions.

a nuisance or because it is moot, every motion filed in a case must be resolved before the case can be closed. If assigned a complex class action, bankruptcy case, or multi-district litigation (MDL), a trial judge can be in the position to issue several orders a week in a single case.[3]

Although every judge uses judicial clerks differently, most clerks draft the first version of orders that judges sign. As a clerk, your job of making the judge reversal-proof begins when you do research at the bench memo stage and continues when you draft orders. Since an appellate court can only review the record that the judge and the attorneys preserved in the trial court, the trial-level record, including all orders issued in the case, must be complete and accurate.

Written orders not only memorialize and explain a judge's rulings in the case, they also create precedent. Although trial court judges cannot bind other courts, and they themselves are of course bound by the appellate courts in their jurisdictions, any written decision can serve as persuasive authority. Orders also become the "law of the case" and may impact future decisions in the same case.

Types of Orders and Their Functions

Trial judges issue several different types of orders. Some are dozens of pages long and address several issues, and some are cursory single-page orders that do nothing more than memorialize

---

3. *See, e.g.,* Chief Judge Michael J. Davis, *Pretrial Orders and Minute Entries,* United States District Court, District of Minnesota, http://www.mnd.uscourts.gov/MDL-Baycol/orders-minutes.shtml (listing some of the pretrial orders in *In re Baycol Product Liability Litigation* MDL and providing links to other orders filed in the same case); Judge Lewis A. Kaplan, *Multi-District Cases,* United States District Court for the Southern District of New York, http://www1.nysd.uscourts.gov/cases.php?form=mdl (listing some of the pretrial orders in the *In re Rezulin* MDL).

what a judge orally ruled from the bench. Some orders address merely procedural issues, and some orders decide the pivotal issues of a case and include an order for judgment that ends the case. Judges can also issue less formal *letter orders*, which are exactly what they sound like—letters written to the parties to resolve issues that have come to the judge's attention. Letter orders are often written to address procedural issues or to establish rules governing deposition practice or access to evidence. See Chapter Ten for a discussion of some of the other types of documents judicial clerks draft, including letters.

Orders on different types of motions have different consequences for cases. Judges issue orders on both dispositive and nondispositive motions. A *dispositive motion* is a motion that, if granted, disposes of all or some of the claims in a case. Examples of dispositive motions are motions to dismiss, motions for summary judgment, and motions to suppress evidence. A *nondispositive motion* is a motion that, if granted, has an effect on the case, but does not end the case. Examples of nondispositive motions are motions to compel the production of evidence, motions to join parties, and motions to extend time for discovery.[4]

The following is a description of some types of orders that a trial-level clerk may be asked to draft. Always check with the judge to see what types of orders the judge issues in certain situations. This list is not comprehensive, since on any day, a judge may need to address a unique issue that requires a unique type of decision.

---

4. In the federal system, magistrate judges usually issue orders on nondispositive motions. 28 U.S.C. §636 (b)(1)(A) (2006). Magistrates also hear dispositive motions and issue reports and recommendations (R and Rs) to district court judges recommending how the district judges should decide the motions. 28 U.S.C. §636 (b)(1)(C) (2006).

R and Rs look like orders and memoranda of law, and you can use the format for orders and memoranda outlined in this chapter if called upon to draft an R and R. In state courts, the trial judges often take turns being the "signing judge" who decides routine nondispositive motions.

Minute orders. In most courts, a minute order memorializes an order issued orally from the bench during a hearing or trial. These orders are often form orders and usually address simple issues that a judge can resolve merely by granting or denying a motion without much written explanation, such as an order denying a motion to withdraw as counsel or an order denying a motion because the issue is moot. Minute orders are usually included in the minutes of the hearing, rather than issued as separate documents.[5] If you are asked to write a minute order for the judge's signature, ask if there is an already-existing form the judge or the clerk of court's office requires.

Orders provided by parties. Not every issue that must be decided in a case is a contentious issue. Very often, parties will jointly provide an order they want the judge to sign. For example, scheduling orders setting the deadlines for the close of discovery, motion practice, and trial dates are often negotiated by the parties and judges merely sign the orders. If the parties agree on the majority of the terms, but need the judge to decide one or two issues, the parties may submit their competing proposed orders, and the judge will then sign one to control the case. For the most part, judges are happy to sign orders agreed to and provided by the parties.

Many judges require parties to submit proposed orders with their motions, and you will likely be the first person to read them. Before you give the order to the judge, make sure the order actually says what the parties say it does and that signing the order will not cause the judge any problems with schedules or other cases. Also, to the extent the order cites any authority, check the authority to ensure the judge can safely rely on it. The judge, of course, does not need to adopt either party's order. Since proposed orders

---

5. *See Black's Law Dictionary* 1207 (9th ed. 2009) (explaining that "[a]lthough practice varies, traditionally when a trial judge is sitting officially, with or without a court reporter, a clerk or deputy clerk keeps minutes. When the judge makes an oral order, the only record of that order may be in the minutes. It is therefore referred to as a minute order.").

are usually cursory, trial court judges often prefer to write their own orders to decide complex issues so they can explain their reasoning.

Orders and memoranda of law. These are the longest orders trial judges issue. They are also the orders judicial clerks spend the most time on. Orders and memoranda of law explain the judge's decisions on contested motions and issues, and contain the analysis and reasoning that supports the decisions. A single order may contain decisions on several motions and issues, and can dispose of the entire case.

Trial Order Preliminaries

If you have already written a bench memo for the judge, you will likely use that as a template for your order. If the issues addressed at oral argument are the same as those addressed in the original papers, you will not need to do any new research beyond updating. Sometimes, however, new issues come up during oral argument and, to the extent those issues were not addressed in your bench memo, you will need to research them. Additionally, if the judge wants to rule differently than you recommended in your bench memo, you will need to change your analysis and conclusions to support the judge's decision. The most challenging aspect of rewriting your analysis in this situation is making sure the law supports the judge's decision. If, after trying to make the order work out the way the judge wants, you find that the law does not support the decision, you must notify the judge immediately and explain why the decision could be reversed on appeal.

Since judges must decide motions in many different cases every week, judges and clerks must decide which motions require lengthy and in-depth orders and memoranda of law that address each issue and subissue, which motions can be disposed of with more cursory orders, and which motions can be ruled on orally from the bench or in short letter orders sent to the parties. Although the judge will make the ultimate decision about what type of order is required in every situation, you will likely be included in the decision-making process. This process should include consideration of the audience for the order.

The primary audiences for a trial court order are the parties and the parties' attorneys. Secondary audiences are the higher court to which the case may be appealed; the public, including the press, legal scholars, law students, and the general public; and attorneys. If the case is complicated or of interest to the general public, a complete order and memorandum will likely be helpful. If, however, the case is not novel or difficult, a more cursory order may suffice since the order will likely be read only by the parties and attorneys involved in the case. As discussed in Chapter Seven, a good bench memo can help you and the judge make these decisions.

The Relationship between Chambers and the Clerk of Court's Office

As discussed in Chapter Two, every court has a clerk of court's office where all filings are received and *docketed*. *Docket* is used in many different ways in the law, both as a noun and a verb.[6] *Docket* literally means "a schedule of cases pending,"[7] thus, attorneys talk about "the court's docket." In addition, the list of filings, orders, and pleadings in a particular case is called *the docket sheet*. Clerk of court employees, called *docket clerks*, maintain the docket sheets for all cases pending in the court. When a docket clerk makes entries on the docket sheet, he or she is *docketing* items in the case. Each docketed item is assigned a docket number that belongs to that document or piece of evidence for the life of the case. Parties' briefs, motions, and exhibits, and judges' orders and other writings are all docketed in the clerk of court's office. Thus, some of the suggestions in the following sections are offered so that the documents you draft can be efficiently docketed.

---

6. Bryan A. Garner, *A Dictionary of Modern Legal Usage* 289 (2d ed. 1995).

7. *Id.*; *see also* Fed. R. Civ. P. 79 (explaining what information must be docketed).

Trial Order and Memorandum of Law Structure

Through orders judges not only decide current disputes, but also communicate to the public how they think similar future disputes should be resolved.[8] Some orders are cursory: "The Court cannot grant the relief Calico Corporation seeks because the issue is moot. Motion denied." Some address several different issues and subissues and include a memorandum of law that contains a thorough analysis of each one. Regardless of the subject matter of the order, thoroughness combined with conciseness is the goal. Keep the focus on the issues; do not address unimportant side issues that will have no bearing on the judge's holding. And, as discussed in Chapter Five, use clear, efficient language to keep the document as short as practicable.

The following is a guide for drafting an order and memorandum of law on an average motion — one that was fully briefed and argued, and now requires a detailed order explaining the judge's decision and the reasons for the decision.[9]

An order and memorandum of law typically contains the following sections: (1) caption; (2) introduction; (3) background; (4) discussion; (5) order; and (6) signature block.[10] Some simple or

---

8. One group of commentators has gone so far as to opine that "[t]he heart of a judge's reputation and function rests with the use of the pen." Gerald Lebovits, Alifya V. Curtin, & Lisa Solomon, *Ethical Judicial Opinion Writing*, 21 Geo. J. Legal Ethics 237, 237 (2008).

9. Judges do not hear oral argument on every motion they must decide. Parties can request oral argument, but it is only granted at a judge's discretion. In addition, certain issues are routinely decided "on the papers" without oral argument. Petitions for writs of habeas corpus and appeals from the decisions of Social Security administrative law judges are examples of motions that are routinely decided without oral argument.

10. If your judge prefers that the order appear before the discussion, the sections of your order and memorandum would appear in this sequence: (1) caption; (2) order; (3) introduction; (4) background; (5) discussion; and (6) signature block.

less contentious issues may require less detail and may not require all these parts or a complete memorandum. You can pick the parts that are necessary for shorter orders.

Caption. The caption contains the following information: the name of the court, the name of the case (including all joined and impleaded parties), the case number, and the title of the document (i.e., "Order" or "Order and Memorandum of Law"). Any order, no matter how cursory or casual in format, must contain this information. This section should also contain the names of the attorneys who argued the motion(s) and who wrote the briefs; these are called the *attorney appearances*. Judges usually have a template for this section, and it customarily looks the same for any order issued by one judge.

Introduction. The introduction is a short statement of the purpose of the order and the nature of the action or motion before the court. The introduction is set apart by an "Introduction" subheading and usually begins with language that lets the reader know what the order is about, such as, "This case is before this Court on Defendant's Motion for Summary Judgment (Docket No. 12) and Plaintiff's Cross Motion for Summary Judgment (Docket No. 15)." It is important that readers know right away what issues the order will address. In some cases, several motions might have the same name (such as "Motion to Compel Discovery"), and readers and docket clerks need to know what specific motions each order resolves. Docket numbers give that information and should be included in the introduction. If, for some reason, docket numbers are not available, the filing dates can help identify the specific motions that the order addresses.

The introduction should tell readers whether the motions are granted or denied. Readers should not have to wait until the end of the order to know the decisions.

Although motions are the usual means for bringing an issue to the court's attention, sometimes issues come up that are not the subject of formal motion practice. For example, questions may come up in oral argument that have not been included in a motion. In that situation, you might be addressing a "request" or an

"issue" that will not have a docket number. Do your best to identify the subject matter in a way that will be clear to the parties.

Background.[11] The background is the first place in the document
where the judge sets the tone for the order, and it is set apart from
the introduction by a "Background" subheading. In this section
you will present the relevant facts the judge relies on to decide the
motion and that readers need to understand the issues addressed
in the document. You might be able to copy this section directly
from your bench memo, or oral argument might change your original idea about what facts are relevant. This section is written in
the past tense and is organized in the way that is most helpful to readers, usually chronological. Most judges prefer a narrative form of
presentation, but some orders may work better if the facts are presented in a numbered list. In this section, you must walk a line between providing enough information and context for a reader to
understand the situation and subsequent decision and overwhelming
the reader with irrelevant information.

You must also address the facts in the appropriate legal context.
For example, when deciding a motion for summary judgment, the
judge must view the facts in the light most favorable to the nonmoving party.[12] Judges must scrupulously adhere to these standards and
state up front that any facts are presented in light of the appropriate legal standard. Failure to do so can result in reversal on appeal.
Unless the parties stipulate to the facts, you should include citations to the record indicating where the information can be found
and should avoid adopting one party's version of disputed facts
without giving reasons for doing so. Failure to independently identify the legally significant facts can leave the judge open to allega-

---

11. Some judges call this section the "Facts" section, but since many orders will actually decide whether there is agreement on the facts, "Background" is a better choice.

12. *See Anderson v. Liberty Lobby, Inc.*, 477 U.S. 242, 247–48 (1986).
When deciding motions for summary judgment, judges must not resolve
factual disputes. Facts must be left for juries to decide at trial.

tions of failure to impartially decide the issues. Most judges prefer to cite within the text of the document, although you should ask the judge you work for if you should cite in the text or in footnotes. Introduce the parties and other pertinent people and entities by telling the reader what role they have in the litigation (plaintiff, defendant, etc.). After that, refer to the parties by name or functional designation (Smith, Jones, landlord, banker, etc.) rather than litigation role. This avoids confusion that may arise at the trial level where generous joinder and interpleader rules can result in many parties on each side of a case. Finally, establish consistent references for parties and use those throughout the order.

Discussion.[13] The discussion is the heart of an order and memorandum, and is set apart with a "Discussion" subheading. As in a bench memo, discussed in Chapter Seven, a judge can frame the issues here. Judges are not bound to articulate the issues in the same way as the parties. Once the issues are framed, the discussion begins with the legal standard the judge will apply to the facts, such as the summary judgment standard of Federal Rule of Civil Procedure 56(c) or the broad relevancy standard of Federal Rule of Civil Procedure 26. If a party has the burden of proof on an issue, that information must be included here. The organization of the rest of the discussion will be determined by the legal issues addressed in the order.

Use subheadings and other visual rhetoric to guide the reader through the order.[14] The legal issues addressed in the order will determine the organization of the order and what subheadings are

---

13. Some judges call this section "Analysis."

14. For an acknowledgment that all judges do not break up their written decisions using subheadings, see Ruggero J. Aldisert, Meehan Rasch, & Matthew P. Bartlett, *Opinion Writing and Opinion Readers*, 31 Cardozo L. Rev. 1, 22–23 (2009) (explaining that although the authors prefer "segmented" discussions of issues, some judges prefer that their decisions "be uninterrupted; … to flow like an essay").

needed. The subheadings should establish an easy-to-follow organization and an easy-to-understand hierarchy of subissues.

For example, when deciding if a plaintiff satisfies the four factor test for establishing a prima facie case of race discrimination under Title VII of the Civil Rights Act of 1964, you will likely break the analysis down into four subissues, one for each factor. A traditional outline format that uses Roman numerals for the highest level subheadings and letters and numbers for lower level subheadings is very effective. Each section should address a single discrete issue or subissue.

The main subheadings act as a roadmap to the order and clarify what issues the order addresses. Thus, they serve as the "I" part of each individual IRAC. Like a good table of contents, good subheadings guide readers through the document, and allow readers to easily find the section that addresses a particular issue. Subheadings can be presented in many different formats: generically — "Marshall's Title VII Claims"; as questions — "Was Marshall's Termination Discriminatory in Violation of Title VII?"; or as conclusions — "Marshall's Termination Was Not the Result of Race Discrimination." To the extent possible, use the same format for all subheadings in a single order.

Use basic IRAC formula to address and resolve each issue. Each subsection should contain one complete IRAC. As in a bench memo, you must address threshold issues first, and then address the remaining issues in an order that will be easily understood, usually starting with the most important issue.

When you present the law that controls each issue (the "R" part of each IRAC), present it in the present tense, but discuss precedent cases in the past tense. Do not waste space discussing precedent cases in depth unless you plan to use the facts from those cases for comparison in your analysis. In addition, one citation to the seminal controlling case is sufficient. Unless you need to demonstrate that a certain view of the law has broad support, such as when you are addressing a case of first impression in your jurisdiction and you need to show the support for the opposing views on the issue, you should avoid string citations in court orders. As discussed in Chapter Six, save string citations for scholarly writing.

The analysis (the "A" part of each IRAC) in a trial court order will often be shorter than the analysis in a trial court bench memo because an order need not fully explain both parties' arguments. It is important to present the losing party's arguments and explain why they were inferior to the winning party's arguments, but the winning party's arguments will often be subsumed in the judge's conclusions and analysis. It would be redundant to discuss the winning party's arguments and then use the same language to explain why the arguments are winners. Thus, although a good bench memo can provide a useful template for an order, there will be significant differences between the two documents.

When drafting the analysis, make holdings and findings clear. Use the words, "the Court finds" and "the Court holds," or "I find" and "I hold," depending upon the judge's preference. Do not make readers guess which side prevails or when analysis ends and conclusions begin.

You must include a "mini conclusion" for each issue and subissue (the "C" part of each IRAC). These can be gathered together at the end to create the "final conclusion," if necessary. For example, if your mini conclusions prove that all four individual elements of a prima facie discrimination case have been satisfied, your final conclusion would be that the plaintiff established a prima facie case of discrimination.

Trial court orders and memoranda are sometimes longer than appellate court opinions because the trial court cannot merely rely on one reason to support any decision. The trial judge should give alternate reasons for a decision, if they exist. That way, the appellate court will have a complete record to review, and if the appellate court decides to reverse on one basis, it may still affirm on another basis. For example, a judge deciding whether a plaintiff has established a prima facie case of gender discrimination must engage in a four-factor analysis.[15] All four factors must be satisfied

15. To establish a prima facie case of gender discrimination under Title VII, a plaintiff must show that "(1) she is a member of a protected class, (2) she was meeting her employer's legitimate job expectations, (3) she suffered an adverse employment action, and (4) similarly situated employees out-

to establish a prima facie case. If the judge finds factors one and two are satisfied, but finds factor three is not satisfied, the judge can dismiss the claim at that point. However, if the judge also finds factor four is not satisfied, you should fully analyze that factor and explain the judge's decision. That way, if the appellate court disagrees with the trial judge's decision on factor three, it can affirm based on factor four. Although an appellate court can affirm for any reason, and does not necessarily have to rely on the reasons given by the trial judge,[16] it is more desirable that the trial judge be affirmed on a basis that the judge first articulated.

Orders should be professional, objective, and unemotional in tone. All litigants must feel they were given a fair hearing and that their issues were fully decided on the merits.[17] Although orders sometimes express judges' displeasure or impatience with parties, this is a decision for a judge, not a clerk, to make.[18] For the most part, the tone of an order should be dispassionate, authoritative, and impartial.

At the judge's discretion, an order can acknowledge that the decision was a close one or that the judge does not necessarily agree with the binding precedent, but the judge's final decision must be unambiguous.

---

side the protected class were treated differently." *Shanklin v. Fitzgerald,* 397 F.3d 596, 602 (8th Cir. 2005) (internal quotation marks omitted).

16. *Horn v. B.A.S.S.,* 92 F.3d 609, 611 (8th Cir. 1996) (citing *B. B. v. Continental Ins. Co.,* 8 F.3d 1288, 1291 (8th Cir. 1993)).

17. Code of Conduct for United States Judges, Canon 3 (2009), http://www.uscourts.gov/library/codeOfConduct/Code_Effective_July-01-09.pdf. ("A judge shall perform the duties of the office fairly, impartially and diligently.").

18. The judge also gets to decide if there should be humor in an order. For discussions of the propriety and effectiveness of using humor in judicial opinions, see Nancy A. Wanderer, *Writing Better Opinions: Communicating with Candor, Clarity, and Style,* 54 Me. L. Rev. 47, 68–69 (2002); Jennifer Sheppard, *The "Write" Way: A Judicial Clerk's Guide to Writing for the Court,* 38 U. Balt. L. Rev. 73, 109–10 (2008) (advising against using humor in judicial writing); Adalberto Jordan, Note, *Imagery, Humor, and the Judicial Opinion,* 41 U. Miami L. Rev. 693 (1987) (exploring the use of various literary devices in judicial opinions).

Order. The order states the final disposition of the motion or motions addressed. Some judges want the order set apart by a subheading, but some prefer to let the unique look of this section create the necessary visual break. Although you have included mini conclusions on the various issues throughout the document (the Cs in the individual IRACs), this is the place where busy readers can look for a quick snapshot of the judge's ultimate decisions on all issues addressed in the document.

You should set off this part of the document with the words "IT IS HEREBY ORDERED" followed by a clear list of the decisions contained in the order.[19] Many judges prefer that "IT IS HEREBY ORDERED" be in bold type and that the actual dispositions also be capitalized and in bold type.

If an order only addresses one issue, the order section can be written in narrative form: "**IT IS HEREBY ORDERED** that Defendant's Motion to Suppress Evidence (Docket No. 45) is **DE-NIED.**"

It is helpful to number the judge's conclusions when an order addresses more than one issue. Thus, an order addressing cross motions for summary judgment and a motion to extend time to file other motions might read as follows:

IT IS HEREBY ORDERED:
1. Defendant's Motion for Summary Judgment (Docket No. 12) is **GRANTED**;
2. Plaintiff's Motion for Summary Judgment (Docket No. 15) is **DENIED**; and
3. Plaintiff's Motion for Extension of Time to File Motions in Limine (Docket No. 16) is **DENIED AS MOOT.**

Although every judge will have a preference for how the order should look, this format is clear and easy to follow. The docket

---

19. If you are drafting a report and recommendation for a magistrate judge, you would set off this section with the words "IT IS HEREBY RECOMMENDED."

numbers are included so the parties know which motions the order resolves and so the docket clerk can match the decisions with the correct motions for easy docketing.

Judgment actually terminates a case.[20] If the order and memorandum disposes of the case entirely, follow the judge's instructions about whether you should mention judgment in the order section.[21] Judgment triggers the next stages in the litigation. A winning party can enforce a judgment and seek any monies awarded or can enforce injunctive or equitable relief. Judgment also starts the clock running on the losing party's right to appeal.

Signature Block. The judge must sign and date all orders, even if they are filed electronically. If filed electronically, affix an approved electronic signature. Orders must be dated because the timing of the rights and obligations established by an order is counted from the date the order is signed.

Post-Drafting Decisions

Once you have drafted any kind of order for the judge's approval, a new phase of drafting begins. During this phase, the document must be edited and proofread not only for accuracy, but also for voice and style; and you and the judge will work together, often sending drafts back and forth, until the judge is ready to release the order.

Proofreading procedure. Even if you have a bench memo that perfectly tracks the final order, you still must carefully proofread the order. First, a bench memo is written in your voice. An order must be written in the judge's voice. Everything that comes out of

---

20. *Black's Law Dictionary* 918 (9th ed. 2009) (providing the following definition of judgment: "A court's final determination of the rights and obligations of the parties in a case").

21. If the order disposes of the case entirely, the judge might want to close with the words, "LET JUDGMENT BE ENTERED ACCORDINGLY." In some jurisdictions, this signals the clerk's office to enter judgment in a case. Federal Rule of Civil Procedure 58 provides for judgments that are separate documents from orders.

one chambers must sound like it was drafted by the judge when, in reality, various documents might be drafted by different judicial clerks. Thus, one of the first and most important tasks you will have as a clerk is learning to write in the judge's voice. Some trial judges refer to themselves as "the Court" in orders. Others refer to themselves as "I." Know which reference the judge prefers, and use it consistently in all documents signed by the judge.[22] Writing in the judge's voice will become second nature after a few months. See Chapter Nine for more information on learning to write in the judge's voice.

Once the first draft is done, the judge and the clerk may pass several mark-up drafts back and forth before the judge decides on the final version of the order, or the judge might give the clerk oral feedback about changes to the order. This process is different for every judge-clerk pair, and you must follow the lead of the judge for whom you work. Remember that until the order is publicly released, you cannot tell anyone what the judge has decided or which way the judge is leaning. Chapter Twelve discusses more limitations on communicating about the judge's decision-making process.

As discussed in Chapter Six, citations to precedent and to the record must be thorough and pristine. Just as trial judges are not required to behave "like pigs, hunting for truffles buried in briefs"[23] when looking for arguments, appellate judges are not required to guess what support trial judges relied on when making their decisions. An order that contains proper citations to the record and proper citations to precedent will help the appellate court understand the issues and the trial judge's reasoning.

_____

22. An exception to this rule might be if the judge signs an order drafted by the parties and submitted for the judge's signature. A judge will rarely ask a clerk to retype this kind of order for two reasons: (1) time constraints do not permit it, and (2) the order will likely not look like an order that originated with the court in anyway, so formatting consistency is not expected.

23. *United States v. Dunkel*, 927 F.2d 955, 956 (7th Cir. 1991).

Privacy concerns. Certain orders should not be available to the public and must be filed under seal.[24] Most of the time, the party requiring confidentiality will request that an order be filed under seal, or the case might be covered by a protective order that requires certain information be excluded from publicly filed documents. However, if there is any question about the confidentiality of the parties or other persons or entities mentioned in an order, a conscientious clerk should ask the judge if the order should be filed under seal.

If potentially personal or embarrassing information is included in the order and the person to whom that information applies is not a party, the judge might want to change the person's name or use initials to identify the person. For example, in support of a discrimination claim, a plaintiff might proffer the employment file of the employee who got the plaintiff's job after the plaintiff was terminated. In most situations, there is no reason this employee should be identified in a publicly filed order. While the employee's work record and certain characteristics such as race or gender might be relevant, the employee's name is rarely relevant. Ask the judge how to handle these issues.

Choosing to publish. State trial court orders are not typically published in regional or state reporters. On the other hand, federal trial court orders are sometimes included in *The Federal Supplement.*

The decision to publish an order is made very intentionally. Orders that merely apply established law to facts are not normally published. However, if an order addresses a new or emerging area of the law or if the order is issued in a case of particular public interest, the judge might decide to publish the order. But be aware that when orders are docketed electronically instead of in paper, electronic legal research sites and repositories can make the orders widely available, even if they are not officially "published." Thus,

---

24. Sealing records means "[t]he act or practice of officially preventing access to particular ... records, in the absence of a court order." *Black's Law Dictionary* 1467 (9th ed. 2009).

every order that comes out of chambers will potentially be read by a wide audience so it must be well-written, well researched, and thoroughly proofread.[25]

Checklist for Trial Court Orders and Memoranda of Law

Caption

- Includes the name of the court?
- Includes the full name of the case?
- Includes the case number?
- Includes the title of the document?
- Includes the names of the attorneys who argued the motion(s) and wrote the briefs?

Introduction

- Clearly identifies the issues before the court?
- Includes docket numbers for all the motions addressed in the order?
- Includes the judge's decision on each issue?
- Includes other information the reader needs to understand the discussion?

Background

- Includes all the pertinent information the judge will rely on to decide the issues addressed in the order?
- Includes relevant background information that readers need to understand the order?

---

25. Citation to unpublished decisions is no longer uniformly banned. Although state rules still vary, Federal Rule of Appellate Procedure 32.1 provides that federal appellate courts cannot prohibit citation to unpublished cases that were decided after January 1, 2007. The trend to loosen up citation rules creates a situation in which any order can potentially be cited as persuasive authority.

- Omits extraneous or irrelevant information?
- Explains where the parties' views of the facts differs?
- Includes information related to the judge's presentation of the facts and the way in which the judge must look at the facts (i.e., in the light most favorable to the nonmoving party when deciding a motion for summary judgment)?
- Contains citations to the record?

Discussion

- Includes the legal standards the judge must apply?
- Includes the burdens of proof the parties must satisfy?
- Addresses all the issues raised in the motions?
- Contains a logical presentation of issues, broken down into subsections, when appropriate?
- Includes subsections that contain complete IRACs on discrete issues?
- Uses consistent format for all subheadings?
- Supports all decisions with citations to good law?
- Fully explains all decisions?
- Explains reasons for rejecting certain arguments, when necessary?
- Has an authoritative, respectful, detached, and professional tone?

The Order

- Includes the judge's decisions on all issues and motions decided in the order?
- Includes docket numbers for all the motions decided in the order?

Signature Block

- Includes the judge's signature and the date?

Writing, Revising, Editing, Proofing, Citation

- Uses topic sentences throughout to help guide readers through the analysis?

- Has been revised for grammar, usage, and style to make the document as clear and concise as possible?
- Has been proofread for spelling and other typographical errors?
- Has been cite checked for form, content, and placement?

Sample Trial Court Order and Memorandum of Law
SUMMERSET COUNTY DISTRICT COURT

STATE OF VERMONT	CASE NO. CRIM. 04-663(1)
Plaintiff,	
v.	
SAMUEL FOLDAY,	ORDER AND
Defendant.	MEMORANDUM OF LAW

Arianna Patel, Summerset County Attorney's Office, on behalf of the State of Vermont.

Calvin Nelson, Office of the State Public Defender, on behalf of Samuel Folday.

I. INTRODUCTION

This matter is before the Court on Plaintiff State of Vermont's Motion to Restrain Defendant During Trial. (Docket No. 117.) For the following reasons, the motion is granted.

II. BACKGROUND

A. Folday's Criminal Background

On July 24, 2004, Defendant Samuel Folday was arrested for first-degree burglary. Although there are no allegations that Folday used violence in the commission of this offense, Folday has a criminal history dating back to 1994, when he was nineteen years old. (Pros. Ex. 9.) Since that time, Folday has been convicted twice for third-degree robbery, once for first-degree robbery, twice for second-degree assault, and once for distribution of methamphetamine. (*Id.*) Folday has served several different terms in prison for these crimes. (*Id.*) While in prison on the drug conviction, Folday joined the Bad Boys, a loosely organized group of men who, since approximately 1995, have engaged in a variety of illegal activities including selling marijuana and methamphetamine, stealing cars, and breaking and entering for the purpose of stealing. (Pros. Ex. 13.) In recent years, the activities of the Bad Boys have expanded to include crimes against people such as assault and fraud. (*Id.*) One member of the organization was recently convicted of planting a pipe bomb under a car owned by an assistant United States attorney. (*Id.*)

Folday denies that the Bad Boys is a gang, and the State Gang Task Force does not identify this group as an organized gang that requires prospective members to commit certain crimes or pass other initiations to join. (Def. Ex. 4.)

Since last being released from prison on December 23, 2001, Folday has violated his parole twice. (Pros. Ex. 11.) On February 22, 2002, Folday tested positive for methamphetamine during a routine drug test and was subjected to weekly drug tests for the next three months. (*Id.*) All those tests were clean. (*Id.*) On December 21, 2003, Folday was arrested for third-degree assault when he pushed a man "for looking at [his] girlfriend" at a concert. (*Id.*) The assault charge is pending in Pine County District Court. (*Id.*) Folday has been working for Grandview Landscaping and Snow Removal since June 2002, and his employer says Folday is a model employee. (Def. Ex. 7.)

B. Folday's Current Trial

Folday's trial for first-degree burglary began on March 21, 2005. The first day of trial was uneventful. However, a court security officer testified that Folday became agitated after the first day of trial when, while being escorted back to jail, the officer would not let Folday linger in the courthouse to visit with his brother who traveled to Vermont from Utah for the trial. The officer said that Folday "took a swing" at the officer and said that if he was not allowed to visit with his brother, he would "make [the officer] sorry." (Cooper Aff. ¶ 6.) The officer laughed this off, though, and said he does not consider Folday a threat. (*Id.* ¶ 7.)

On the morning of what should have been the second day of trial, the State moved to have Folday restrained for the remainder of the trial. The State based its motion on an unsigned note the Summerset County Sheriff received early that morning stating that people were planning to storm the courtroom to help Folday escape during trial. During an in-chambers meeting, both Folday and his counsel denied knowing anything about the note. The Court canceled trial for the day and heard oral argument on the State's motion.

III. DISCUSSION

The State proposes restraining Folday using a leg restraint. The restraint is designed to look like a medical device and will lock should Folday try to run. Folday has tried on the brace and, although it technically fits, it is uncomfortable. Folday opposes the State's motion and argues that restraining him in the courtroom would violate his constitutional right to a fair trial. Folday is also afraid that since the restraint is uncomfortable, he might end up adjusting it during trial and calling attention to the restraint. This, Folday asserts, might prejudice the jury against him. Folday first argues that restraints are not necessary since he does not know anything about the note. He further argues that even if some extra security measures should be taken, restraints are the wrong choice. Folday suggests posting extra security officers in the courtroom in lieu of restraining him.

The Sixth and Fourteenth Amendments guarantee a state criminal defendant's right to a fair trial. *Holbrook v. Flynn*, 475 U.S. 560, 567 (1986). The right to a fair trial includes the right to appear before a jury "without the badges of custody." *Hightower v. State*, 428 A.2d 562, 570 (Vt. Ct. App. 1987). Thus, the use of bodily restraints visible to a jury risks denying the defendant a fair trial because restraints may influence the jury to determine guilt on the basis of external factors rather than probative evidence. *Holbrook*, 475 U.S. at 567.

Restraints are discouraged because they can affect jurors' feelings about a criminal defendant's presumed innocence. *Illinois v. Allen*, 397 U.S. 337, 344 (1970). Unless no other alternative exists, restraints must not be used in a courtroom because using restraints can call into question the fairness of a criminal trial. *Brody v. State*, 766 A.2d 893, 899 (Vt. 2000). However, trial judges are not without discretion in these matters, and under some circumstances, binding and gagging might be the "fairest and most reasonable way" to control a criminal defendant. *Allen*, 397 U.S. at 344. Realistically, jurors understand that criminal defendants are never in court by their own choice, and therefore, there is no reason to disallow "every practice tending to single out the accused from everyone else in the courtroom." *Holbrook*, 475 U.S. at 567.

Whether a restraint or other device can impermissibly influence the jury is an issue subject to close judicial scrutiny. *See Estelle v. Williams*, 425 U.S. 501, 504 (1976). To survive close scrutiny, the restraint must be related to accomplishing an essential state interest, such as courtroom security, and must be the least restrictive and least visible means available to accomplish that interest. *See Holbrook*, 475 U.S. at 568–71. Even essential state interests "cannot be promoted at the expense of violating an individual's right to a presumption of innocence." *Brody*, 766 A.2d at 901.

A. Need for Restraint

Restraints are acceptable to prevent a criminal defendant's escape, to protect the safety of people in the courtroom, and to protect the "conduct of the court's important business." *Hightower*, 428 A.2d at 571.

For example, in *Hightower*, the court found no abuse of discretion when a criminal defendant was placed in leg restraints during his first-degree murder trial on days when extra court security officers were not available. *Id.* at 577. The trial court judge based the decision to restrain the defendant on the defendant's criminal history, which included three convictions for first-degree robbery, three assaults involving firearms, two second-degree sexual assaults, and arson. *Id.* The court also expressed concern that the defendant, who was a member of the South Side Princes gang, would try to wreak havoc in the courtroom to further the gang's goal of "disrupting the courts of the land." *Id.*

Restraints were also justified when a criminal defendant who had previously escaped from custody kept trying to stand up and object to testimony during her trial. *Lynn v. State*, 779 A.2d 451, 465 (Vt. 2001). The defendant also had previous convictions for rob-

robbery, attempted murder, and kidnapping. *Id.* The court reasoned that the defendant's dangerous criminal past and inability to stay seated justified the use of restraints in order to protect not only the people in the courtroom, but also "the dignity and decorum of the court, itself." *Id.* at 466.

The Court finds that it is necessary to restrain Folday during trial. Folday's admitted affiliation with the Bad Boys is particularly troubling. The group's activities have been escalating in violence in recent years, and the Court cannot risk this courtroom becoming one of the group's targets. The Court must protect courtroom security. On the first day of trial, four attorneys, twelve spectators, twelve jurors, and six court staff were present in the courtroom. The Court cannot guarantee the safety of all these people without doing something to discourage a potential breakout. While the facts in this case are somewhat less egregious than the facts in many of the reported cases, the definition of "need" in the case law is fairly broad, including even the protection of the "decorum" of the court. The Court takes its responsibility to protect the people in its courtroom very seriously, and finds that if a group the size of the Bad Boys tried to take Folday out of the courtroom, the current security officers would likely be unable to protect both Folday and the public. This is especially true since the court is currently short-staffed and there are no extra court security officers available to help control the courtroom.

Folday's history of assault also justifies the restraints. The case law allows a court to base its decision to restrain a defendant on the defendant's criminal record, especially if other factors augment the need for the restraint, such as a threat of escape. While Folday is not on trial for murder, as were many of the defendants in other cases, burglary is a serious crime of violence. In addition, Folday threatened and attempted to strike an officer of this court. Although the officer said he does not fear Folday, the fact remains that Folday lashed out and made a threat with no provocation. Folday has been in court often enough to know the rules: visits between criminal defendants and family members do not take place in the courtroom. However, even with this knowledge, Folday not only threatened violence, but also acted in a violent manner. This, alone, might justify the use of restraints even if the court was not faced with the broader threat presented by the anonymous note. Thus, the fact that Folday claims ignorance about the source of the note is not persuasive.

The Court is not required to wait until action is taken on a threat, or until a defendant acts out before ordering additional security measures if they are otherwise indicated. Rather, the Court has the discretion to act quickly to protect the security and decorum of the courtroom. Accordingly, the Court finds that restraints are necessary in this case.

B. Least Restrictive Alternative

Once a court determines that restraints are necessary, the court has a duty to use the least restrictive alternative possible. In general, if the court conceals the restraints from the jury, the restraints will pass constitutional muster. *See Brody*, 766 A.2d at 900. In cases where criminal defendants were ordered to wear leg restraints, the use of the restraints was affirmed when the restraints were hidden from the jury. *Tyler v. State*, 356 A.2d 888, 892 (Vt. Ct. App. 1985) (paper curtain covering front of open counsel table sufficient to conceal restraint); *Lynn*, 779 A.2d at 466 (counsel table with solid front sufficient to conceal restraint).

In *Tyler,* the criminal defendant complained that the paper covering the front of the counsel table fell down and made her brace visible to the jury. 356 A.2d at 891. The appellate court upheld the trial court's use of the paper because the defendant's brace was still sufficiently hidden from the jury. *Id.* Likewise, in *Lynn,* the court held that any noise the jury might have heard when the defendant's ankle chains and shackles rattled as she crossed and uncrossed her ankles was due to the defendant's own behavior. 779 A.2d at 467. The court reasoned that the defendant had been warned about the noise, that a mat was placed under the table to muffle any noise, and that the defendant seemed to be crossing her ankles on purpose to call attention to her restraints. *Id.*

The Court finds that there is no less intrusive means of restraining Folday. First, as discussed above, posting more security, as Folday suggests, is not possible since all the court security officers have assignments elsewhere in the courthouse. Even if security officers are available, posting them in the courtroom may draw more attention to Folday than this unobtrusive device, especially since extra security officers were not present on the first day of trial. The Court would not want to prejudice Folday by suggesting that a major show of force is necessary to keep him in line.

Second, the leg brace will be hidden under Folday's clothing. The jury will never see the brace unless Folday, himself, draws attention to it. The brace is also designed to look like a medical device, not a security restraint, which lessens the chance that jurors will realize Folday is restrained if, in some way, the jury sees the restraint or realizes that Folday is wearing it.

Finally, Folday will be seated at counsel table before the jury enters the courtroom, so the jury should never see the brace or any effect it has on Folday's mobility, unless Folday purposely calls attention to the device. Thus, a leg restraint is the least restrictive alternative in this situation.

C. Conclusion

The Court finds it is necessary to restrain Folday for the remainder of his trial. The Court further finds that using a leg restraint designed to look like a medical device is the least restrictive way to restrain Folday. Folday will be restrained during the remainder of his trial.

IV. ORDER

Based on all the filings and arguments of the Parties, and on the reasoning contained in this memorandum of law, **IT IS HEREBY ORDERED:**

1.   Plaintiff State of Vermont's Motion to Restrain Defendant During Trial (Docket No. 117) is **GRANTED;**

2.   Defendant Folday shall wear a leg restraint during the remainder of his trial. The restraint shall be hidden under Folday's clothing and shall be adjusted to make it as comfortable as possible; and

3.   Defendant Folday shall be escorted in and out of the courtroom out of the view of the jury.

Dated: March 23, 2005   _____

                                              Judge James B. Gonzalez
                                              Summerset County District Court

8.2 Findings of Fact and Conclusions of Law

Not every matter that comes before a court does so on a motion. Judges often preside over bench trials in which the judge, rather than a jury, acts as the fact finder. A criminal defendant can waive the right to a jury trial and have a judge decide the case.[26] Similarly, the parties to a civil dispute can agree to have a judge, rather than a jury, resolve factual and legal issues raised in the case, or a judge might decide that a nonjury trial is required in a certain situation.[27] When judges act in this capacity, they may issue written findings and conclusions.[28] The resulting document has the title "Findings of Fact and Conclusions of Law."[29]

Findings of fact and conclusions of law tell readers which version of the facts the judge adopts and what conclusions the judge reaches when applying the law to those facts. Findings of fact and conclusions of law contain many of the same sections as orders and memoranda of law: caption; introduction; background (if the introduction does not sufficiently convey all the relevant informa-

---

26. Fed. R. Crim. P. 23(a).

27. Fed. R. Civ. P. 39(a).

28. *See* Fed. R. Crim. P. 23(c) ("In a case tried without a jury, the court must find the defendant guilty or not guilty. If a party requests before the finding of guilty or not guilty, the court must state its specific findings of fact in open court or in a written decision or opinion."); Fed. R. Civ. P. 52(a)(1) ("In an action tried on the facts without a jury ... the court must find the facts specially and state its conclusions of law separately. The findings and conclusions may be stated on the record after the close of the evidence or may appear in an opinion or a memorandum of decision filed by the court.").

29. The final document might have a longer name such as "Findings of Fact, Conclusions of Law, and Order" or "Findings of Fact, Conclusions of Law, and Order for Judgment" depending upon the effect of the actual document.

tion); signature block; and order.[30] If you include a background section, it will often be shorter than its order and memorandum of law counterpart since one of the purposes of findings of fact and conclusions of law is to determine what the facts are. Thus, you might not be able to tell the whole story right up front. The checklist at the end of this section contains questions about information typically included in the background section. The document will also contain two different sections: (1) findings of fact, and (2) conclusions of law.

Sometimes findings of fact and conclusions of law overlap. Therefore, in the introduction, many judges include boilerplate language acknowledging the situation: "To the extent the findings of fact may be considered conclusions of law, they will be deemed conclusions of law. Similarly, to the extent that matters expressed as conclusions of law may be considered findings of fact, they will be deemed findings of fact."

Drafting Findings of Fact

Findings of fact (findings) state the facts that the court adopts. In most trials, some legally significant facts are uncontested. If the judge relies on an uncontested fact when making a decision, the judge may tell readers that the fact is uncontested or may just state it as a fact. Findings should state the reasons for adopting a certain contested version of the facts over another version. The explanation need not include a full discussion of every fact, but can merely state that "the following facts have been proven by a preponderance of the evidence." However, findings that resolve contested issues should be supported with citations to the record—

---

30. If the findings of fact and conclusions of law dispose of a case in its entirety, the document may include a judgment, or the judgment can be a separate document. *See* Fed. R. Crim. P. 23(c) ("In a case tried without a jury, the court must find the defendant guilty or not guilty."); Fed. R. Civ. P. 52(a)(1) ("Judgment must be entered under [Federal] Rule [of Civil Procedure] 58.").

either the exhibits or the trial transcript. If you are drafting findings, make it easy for an appellate court to understand the basis for the decisions, so it is easy to affirm those decisions.

Findings are typically written as numbered paragraphs rather than in narrative paragraph form. For example, if criminal defendant Michael Quinn is on trial for burglary, with the underlying crime being the theft of Alex Smith's unique wallet, whether Quinn had Smith's consent to be in Smith's home might be an unresolved fact issue. If the judge determines that Quinn did, indeed, enter the home without Smith's consent, the finding might look like this:

> 1. Smith did not give Quinn permission to enter his home on May 17, 2009. (Tr. R. at 7:3.) In fact, Smith had not spoken to Quinn for five months at the time of the break-in (Tr. R. at 7:15; 45:20–21.)

If the parties stipulated that Smith was upstairs sleeping during the time Quinn was in Smith's home, it is not necessary to elaborate on this fact:

> 2. Smith was in his home and asleep in his upstairs bedroom when Quinn entered Smith's home on March 17, 2009. (Tr. R. at 8:12–13.)

Likewise, if the unique look of the stolen wallet is undisputed, but still relevant to the case, and if the wallet contained Smith's ATM card, the finding may look like this:

> 3. Smith's wallet is unique. It is a green canvas pouch that his grandfather carried in World War I. (Tr. R. at 7:20–21.) The pouch is approximately six inches long by three inches high, and has the initials "J.L.S." stamped on one side in black ink. (Tr. R. at 7:22.) On May 17, 2009, the wallet contained Smith's ATM card and driver's license. (Tr. R. at 23:11.)

If the judge determines that Quinn took Smith's wallet, the finding and the support for it might look like this:

4. Quinn took Smith's wallet from Smith's kitchen table. Smith noticed his wallet was missing when he woke up and went to the kitchen for breakfast. (Tr. R. at 8:6–12.) Smith immediately reported his missing wallet to the police. (Tr. R. at 8:15.) Four hours after Smith reported his wallet missing, Quinn was seen on the Valley Area Bank drive-up teller videotape trying to withdraw money using Smith's ATM card. (Pros. Ex. 7.) One hour later, Quinn was pulled over for speeding, and the arresting officer, who had seen a picture of Smith's wallet at a morning briefing at the beginning of his shift, noticed Smith's wallet on the dashboard of Quinn's car. (Tr. R. at 16:18.) Although Smith's driver's license had been removed from the wallet, the Court finds Smith's in-court identification of the wallet (Tr. R. at 10:6) credible and Quinn's uncorroborated story that he received the wallet as a gift (Tr. R. at 40:15–18) untenable.

As with bench memos and orders, findings of fact and conclusions of law should be broken up with subheadings to help flow and readability. In addition, some judges prefer that each numbered paragraph contain only one sentence.

Drafting findings can be a tedious process. Be prepared to spend time combing through the trial transcript and your notes to find the testimony and evidence that is most credible. Drafting findings will be easier if the judge allows parties to submit any stipulated facts prior to trial. This will not only lessen your burden during the drafting stage, but may also make the trial move more quickly since testimony will be unnecessary on certain issues.

Drafting Conclusions of Law

Conclusions of law (conclusions) explain the judge's decisions based on an analysis of the law in light of the facts of the case. Sometimes the facts and the legal conclusions will be one and the same, but most times a judge must apply the law to the facts to come to a legal conclusion. For example, in the burglary scenario, suppose the judge found that Quinn entered Smith's home while Smith was asleep and stole a wallet from the kitchen table. In the conclusions, the judge would state that Quinn's conduct satisfied Minnesota's first-degree burglary statute because Quinn entered a dwelling while someone other than an accomplice was in the building and committed the crime of robbery therein.[31] Like findings, conclusions are usually written as numbered paragraphs. Although the numbered paragraphs may look somewhat informal, citations to precedent and to the record are as necessary here as they are in any legal analysis. Thus, a conclusion in the burglary case may look like the following:

> 1. Quinn entered Smith's home without Smith's consent. Although Smith and Quinn knew each other, Quinn had only been in Smith's home twice in five years. (Tr. R. at 6:11.) More importantly, Smith never gave Quinn permission to enter his home on May 17, 2009. (Tr. R. at 7:2.) Although Smith let Quinn stay at his home when Quinn first arrived in town, Quinn could not possibly rely on Smith's statement, "We have an open door policy for friends," (Tr. R. at 39:20–21) to mean that any acquaintance could enter Smith's home at will without an invitation or specific permission.

Note how the fact that Smith did not give Quinn permission to enter his home is both a fact and an ultimate legal conclusion that satisfies one element of burglary under the Minnesota statute. This

---

31. Minn. Stat. § 609.582(1) (2008) provides, in part, that "[w]hoever enters a building without consent and with intent to commit a crime, or enters a building without consent and commits a crime while in the building ... commits burglary in the first degree ... if ... the building is a dwelling and another person, not an accomplice, is present in it when the burglar enters or at any time while the burglar is in the building."

overlap means that there is not always a clean line between the two parts of the document. To the extent that a fact also constitutes a legal conclusion, the better practice is to state it twice—once in each section. That way, each section of the document will be complete on its own. If the judge finds this approach redundant, the judge will tell you where the information should be included. Also, as with any document that comes out of chambers, the clerk must ensure that all issues that should be resolved by the document are actually resolved and that there are no loose ends. Including the information in both sections, at least in a first draft, will help ensure that no issues or subissues are missed.

Checklist for Findings of Fact and Conclusions of Law

Caption
- Includes the name of the court?
- Includes the full name of the case?
- Includes the case number?
- Includes the title of the document?
- Includes the names of the attorneys who appeared at trial?

Introduction
- Clearly identifies the issues at trial?
- Includes information readers need to understand the situation before the court, such as an acknowledgment that a civil case is being tried to the bench by the consent of both parties or that a criminal defendant properly waived his right to a jury trial?
- Includes context that readers need in order to understand the findings and conclusions?

Background (if necessary)
- Includes information not included in the introduction that readers need to understand the findings and conclusions?

Findings of Fact

- Includes the version of the facts the judge finds most credible?
- Includes citations to the record that support the judge's findings on contested facts?
- Includes uncontested facts if relevant to the legal conclusions?
- Breaks up findings with subheadings, if necessary?
- Presents findings as numbered paragraphs?

Conclusions of Law

- Includes relevant statutes or case law that governs the issues in the case?
- Applies the governing law to the facts adduced in the findings of fact to reach legal conclusions?
- Breaks up conclusions with subheadings, if necessary?
- Presents findings as numbered paragraphs?

The Order

- Includes the judge's decisions on all the issues decided at trial?
- Clearly specifies whether criminal defendants are guilty or not guilty?
- Delineates any further actions that must be taken or that a party is entitled to take?
- Includes timelines and deadlines, if necessary?

Signature Block

- Includes the judge's signature and the date?

Writing, Revising, Editing, Proofing, Citation

- Has been revised for grammar, usage, and style to make the document as clear and concise as possible?
- Has been proofread for spelling and other typographical errors?
- Has been cite checked for form, content, and placement?

Sample Findings of Fact, Conclusions of Law, and Order

TREVOR COUNTY DISTRICT COURT

STATE OF MINNESOTA, Plaintiff, v.	CASE NO. 09-CR-567
CHARLES MICHAEL QUINN, a/k/a Charlie Michaels, Defendant.	FINDINGS OF FACT, CONCLUSIONS OF LAW, AND ORDER

Susan Nyguen, Esq., Assistant Trevor County Attorney, on behalf of the State of Minnesota.

Emmett Garcia, Garcia & Assoc., L.L.P., on behalf of Charles Michael Quinn.

I. INTRODUCTION

This matter came before the Court for a bench trial on July 6, 2009, pursuant to Defendant Charles Michael Quinn's knowing written waiver of his right to a jury trial in compliance with Minnesota Rule of Criminal Procedure 26.01. (Docket No. 25.) Quinn is charged with first-degree burglary, and has been free on bail pending trial. During the one-day trial, the Prosecution called two witnesses: William Smith and Officer Silas Kuzo of the Olsonville, Minnesota Police Department. Charles Michael Quinn testified on his own behalf.

Based on the evidence adduced at trial, the Court makes the following Findings of Fact and Conclusions of Law. To the extent findings of fact may be considered conclusions of law, they will be deemed conclusions of law. Similarly, to the extent that matters expressed as conclusions of law may be considered findings of fact, they will be deemed findings of fact.

II. FINDINGS OF FACT

The Court finds that the State has proven the following facts beyond a reasonable doubt.

A. The Parties' Relationship

1. Mr. William Smith owns a home located at 347 Greenway Drive in Olsonville, Minnesota. (Tr. R. at 5:7.) The home contains a dining room that has one window. (Tr. R. at 5:8.)

2. Smith and Defendant Charles Michael Quinn both work at the Icon Software Company, although they work in different departments and only know each other slightly. (Tr. R. at 6:1.)

3. At Icon, Smith has a reputation for being a friendly, helpful person who has an "open door policy for friends." (Tr. R. at 45:20–21.)

4. Before the alleged theft at issue in this case, Quinn had been in Smith's home twice: once in April 2004, when he first arrived in town and his apartment was being painted, and once on December 12, 2008, when Smith hosted a retirement party for another Icon employee. (Tr. R. at 6:14–17.)

5. At the time of the 2008 retirement party, a large Christmas tree stood in front of Smith's dining room window, preventing people from getting near the window. (Tr. R. at 7:3–5; Pros. Ex. 4.)

B. Events of January 16 and January 17, 2009

6. On the evening of January 16, 2009, Smith left his wallet on his kitchen table when he retired to bed at approximately 9:45 p.m. (Tr. R. at 12:6.) The wallet contained $300, Smith's driver's license, and Smith's ATM card, among other things. (Tr. R. at 12:10–11.)

7. Smith fell asleep at approximately 11:00 p.m. (Tr. R. at 13:1.)

8. Smith's wallet is unique. It is a green canvas pouch that his grandfather carried in World War I. The pouch is approximately six inches long by three inches tall and has the initials J.L.S. stamped on one side in black ink. (Pros. Ex. 1.)

9. At approximately 12:30 a.m. on January 17, 2009, Smith heard a noise, but ignored it at first because he thought it was his furnace, which had been making unusual noises for about a week at that time. (Tr. R. at 6:13.) Smith dozed off. (Tr. R. at 6:14.)

10. Smith awoke about ten minutes later when he heard another noise coming from the dining room. (Tr. R. at 6:24.)

11. Smith went downstairs to investigate and saw that the dining room window was partially open. (Tr. R. at 7:12.) Smith closed the window, did a cursory look around the dining and living rooms, checked the safe he kept in the coat closet, checked that the back door was still locked, and decided nothing was amiss. (Tr. R. at 7:22.)

12. At that time, Smith concluded that he must have forgotten to close the window after opening it earlier in the day to let in some fresh air during the day's "January thaw." (Tr. R. at 8:4–6.)

13. Smith's back door is located through the kitchen, but he did not turn on any lights when he walked through the kitchen. (Tr. R. at 7:17–18.)

14. Smith awoke at 6:00 a.m. on January 17, 2009, and went downstairs to his kitchen at approximately 6:30 a.m. At that time, he noticed his wallet was missing from the kitchen table. (Tr. R. at 18:23–34.)

15. Defendant Charles Michael Quinn entered Smith's home through the open dining room window. Quinn's partial palm print was found on Smith's dining room windowsill. (Tr. R. at 23:6–9.) Although Quinn testified that the print "could have gotten there at Pete's retirement party," the Court finds that the State has proved beyond a reasonable doubt that Quinn entered Smith's home through the dining room window on January 17, 2009.

16. Officer Silas Kuzo of the Olsonville, Minnesota Police Department testified that part of the print was located on the outside of the window frame and "kind of wrapped around to the inside, you know, like someone grabbed onto the frame and sill from the outside." (Tr. R. at 24:16–17.) The scientific report evaluating the print corroborates this testimony. (Pros. Ex. 6.) Furthermore, since the Christmas tree was standing in front of the dining room window during the 2008 retirement party (Tr. R. at 7: 3–5), Quinn could not have left the print on that occasion. Moreover, Smith's cleaning lady dusted and wiped down the windowsill on January 15, 2009. (Pros. Ex. 8, Soffy Aff. ¶ 14.)

17. Smith never gave Quinn permission to enter his home on January 16 or 17, 2009. (Tr. R. at 8:30.) Although Smith and Quinn knew each other, Quinn had only been in Smith's home twice in five years. Quinn could not reasonably rely on Smith's statement, "We have an open door policy for friends," (Tr. R. at 22:16) to mean that any acquaintance could enter Smith's home at will without an invitation or specific permission. Thus, Smith's testimony that he thought he had permission to be in Smith's home (Tr. R. at 23:17) is not credible.

18. At 10:42 a.m. on January 17, 2009, Quinn was seen on the Valley Area Bank drive-up-teller videotape trying to withdraw money using Smith's ATM card. (Pros. Ex. 7.)

19. At 11:45 a.m. on January 17, 2009, Quinn was driving on Maple Street in Olsonville and was pulled over for having expired license plate tabs. (Pros. Ex. 3.)

20. During the traffic stop, Officer Kuzo noticed Smith's wallet on the dashboard of Quinn's car. (Tr. R. at 22:14.) Officer Kuzo had heard a description of the missing wallet when he started his shift earlier that morning. (Tr. R. at 22:15–18.)

21. When he inspected the wallet, Officer Kuzo found that it matched the description he had been given of Smith's wallet and that the wallet contained Smith's ATM card. (Tr. R. at 22:19.)

22. Although Smith's driver's license and cash had been removed from the wallet, the Court finds Smith's in-court identification (Tr. R. at 11:6) of the wallet credible and Quinn's uncorroborated story that he received the wallet from a friend who collects military memorabilia (Tr. R. at 40:15–18) not credible.

III. CONCLUSIONS OF LAW

Quinn is charged with first-degree burglary with the underlying crime being theft of Smith's wallet.

A. Did Quinn Commit Theft?

In Minnesota, a person commits theft when he "intentionally and without claim of right takes ... possession of movable property of another without the other's consent and with intent to deprive the owner permanently of possession of the property." Minn. Stat. § 609.52(2)(1).

1. Quinn committed the crime of theft while in Smith's home by taking Smith's wallet without Smith's consent.

B. Did Quinn Commit First-degree Burglary?

A person commits first-degree burglary when he "enters a building without consent and commits a crime while in the building ... if ... the building is a dwelling and another person, not an accomplice, is present in it when the burglar enters or at any time while the burglar is in the building." Minn. Stat. § 609.582.

2. Quinn entered 347 Greenway Drive at approximately 12:30 a.m. on January 17, 2009.

3. 347 Greenway Drive is a dwelling.

4. Smith was in the dwelling during the entire time that Quinn was in the dwelling.

5. Quinn entered Smith's home without Smith's consent.

6. As concluded above, Quinn committed theft while in Smith's home.

7. Therefore, all the elements of first-degree burglary have been satisfied.

IV. ORDER

1. Pursuant to the above Findings of Fact and Conclusions of Law, the Court finds Defendant Charles Michael Quinn, a/k/a Charlie Michaels, **GUILTY** of burglary in the first-degree in violation of Minnesota Statutes Section 609.582;

2. The probation office shall prepare a presentence report ("PSR") in this case. Once both Parties have had the opportunity to object to the PSR, the Court will set a sentencing date; and

3. Charles Michael Quinn is free on bail pending sentencing. All conditions of the Court's February 3, 2009, conditional release order (Docket No. 3) remain in force.

Dated:
July 12, 2009   _____
                                 Judge Christina J. Sullivan
                                 Trevor County District Court

8.3 Jury Instructions

The Constitution provides the right to a jury trial in both criminal and civil matters.[32] Early in American history, judges did not instruct juries; rather, jurors were supposed to "use their common sense" to decide cases.[33] As life became less rural and disputes became more complicated, the need for uniformity in legal rules became more important.[34] Jurors ultimately lost the right to decide the law, and the "modern division of labor" between judge and jury was firmly established by the end of the nineteenth century.[35] Judges now instruct jurors on the law, and jurors decide the facts of the case.[36]

Juries serve two important roles in the American legal system. As discussed above, the jury's most obvious role, and the one law students learn about, is to act as the fact finder in a trial. Jurors decide whose story is more credible and which version of the facts is most believable. In doing so, jurors subtly exercise their other role: bringing society's values into the courtroom.

Although jurors sit through an entire trial, hear all the testimony, and see all the exhibits and evidence, their most important work does not begin until after the end of closing arguments. At that point, the judge will *charge* the jury. When charging a jury, the judge will give the jurors the instructions that will govern their deliberations and the law that must be applied in the case. The judge will tell the jurors that if they believe one version of the facts, one party will prevail, and if they believe another version of the facts, the other party will prevail. Judicial clerks bear much of the re-

---

32. U. S. Const. amend. VI, amend. VII.
33. Peter Tiersma, *The Rocky Road to Legal Reform: Improving the Language of Jury Instructions*, 66 Brook. L. Rev. 1081, 1083 (2001).
34. *Id.*
35. *Id.*
36. *Id.*

sponsibility for drafting the instructions that will eventually be given to jurors. In addition, judicial clerks draft the verdict forms upon which jurors answer the questions raised during trials.[37]

Allegedly incorrect jury instructions are common foundations for appeals. Thus, jury instructions are the source of much debate among litigating parties, and judges must often decide between opposing versions of instructions proffered by the parties.

Although the judicial clerk's role in drafting jury instructions will vary from judge to judge and from case to case, in all jurisdictions parties must be allowed to propose instructions in some way, and must also be allowed to object to instructions they do not want given to the jury. Check with the judge to see what procedure the judge follows for accepting proposed jury instructions and for deciding on the final instructions. The process described below is typical in many courts.

Types of Jury Instructions

When most people think of jury instructions, they think about the final *charge,* or *post-instructions,* the judge will give the jury at the end of the trial. In reality, a judge usually instructs the jury twice: once at the beginning of the trial before opening arguments and once at the end of the trial after closing arguments.[38]

The instructions given orally at the beginning of the trial, after the jury has been empanelled and sworn in, are called *pre-instructions* and are typically not a source of conflict between the parties. Pre-instructions usually include information about the procedures that will be followed during trial; the daily trial schedule; the na-

37. The instructions and verdict form are not always separate documents. Sometimes they are incorporated into one document, which is usually referred to as "the jury instructions."

38. *See* Fed. R. Civ. P. 51; Fed. R. Crim. P. 30 (allowing judges to give both pre-trial and post-trial jury instructions). A judge may also instruct the jury at any other time during the trial when the judge feels it is ap-

ture of the jurors' duties; communication restrictions; and what does and does not constitute evidence the jury can consider.

Pre-instructions might also include information about the law, such as an overview of the causes of action or the crimes at issue in the trial, the defenses proffered by the parties, and the burdens of proof each party bears in the case. Although not required to do so, many judges give this information to jurors at the beginning of trials because it helps jurors listen more effectively and better understand what testimony is relevant. Most judges have standard pre-instructions that they give in all their trials, so unless the trial is about an issue of first impression, you will likely not need to draft many pre-instructions, if any.

Final charge instructions are usually the cause of any controversy between the parties' attorneys. In the final jury charge, the judge explains the law the jury must apply to the facts and instructs the jury to reach its final conclusions based on that law. There are many different sources of jury instructions, including holdings from case law; standard instructions the judge uses over and over again; and books of *pattern jury instructions* issued by bar associations, courts, and legal scholars.[39] These pattern instructions are sometimes called *model jury instructions* or *JIGs,* an acronym for "jury instruction guide." With all these resources available, you will rarely be asked to draft jury instructions from scratch.

---

propriate to do so. For example, immediately after sustaining an objection to testimony, a judge will tell the jury to disregard the testimony. This instruction is usually reiterated during the jury charge instructions. *See also, e.g.,* Minn. R. Civ. P. 51.02(c) (allowing the trial judge to instruct the jury "at any time after the trial begins and before the jury is discharged").

39. *See, e.g.,* ABA Section of Litigation, *Model Jury Instructions: Copyright, Trademark and Trade Dress Litigation* (2008); ABA Section of Litigation, *Model Jury Instructions: Employment Litigation* (2d ed. 2005); Committee on Model Jury Instructions Within the Eighth Circuit, *Manual of Model Civil Jury Instructions for the District Courts of the Eighth Cir-*

Pattern instruction books are usually organized by statute or common law causes of action. Judges can easily find the crimes or causes of action at issue in these pattern instruction books and copy the appropriate instructions into the final jury charge. In theory, this makes the process of drafting jury instructions more streamlined and cuts down on appeals since the instructions in the books have usually been affirmed by appellate courts. Although this works to a certain extent, as discussed below, the better practice is to adapt pattern instructions to fit the needs of a particular trial.

Drafting Jury Instructions

Most judges require attorneys to submit proposed jury instructions at some point either before or during the trial. Not surprisingly, attorneys all want instructions that favor their clients. These proposed instructions are the starting point from which a clerk begins drafting final charging instructions. Although judges' procedures for accepting proposed jury instructions vary widely, many judges require that parties submit joint instructions when possible, and only submit separate instructions when they disagree.

In addition, most judges have standard instructions they give all their juries and standard instructions they give in trials involving frequently litigated causes of action such as burglary or Title VII race discrimination. Always ask the judge or more experienced clerks if such instructions exist. The judge may prefer to use these tried-and-true instructions instead of instructions submitted by the parties. Re-using these instructions saves time and ensures that the judge is comfortable with the instructions.

cuit (2001); Kevin F. O'Malley, Jay E. Grenig, Hon. William C. Lee, *Federal Jury Practice and Instructions Criminal* (5th ed. 2000).

Once the parties have submitted proposed instructions, the clerk must draft final instructions that serve two purposes. First, the instructions must correctly convey the law. Second, the instructions must be easily understood by the jurors. When drafting, remember that the judge's "primary concern should be an effort to empower the jury to understand and apply the law in a holistic and contextual way."[40]

As with any legal writing, you must keep your audience in mind as you draft jury instructions. Most jurors have not had legal training and many have not had any formal education beyond high school. Although the parties submit proposed instructions, the judge has the ultimate responsibility for giving understandable and legally correct jury instructions. Therefore, you should resist any temptation to adopt a jury instruction that the parties agree on without reviewing it for correctness and comprehension.

Using pattern jury instructions. As discussed above, pattern jury instructions are very helpful, and most judges have particular pattern sources on which they like to rely. However, pattern jury instructions have some potential problems. First, there may be more than one set of applicable pattern instructions for your jurisdiction, so there may not be one obviously correct version that should be adopted.

Second, pattern instructions are written by lawyers, they are proffered to the court by lawyers, and former lawyers (judges) decide what the jury instructions will be in any particular case. But since most jurors are not lawyers, they may not understand terms that law-trained readers understand. Accordingly, you should remove legalese from jury instructions whenever possible.

For example, the words "mitigate," "proffer," "foreseeable," and "breach" are all familiar to first-year law students. However, average citizens do not use these words in daily conversation. Even more

---

40. Elizabeth G. Thornburg, *The Power and the Process: Instructions and the Civil Jury*, 66 Fordham L. Rev. 1837, 1839 (1998).

problematic, some words such as "reasonable" are used in non-legal settings, but can have different meanings under the law. To the average non-lawyer juror, a "reasonable person" might be one who possesses "good sound judgment."[41] More specifically, a "reasonable" person might be a person who possesses judgment similar to an individual juror's judgment. However, under the law, a "reasonable person" is one who "acts sensibly, takes proper but not excessive precautions, does things without serious delay, and weighs evidence carefully but not overskeptically. The reasonable person is neither perfect nor indifferent."[42] Although this definition might not articulate a specific juror's definition of what is reasonable, this is the definition the juror must apply to the facts of the case.

In addition, pattern instructions, which are either written by lawyers or are taken directly from judicial opinions, may make sense when read silently, but not when read out loud. When judges charge juries, they typically read the instructions out loud. In most jurisdictions, jurors can refer to hard copies of the instructions during deliberations, but in some jurisdictions, jurors cannot have hard copies of the instructions or are only allowed copies when requested by the parties.[43] Thus, the instructions must not only be written using words that jurors can easily comprehend and remember, they must

---

41. *Webster's Third New International Dictionary* 1892 (1971).

42. Bryan A. Garner, *supra* note 6, at 737.

43. *See, e.g.,* Pa. R. Crim. P. 646(B)(4) (2008 update) (jury not allowed to have written instructions); Ala. R. Crim P. 21.1 (LexisNexis 2003) (jury generally not allowed to have written instructions or copy of charges against the defendant, except that a judge can provide the charges in a complex case); La. Code Crim. Proc. Ann. art. 801 (Supp. 2009) (allowing jurors a copy of the written charge only if consented to by both parties). *But see* Douglas G. Smith, *Structural and Functional Aspects of the Jury: Comparative Analysis and Proposals for Reform*, 48 Ala. L. Rev. 441, 529 (1997) (citation omitted) (stating that appellate courts generally find the practice of giving jurors written jury instructions "acceptable" as long as jurors are properly instructed to consider the charge instructions as a whole and not to focus on one part of the instructions).

also be punctuated to accurately convey the meaning and allow the judge to communicate the meaning orally. Adding bullet points and organizing in list form rather than paragraph form can help make information easier to understand because these visual breaks will force the judge to slow down and pause in certain places when reading the instructions out loud to the jury. Bullet points and lists will also make the instructions easier for jurors to follow if they are allowed to have copies of the instructions with them during deliberations.

Third, many pattern jury instructions, and many statutes that eventually become part of jury instructions, use archaic language that makes no sense to the ordinary person, or even to most attorneys. For example, using the terms "master" and "servant" to describe employers and employees, or using the word "infant" to describe any person who has not reached the age of legal majority, would seem ridiculous to a non-lawyer. No twenty-first century person applying the modern-day use of the word would consider a fifteen-year-old boy an "infant." As long as changing a word adds clarity and does not change the meaning of the instruction, you should change potentially confusing language. Flag all changes for the judge because the judge must make the final decision.

Fourth, many pattern instructions contain double negatives, rambling sentences, and passive voice. Both double negatives and passive voice make it difficult to identify who is the actor in a particular sentence. Since trials are usually about who did what to whom, ambiguity about when a defendant is liable, guilty, or responsible is problematic. Long rambling sentences are simply hard to follow and can confuse jurors. You should redraft instructions that contain structural and grammatical errors so they will be easily understood by the jury. Do not feel constrained by the pattern instructions — improve upon them if you can.

In reality, not all legal or potentially ambiguous terms are avoidable. When you must use such words, you should define them. Failure to define common words such as "reasonable" or uncommon terms such as "fraudulent conveyance" can lead to juror confusion, which in turn can lead to distrust of the verdict and, eventually, distrust of the entire jury system.[44]

Fifth, pattern instructions are often written either too generally or too specifically to be workable in every case. Pattern-instruction authors either have the statutes or case holdings in front of them and write instructions that fit the cold words of the statute or holding, or copy instructions that have worked in other cases. However, real trials involve unique people in unique situations. "One size fits all" jury instructions do not always work for the distinct nuances of a given case and may need to be re-written to make sense for your situation. Gender-specific or other specific references can be changed or added as necessary to make the instructions relevant to the present case if doing so does not change the instruction's meaning. Avoid pronouns whenever possible, even if pattern instructions include them, because they can lead to confusion.

Even though pattern jury instructions are good resources and good time savers, you must make sure every instruction is correct and works in the context of your case. To the extent the parties propose pattern instructions that meet these criteria, you can probably include them in your first draft of the jury instructions. If the

----

44. For example, during a California murder trial, a judge told the jurors that for the defendant to be found guilty, the jury had to find that the killing had been committed with "malice aforethought." Apparently no one defined "malice aforethought" for the jury, and this omission led the jury to conclude that "the murder had to be committed with a mallet." Aaron Lauchheimer, *Giving Jurors the Law in Plain English*, 25 The Nat'l L. J., July 28, 2003, at 48, 48; *see also* David Barron, Note, *I Did Not Want to Kill Him But Thought I Had to: In Light of Penry II's Interpretation of Blystone, Why the Constitution Requires Jury Instructions on How to Give Effect to Relevant Mitigating Evidence in Capital Cases,* 11 J. L. & Pol'y 207, 240–53 (2002) (internal citations in title omitted) (discussing jurors' failure to understand the concept of mitigation in capital cases); Hon. Arthur J. Hanes, Bert S. Nettles, & Leila H. Watson, *The "Plain English" Project of the Alabama Pattern Jury Instructions Committee—Civil,* Ala. Law., Sept. 2007, at 369, 371 (explaining that poor instructions can lead to unreliable verdicts).

law is correct and the instruction is clear, most judges will happily adopt instructions that satisfy both parties.

Choosing from competing proposed instructions. After you have dealt with any joint proposed jury instructions, flag the contested instructions, let the judge know what the competing versions say, and then recommend instructions based on your own research and analysis.

In a case of first impression, the parties will likely disagree about what law should be applied to the facts. In this situation, you may be called upon to do the same type of research you would do for a bench memo. Parties will often file supplemental briefs explaining why the judge should adopt their proposed instructions over their opponents' proposed instructions. However, parties sometimes file the dueling jury instructions without any briefs. In this situation, you must do independent research before you can make your recommendation to the judge. Since judges commonly require citations to authority with proposed instructions, the parties have probably cited at least one source for support, giving you a starting point for your research.

Proofreading jury instructions. Once you have a draft of the jury instructions, you must carefully proofread the instructions for accuracy, internal consistency, and clarity. When proofreading jury instructions, keep in mind the most important writing rule you learned during your first year of law school and reiterated above. Remember your audience — non-law-trained citizens of average intelligence. Therefore, you should avoid legalese whenever possible. Write in short declarative sentences, and use strong verbs that leave no doubt about the meaning of the sentence. Avoid confusing, long-winded, clause-filled sentences — break them up into shorter sentences when possible. Punctuate properly — a stray or missed comma can change the meaning of a sentence. Establish and use consistent references for parties and entities.

In addition, present the instructions in a logical order. Judges usually like to give "generic" instructions up front so that jurors are aware of evidentiary rules and burdens of proof when they hear the claim-specific instructions. Number each instruction and put each instruction on its own page with a title so the attorneys and the judge can easily refer to specific instructions during discussions, and so jurors get a visual break from reading too much text on a page. Good organization will also make jury instructions easy to understand. Visual rhetoric, in the form of roadmaps, bullet points, and numbered lists, will all help jurors understand instructions and, as discussed above, may force the judge to slow down and read the information systematically instead of flying through each sentence. For example, if you are working on a case involving civil negligence claims, you might want to explain the basic law in the following way. (For purposes of this example, assume that "duty," "breached," "caused," and "damages" are defined elsewhere in separate jury instructions.)

> In order for Yex Corporation to be found negligent in this case, you must find that four things were true on the afternoon of April 14, 2008:
>
> 1. Yex Corporation owed Martin Zobst a duty to maintain Yex's lawn sprinkler system in such a way that no customer could trip over the in-ground sprinkler heads;
>
> 2. Yex Corporation breached that duty by failing to maintain Yex's lawn sprinkler system in such a way that no customer could trip over the in-ground sprinkler heads;
>
> 3. Yex Corporation's failure to maintain Yex's lawn sprinkler system in such a way that no customer could trip over the in-ground sprinkler heads caused Martin Zobst to trip over a sprinkler head and fall;
>
> AND
>
> 4. Martin Zobst suffered damages as a result of his fall.

This short example contains a roadmap (i.e., there are four things to come); numbered points for easy tracking; common repeated language; consistent references to parties; no pronouns; and emphasis in the form of "AND" written in all capital letters to visually remind the jury that all four elements must be satisfied for the defendant to be found negligent, or to cause the judge to give the word emphasis when reading the instruction out loud. Given in conjunction with the other instructions, this instruction would help a jury stay on track.

Drafting Verdict Forms

Verdict forms are drafted at the same time as jury instructions. On a verdict form, the jury (1) answers the questions the judge poses, and (2) renders its official verdict. Like jury instructions, verdict forms can be a source of contention between parties.

Judges have broad discretion in framing the questions on verdict forms.[45] Juries can be asked to render *general verdicts* or *special verdicts*. A *general verdict* is merely the answer to the ultimate legal question in the case:

"We, the jury, find for _____."[46]

(Fill in party name.)

When asking for a general verdict, the jury charge will include a long narrative about the issues in the case, the parties' theories and defenses, and the law, and then conclude with the ultimate legal question.[47] With a general verdict, it is possible for a jury to find a defendant liable even though there is not unanimous agreement as to which of the plaintiff's legal theories was proven.[48] As long as each juror decides that the plaintiff proved the defendant's conduct satisfied the elements of any single claim the defendant will be found liable—even if six jurors found only Claim 1 proved liability and six jurors found only Claim 2 proved liability.[49] As long as each of the twelve jurors found that some claim was proved, the defendant is liable.

A *special verdict* is one in which the jury must return "a special written finding on each issue of fact."[50] Judges may also require the

---

45. *See* Fed. R. Civ. P. 49.
46. Thornburg, *supra* note 40, at 1844.
47. *Id.*
48. *Id.*
49. *See id.* at 1844–46.
50. Fed. R. Civ. P. 49(a)(1).

jury to answer *special interrogatories*, which are narrow factual questions such as "Was Plaintiff Anne Goody assaulted by an unidentified attacker on May 14, 2008? Yes or No."[51] Because special verdict forms contain narrow questions, they tend to elicit unanimous verdicts. However, they are longer and contain more questions than general verdict forms. The judge will make the ultimate decision about the level of detail to include in the verdict form.

Regardless of the level of detail, good verdict forms ask questions that can be answered with one- or two-word answers or that can be answered in a "yes/no" check-box manner. Even general verdicts, which require a significant amount of narrative information up front, should ask pointed final questions.

Good verdict forms also make the relationship between certain questions clear. For example, if you are drafting jury instructions in a negligence case that includes a claim for punitive damages, the jurors will not need to decide if punitive damages are appropriate unless, and until, they decide there was negligence in the first place.

Assume you have drafted a verdict form that includes the following questions. Question 1 asks whether the defendant was negligent, Question 2 asks whether punitive damages are appropriate, and Question 3 asks what amount of punitive damages are appropriate. If the jury answers "No" to Question 1, then the jury must not answer Question 2 and Question 3. Thus, after Question 1, you should include instructions that say, "If you answer 'yes' to Question 1, answer Question 2. If you answer 'no' to Question 1, skip Question 2 and Question 3. Move on to answer Question 4."

Failure to properly instruct the jury about the effect of its answers in this way could result in inconsistent verdicts, such as a jury finding that a defendant was not negligent, but that the plaintiff was nevertheless entitled to punitive damages. Federal Rule of

---

51. Question format modeled in Ronald W. Eades, *The Problem of Jury Instructions in Civil Cases*, 27 Cumb. L. Rev. 1017, 1024 (1996–1997). For a discussion of the effect that framing the verdict form and jury questions in particular ways can have on the outcome of the trial, see Thornburg, *supra* note 40, at 1843–73.

Civil Procedure 49 provides judges guidance for dealing with inconsistent verdicts, but the result is often a new trial. Obviously the interests of judicial economy are best served by avoiding retrials whenever possible.

Thus, if you were drafting a verdict form in the negligence case in which Plaintiff Martin Zobst sought actual and punitive damages from Yex Corporation, you might draft part of the verdict form in the following way. (For purposes of this example, assume that the jury has been instructed on both the elements of negligence and the standard for proving entitlement to punitive damages.)

1. Was Yex Corporation negligent towards Martin Zobst on April 14, 2008?

_____Yes OR _____No

(Check one answer.)

If you answer "Yes" to Question 1, answer Question 2.

If you answer "No" to Question 1, Stop.

2. Is Martin Zobst entitled to monetary compensation for the actual damages he suffered as a result of Yex Corporation's negligence of April 14, 2008?

_____Yes OR _____No

(Check one answer.)

If you answer "Yes" to Question 2, answer Question 3 and Question 4.

If you answer "No" to Question 2, Stop.

3. What monetary amount fairly compensates Martin Zobst for the actual damages caused by Yex Corporation's negligence of April 14, 2008?

_____

(Insert amount in U.S. dollars and cents.)

4. Is Martin Zobst entitled to punitive damages because of Yex Corporation's negligence of April 14, 2008?

_____Yes OR _____No

(Check one answer.)

If you answer "Yes" to Question 4, answer Question 5.

If you answer "No" to Question 4, Stop.

5. What amount of punitive damages is appropriate in this case?

_____

(Insert amount in U.S. dollars and cents.)

As you can see, even the jury instructions in a simple negligence action can be confusing if roadmaps and stop signs are not used to guide the jurors. Make sure you include instructions telling the jury what to do next if the jury's answer to a question will affect the jury's next task.

Charge Conferences

Once the judge has approved a draft of the instructions and verdict form, the judge and the attorneys will discuss the draft on the record and out of the jury's hearing. This discussion is called a *charge conference.* The judge must give the attorneys the opportunity to argue for their proposed instructions on the record so the issues are preserved for appeal.[52] The judge will decide on the record which version of the instructions will be used, and the clerk will usually create the final draft of the instructions, incorporating any changes that were made as a result of the charge conference.

Charging the Jury

Judges usually read the instructions to the jury. As discussed above, most juries are allowed to take copies of the charge instructions into the deliberation room. In addition, the judge can present the instructions in alternative ways to increase the likelihood that all the jurors understand the charge, such as projecting the instructions using a document camera. Many courtrooms have this technology. Attorneys use it for their advantage, and judges should use it for jurors' advantage also.

Once the jury has been charged, the jurors retire to the deliberation room to do their important work, and the judge, the clerk,

_____

52. Fed. R. Crim. P. 30(d); Fed. R. Civ. P. 51(b)(2).

the attorneys, and the parties wait for the verdict. During deliberations, the judge may need you to do additional research if the jury has any questions about its job or the instructions.

Checklist for Jury Instructions and Verdict Forms

Jury Instructions

- Correctly state the law?
- Avoid legalese whenever possible?
- Change even common words to simpler words to avoid confusion?[53]
- Define legal terms and uncommon words?
- Use short declarative sentences, whenever possible?
- Use clear strong verbs, whenever possible?
- Written in active voice, whenever possible?
- Are correctly punctuated?
- Use consistent references to parties, places, and things?
- Avoid pronouns?
- Present each instruction on a separate page with a title at the top of the page?
- Present instructions in a logical order?
- Incorporate roadmaps, lists, and bullet points to make instructions visually pleasing and easy to follow?

Verdict Form

- Easy to understand and follow?
- Solicits simple one- or two-word answers or "yes/no" answers to questions, whenever possible?

---

53. For example, "adjacent to" can be changed to "next to." Byran A. Garner, *The Redbook: A Manual on Legal Style* § 11.2(b) (2d ed. 2006) (providing simple substitutes for potentially confusing words). See also the editing tables at the end of Chapter Five.

- Tells jurors what questions to answer next and what questions to skip, depending on answers to specific questions?
- Clearly presents places for juror answers by using check boxes for "yes/no" answers and blank lines for narrative answers or money amounts?

Writing, Revising, Editing, Proofing

- Easy to understand and follow?
- Solicits simple one- or two-word answers or "yes/no" answers to questions, whenever possible?
- Tells jurors what questions to answer next and what questions to skip, depending on answers to specific questions?
- Has been revised for grammar, usage, and style to make the document as clear and concise as possible?
- Has been proofread for spelling and other typographical errors?

Sample Jury Instructions[54]
United States District Court
District of Minnesota

United States of America,
  Plaintiff,
  v.
Malcolm Jones,
  Defendant.
	No. 07-CR-118
	
	JURY INSTRUCTIONS

JURY INSTRUCTION NO. 1
READ INSTRUCTIONS AS A WHOLE

It is your duty as jurors to follow the law as stated in all of the instructions of the Court and to apply the law to the facts as you find them. You are not to single out any one instruction alone as stating the law, but must consider the instructions as a whole in reaching your decisions.

No matter what you think the law ought to be, you must base your verdict on the law contained in these instructions. In decid-

---

54. This sample is edited for space. Not every instruction that would be included in a real set of instructions is included, and not every instruction that is included is complete. The purpose of this sample is to help new judicial clerks understand the kind of language used to convey legal concepts and the kind of detail required when charging a jury. Ideally, each instruction should appear on its own page. To save space, these instructions are presented together.

These sample jury instructions are adapted from the jury instructions in *United States v. Williams*, No. 04-CR-313 (MJD/FLN) (D. Minn. Mar. 23, 2005) (Doc. No. 129). Some of the instructions appear exactly as they did in the *Williams* instructions and some have been re-drafted for educational purposes. Since many of these instructions were drafted or re-drafted for educational purposes, readers should not rely on the instructions as accurate statements of the law. No attempt has been made to determine the original source of any particular instruction, such as a pattern instruction book, JIG, dictionary, or case holding.

ing the issues in this trial you must not be persuaded by bias, prejudice, or sympathy for or against any of the parties to this case or by any public opinion.

JURY INSTRUCTION NO. 2
PRESUMPTION OF INNOCENCE

You must presume the defendant, Malcolm Jones, to be innocent of the crime charged. Even though he is accused of a crime in an indictment, he begins the trial with a "clean slate," with no evidence against him. An indictment is not evidence of any kind. You can only consider legal evidence presented during the trial. The presumption of innocence alone, therefore, is sufficient to acquit Jones.

JURY INSTRUCTION NO. 3
BURDEN OF PROOF

The burden is always upon the Government to prove guilt beyond a reasonable doubt. This burden never shifts to Jones. Jones has no duty to call witnesses or even to produce evidence. Jones is not even obligated to cross-examine the witnesses for the Government.

It is not required that the Government proves guilt beyond all possible doubt. The test is one of reasonable doubt. A reasonable doubt is a doubt based upon reason and common sense — the kind of doubt that would make a reasonable person hesitate to act.

"Proof beyond a reasonable doubt" is proof of such a convincing character that a reasonable person would not hesitate to rely and act upon it in his or her own most important affairs.

Unless the Government proves beyond a reasonable doubt that Jones has committed each and every element of the crime charged in the indictment, you must find Jones not guilty.

If you view the evidence in the case as reasonably permitting either of two conclusions — one of innocence, the other of guilt — you must find Jones innocent.

JURY INSTRUCTION NO. 4
WHAT CONSTITUTES EVIDENCE

The evidence in this case consists of the following:

- sworn testimony of the witnesses, regardless of who may have called them;
- all exhibits received in evidence, regardless of who may have produced them; and
- all facts that may have been admitted to or agreed to in court.

Anything you may have seen or heard outside the courtroom is not proper evidence and cannot be considered.

Questions, objections, statements, and arguments of attorneys are not evidence in the case, unless made as an admission or an agreement. You are to base your verdict only on the evidence received in the case.

In your consideration of the evidence received, however, you are not limited to the bald statements of the witnesses or to the bald assertions in the exhibits. In other words, you are not limited solely to what you saw and heard when the witnesses testified or as the exhibits were admitted. You are permitted to draw from the facts that have been proven any reasonable inferences you feel are justified in light of your own experience and common sense.

JURY INSTRUCTION NO. 5
DETERMINING CREDIBILTY

You, as jurors, are the sole and exclusive judges of the credibility of each of the witnesses called to testify in this case, and only you determine the importance or the weight that their testimony deserves. After making your assessment concerning the credibility of a witness, you may decide to believe all of that witness's testimony, only a portion of it, or none of it.

In making your assessment, you should carefully scrutinize all of the testimony given, the circumstances under which each witness has testified, and every matter in evidence that tends to show whether a witness, in your opinion, is worthy of belief. Consider each witness's intelligence, motive to falsify, state of mind, and appearance and manner while on the witness stand. Consider the witness's ability to observe the matters as to which he or she has testified and consider whether he or she impresses you as having an accurate memory or recollection of these matters. Consider also any relation a witness may bear to either side of the case, the manner in which each witness might be affected by the verdict, and the extent to which, if at all, each witness's testimony is either supported or contradicted by other evidence in the case.

Inconsistencies or discrepancies in the testimony of a witness or between the testimony of different witnesses may or may not cause you to disbelieve or discredit such testimony. Two or more persons witnessing an incident or a transaction may simply see or hear it differently. In weighing the effect of a discrepancy, however, always consider whether it pertains to a matter of importance or an insignificant detail and consider whether the discrepancy results from innocent error or intentional falsehood.

After making your own judgment or assessment concerning the believability of a witness, you can then attach as much importance or weight to that testimony, if any, that you feel it deserves. You will then be in a position to decide whether the Government has proven the charge beyond a reasonable doubt.

JURY INSTRUCTION NO. 6
JONES'S RIGHT NOT TO TESTIFY

The defendant in a criminal case has an absolute right under our Constitution not to testify. The fact that Jones did not testify must not be discussed or considered by the jury in any way when deliberating and in arriving at your verdict. No inference of any kind may be drawn from the fact that Jones exercised his privilege under the Constitution and did not testify.

JURY INSTRUCTION NO. 7
ELEMENTS OF THE CRIME CHARGED

Defendant Malcolm Jones is charged with being a convicted felon in possession of a firearm in violation of 18 United States Code,

Section 922(g). The crime of being a convicted felon in possession of a firearm has three essential elements:

1) Jones had previously been convicted of a crime punishable by imprisonment for a term exceeding one year;
2) After that conviction, Jones knowingly possessed the firearm described in the indictment; and
3) The firearm was transported in interstate commerce either before Jones possessed the firearm or during the time Jones owned the firearm.

If all of these essential elements have been proven beyond a reasonable doubt, then you must find Jones guilty of the crime charged; otherwise, you must find Jones not guilty of this crime.

The Government and Jones have agreed that Jones has been convicted of a crime punishable by imprisonment for more than one year under the laws of the State of Minnesota. Therefore, you must consider the first essential element as proven.

JURY INSTRUCTION NO. 8
"KNOWINGLY POSSESSED"

The second element of the crime charged prohibits a person from having "knowingly possessed" a firearm. The Government is not required to prove that Jones owned the firearm. Taking a firearm or having temporary possession of a firearm may be the basis for a conviction of possessing a firearm.

JURY INSTRUCTION NO. 9
"KNOWINGLY" DEFINED

In the second element of the crime charged, the term "knowingly" means that Jones was conscious and aware of his actions, that he realized what he was doing or what was happening around him, and that he did not act or fail to act because of ignorance, mistake, or accident.

JURY INSTRUCTION NO. 10
"POSSESSION" DEFINED

The law recognizes several kinds of possession. A person may have "actual possession" or "constructive possession."

A person has actual possession of a thing when he has direct physical control over the thing. Ownership is not required.

A person has constructive possession of a thing when, although not in actual possession, he has both the power and the intention to exercise control over a thing, either directly or through another person or persons. Ownership is not required.

Whenever the words "possessed" or "possession" are used in these instructions, they include actual as well as constructive possession.

JURY INSTRUCTION NO. 11
"FIREARM" DEFINED

The term "firearm" means any weapon (including a starter gun)

- that will,
- is designed to, or
- may be easily converted to

expel a projectile by the action of an explosive.

JURY INSTRUCTION NO. 12
"COMMERCE" DEFINED

The phrase "commerce" means the exchange of goods or services.

JURY INSTRUCTION NO. 13
"IN INTERSTATE COMMERCE" DEFINED

In the third element of the crime charged, traveled "in interstate commerce" includes commerce between any place in a State and any place outside of that State.

The Government may meet its burden of proof on the question of being "in interstate commerce" by proving beyond a reasonable doubt that the firearm identified in the indictment had traveled at any time across a state boundary line.

If you find beyond a reasonable doubt that the firearm in question was manufactured in a state other than Minnesota and Jones possessed that firearm in the State of Minnesota then you may, but are not required to, find that it was transported across a state line.

Jones did not have to personally participate in the interstate movement of the firearm in order for the third element to be proven. Therefore, the Government does not have to prove that Jones knew that the firearm traveled in interstate commerce in order to prove the offense.

JURY INSTRUCTION NO. 14
PROVING INTENT OR KNOWLEDGE

Intent or knowledge may be proven like anything else. You may consider any statements Jones made and acts Jones did along with all the facts and circumstances in evidence. You may, but are not required to, infer that a person intends the natural and probable consequences of acts knowingly done or knowingly omitted.

Sample Verdict Form

United States District Court
District of Minnesota

United States of America,   No. 07-CR-118
    Plaintiff,
      v.
Malcolm Jones,   VERDICT FORM
    Defendant.

We, the jury, unanimously find the Defendant Malcolm Jones

_____ or _____
     Guilty   Not Guilty
      (Choose one.)

of being a Convicted Felon in Possession of a Firearm in violation of 18 United States Code Section 922(g) as charged in the indictment.

_____   _____

Dated   Signature of Jury Foreperson

_____

Printed Name of Jury Foreperson

8.4 Statements of Reasons for Imposing Sentence

A statement of reasons for imposing sentence is exactly what the title suggests — a document in which a trial judge explains why, based on a convicted criminal's past history and recent conviction or guilty plea, the judge imposed a certain sentence. These documents contain confidential information and are usually filed under seal.[55] Some judges choose to issue written statements of reasons for all sentencings, and some judges issue statements of reasons only when they depart either upward or downward from the presumptive sentence under the appropriate sentencing guidelines.[56]

Sentencing criminals is one of a trial judge's most serious duties. Thus, the judge must justify the sentence imposed and must explain why certain defense arguments were rejected in favor of the opposing prosecution arguments or vice versa. When deciding on an appropriate sentence, the judge must state that the prosecution met its burden by proving the elements of the crime beyond a reasonable doubt or that the defendant admitted on the record to committing the crime, and must state the reasons for imposing a certain sentence.[57] The judge should always do this on the record in court,

---

55. *See supra* note 24 for an explanation of sealing records.

56. In *Blakely v. Washington,* 542 U.S. 296 (2004) and *United States v. Booker,* 543 U.S. 220 (2005), the Supreme Court announced that the federal sentencing guidelines and state guidelines modeled on them were no longer mandatory, but were merely advisory. Although the guidelines are now advisory, they are still the basis for the sentencing recommendations made by probation officers and a starting point for arguments about the appropriate sentence in any given case.

57. In the federal system, the reasons may also be included in the order of judgment and commitment, the document that outlines how much prison time, if any, the convicted person must serve, and the length and limitations of any subsequent supervised release. *See* Federal Judicial Center, *Law Clerk Handbook: A Handbook for Law Clerks to Federal Judges* 35 (Sylvan A. Sobel ed., 2d ed. 2007), *available at* http://www.fjc.gov/public/

but may also need to put the reasons into writing in a statement of reasons.

Ask the judge or a more experienced judicial clerk for old statements of reasons to use as templates if you are called upon to draft a statement of reasons. Statements of reasons usually follow the same basic format as orders, so you can also use an order as a template if no statements of reasons are available.

8.5 Additional Resources

Ruggero J. Aldisert, *Opinion Writing* (1990)

Amiran Elwork, Bruce D. Sales, & James J. Alfini, *Making Jury Instructions Understandable* (1982)

Federal Judicial Center, *Law Clerk Handbook: A Handbook for Law Clerks to Federal Judges* (Sylvan A. Sobel ed., 2d ed. 2007), *available at* http://www.fjc.gov/public/pdf.nsf/lookup/law clhbk.pdf/$file/lawclhbk.pdf

Federal Judicial Center, *Judicial Writing Manual* (Sylvan A. Sobel ed., 1991), *available at* http://www.fjc.gov/public/pdf.nsf/lookup/ JudicialWritingManual.pdf/$file/JudicialWritingManual.pdf

Bryan A. Garner, *The Redbook: A Manual on Legal Style* (2d ed. 2006)

Jill S. Gelineau, *Using Jury Instructions to Shape the Trial* (ALI-ABA Course of Study Materials, Course No. SM102, Jan. 4–6, 2007) (available at Lexis, CLE library, ALLCLE file)

Joyce J. George, *Judicial Opinion Writing Handbook* (5th ed. 2007)

Thomas Gibbs Gee, *A Few of Wisdom's Idiosyncrasies and a Few of Ignorance's: A Judicial Style Sheet*, 1 Scribes J. Legal Writing 55 (1990)

---

pdf.nsf/lookup/lawclhbk.pdf/$file/lawclhbk.pdf. Both the statement of reasons and the order of judgment and commitment must be provided to the probation office, the Sentencing Commission, and, if imprisonment is ordered, the Bureau of Prisons. *Id.*

Gerald Lebovits, Alifya V. Curtin, Lisa Solomon, *Ethical Judicial Opinion Writing*, 21 Geo. J. Legal Ethics 237 (2008)

Kevin O'Malley, Jay E. Grenig, & Hon. William C. Lee, *Federal Jury Practice and Instructions Civil* (5th ed. 2000)

Kevin O'Malley, Jay E. Grenig, & Hon. William C. Lee, *Federal Jury Practice and Instructions Criminal* (5th ed. 2000)

Todd C. Peppers, Micheal W. Giles, Bridget Tainer-Parkins, *Inside Judicial Chambers: How Federal District Court Judges Select and Use Their Law Clerks*, 71 Alb. L. Rev. 623 (2008)

Chapter 9

Drafting Appellate Opinions

One of an appellate court clerk's main duties is drafting opinions. Producing an appellate opinion is a collaborative process, and when you draft an opinion you are just one of the collaborators. By the time you draft an opinion for a case you have probably already written a bench memo, the parties' attorneys have made oral arguments, and the judges assigned to the case (the "panel") have held a conference at which they came to a preliminary agreement about how to decide the case. After you draft the opinion, the draft is reviewed by your judge and by the other judges on the panel, and then finalized by you and the judge. Finally, you (and perhaps other clerks) will do final proofreading and citation checking. Throughout the entire process you will be conferring with your judge about the law, the parties' arguments, the judge's reasoning, and the language the judge wants to use to express the reasoning.

The collaborative process involved in opinion drafting will probably differ from the writing process you have used in the past. There will be other important differences as well. First, you will be drafting a document that will have a broader audience than you have written for previously. While you undoubtedly did quite a bit of writing before and during law school, and you may have written a bench memo for the court, that writing was for yourself, a professor, or a judge. Now you are going to write the draft of a document that will likely have a much broader audience and a much longer lifespan—it may be published in books and on the internet, where it can be read by generations of law students and attorneys. The opinion won't have your name on it, but you will know that some of the analysis and writing in the opinion are yours.

Second, opinion drafting places a great deal of responsibility on the clerk, because the first draft influences everything that follows. Even though judges work with drafts to make them their own, they often adopt the authorities, organization, and language from their clerks' drafts. In this way, the clerk's draft opinion may affect the individual parties of the case and may ultimately affect the course of the law itself.

Finally, drafting opinions differs from other writing because you will be writing to express the ideas of a judge or a panel of judges. Even if you do not agree with the opinion, you must write it convincingly. And you must learn how to write in the voice of another person— a judge who is much more experienced than you are. Perhaps even more challenging will be incorporating into an opinion the ideas and words of the other judges who are joining the opinion.

Your role in the process of producing an opinion will vary depending on the judge and court you clerk for. While some appellate court judges expect their clerks to merely edit and cite check opinions, most appellate judges ask their clerks to write drafts of the full opinions the court produces. And judges give their clerks different amounts of direction: some judges explain their reasoning in depth and give their clerks detailed outlines from which to work, while others tell their clerks how they want to rule, but give little guidance about how to organize and analyze the issues. If you are unsure of your role, ask the judge or other clerks for guidance.[1]

9.1 Types of Appellate Opinions

As a clerk to an appellate judge, you may draft several different kinds of opinions. Most of your time will be spent drafting the most comprehensive of these: full majority opinions. But you may

---

1. Remember that the judge has the ultimate responsibility for writing opinions. Thus, no matter how much responsibility the judge gives you, you should always refer to your role as "drafting," not "writing" opinions.

also work on shorter majority opinions such as per curiam and memorandum opinions, or on minority concurring or dissenting opinions. Courts title and categorize opinions in different manners,[2] so you should check with another clerk and ask to see examples to learn the nature and names of the opinions your court produces. The following sections describe several types of opinions and the circumstances in which each is produced.[3]

Full Majority Opinions

You are familiar with full appellate opinions, because these are the published, precedential cases you have been reading since you entered law school. They are written for the most important cases—cases that consider "issues of precedential, institutional, jurisprudential, or social significance."[4] These opinions are important to audiences beyond the parties in the cases because they address new or unsettled legal questions, or involve complex facts, and contribute to the "progressive development of the law."[5] Although ap-

---

2. For example, some courts do not categorize per curiam and memorandum opinions separately.

3. Appellate courts also announce decisions in summary orders. A summary order may simply state the court's disposition of the case in a sentence or two, or may include a short statement of findings and conclusions, but usually will not include an explanation for the decision. Most summary orders are not published. They are not intended to create precedent, but merely to announce the court's decision to the parties. *See* Federal Judicial Center, *Judicial Writing Manual* 3 (Sylvan A. Sobel ed., 1991), *available at* http://www.fjc.gov/public/pdf.nsf/lookup/JudicialWritingManual.pdf/$file/JudicialWritingManual.pdf (includes an example of a summary order on page 35). If you are assigned the task of drafting a summary order, ask another clerk for a form to follow.

4. Elizabeth Fajans et al., *Writing for Law Practice* 340 (2004).

5. Ruggero J. Aldisert, Meehan Rasch, & Matthew P. Bartlett, *Opinion Writing and Opinion Readers*, 31 Cardozo L. Rev. 1, 12 (2009).

pellate judges and clerks spend a great deal of time producing full opinions, not all appellate court decisions are announced in full opinions. For example, in the federal appeals courts, only about thirty-seven percent of opinions and orders the courts produce are full published opinions.[6]

Full opinions are the longest and most fully explained opinions written by appellate courts. A full opinion describes the important facts of the case, analyzes and applies precedent, and explains the reasons for the court's decision. While a full opinion is authored and signed by a single judge, it reflects the decision of the other panel members as well. It may be accompanied by a concurring or dissenting opinion if not all the judges on the panel agree with the reasoning used or the result reached by the majority.

Other Majority Opinions

Intermediate courts of appeals hear many cases brought by parties who have the right to appeal, but which do not have much merit. These cases are easily disposed of, and their decisions are therefore appropriately announced in memorandum or per curiam opinions. (A smaller number of cases decided per curiam are important cases that the court wishes to speak about in one voice.) About sixty percent of opinions and orders filed in federal courts of appeals cases are unsigned per curiam or memorandum opinions.[7]

Per Curiam Opinions. Per curiam means "[b]y the court as a whole,"[8] and a per curiam opinion is "a joint, unexceptional, and

---

6. *See* Administrative Office of the United States Courts, *2008 Annual Report of the Director: Judicial Business of the United States Courts* 44, tbl.S-3 (2009) [hereinafter *Judicial Business of the United States Courts*] (statistics for the United States Courts of Appeals, excluding the Federal Circuit, for the twelve-month period ending September 30, 2008).

7. *See id.*

8. *Black's Law Dictionary* 1251 (9th ed. 2009).

monolithic decision rendered by all members participating."[9] A per curiam opinion is not signed by a particular judge because it is considered the opinion of the whole panel.[10] Per curiam opinions are most often produced in two different circumstances. First, a court produces a per curiam opinion if it determines the case does not warrant a full opinion, for example if the law and its application are clear, either because the case is relatively simple or because the issue has recently been decided by that court or a higher court. Second, if the court determines it should "speak with a single voice" in addressing an issue that is of great importance to the public or that has significant precedential value, it may produce a per curiam opinion.[11]

Per curiam opinions are usually shorter than full opinions — some are as short as a sentence or two — so they are generally less time consuming to produce than full opinions. They are usually published and precedential.

Memorandum Opinions. Unlike full and per curiam opinions, memorandum opinions usually are not published and have no precedential value, and their intended audiences are only the parties and the parties' attorneys. A memorandum opinion is intended to announce the decision of the court but not create binding precedent, generally in a case in which the issues are not of broad importance and can be easily decided by application of settled law. Memorandum opinions are usually shorter than full opinions. Because the facts are familiar to the parties, they are often stated summarily or omitted. The court's analysis may be conclusory; the

---

9. Joyce J. George, *Judicial Opinion Writing Handbook* 323 (5th ed. 2007).

10. Although a per curiam opinion is generally the opinion of the entire panel, some courts, including the United States Supreme Court, occasionally attach a concurring or dissenting opinion to a per curiam opinion. *See, e.g., CSX Transp., Inc. v. Hensley*, 556 U.S. ___, 129 S. Ct. 2139 (2009) (per curiam opinion and two dissenting opinions).

11. George, *supra* note 9, at 325.

court may cite cases but not explain its reasoning in detail. Memorandum opinions are not signed by individual judges.

Concurring and Dissenting Opinions

Most judges approach writing a concurrence or dissent with caution. Unanimous opinions are stronger than opinions of fewer than the whole panel or court, and concurring and dissenting opinions can confuse readers. In addition, dissents can create ill will between judges on the court and undermine the authority of the court's decisions or the court itself. Thus, most courts attempt to reach a consensus — they try to incorporate the ideas of would-be concurring and dissenting judges into the majority opinion. But if a judge feels strongly that the majority's analysis or ultimate conclusion is erroneous and the case will have application beyond the current controversy, the judge may write a concurrence or dissent.

Concurrences and dissents are usually much shorter than full opinions and are often written in a less formal style. Judges are less likely to have their clerks draft these opinions, but as a clerk you may have the opportunity to work on a concurrence or dissent.

Published and Unpublished Opinions

As a judicial clerk you may draft opinions that will be designated as either published or unpublished. *Published* means that the opinion will be included in the jurisdiction's official reporter and will be precedential. A published, precedential opinion potentially has a broad audience and must explain how the court came to its decision, thus most published appellate court opinions are full opinions.[12] In contrast, *unpublished* means that the opinion will not be

---

12. In the twelve-month period ending September 30, 2008, full opinions accounted for nearly ninety-three percent of published opinions in the U. S. Courts of Appeals (excluding the Federal Circuit). *See Judicial Business of the United States Courts, supra* note 6.

included in an official reporter and may not be considered precedential. Unpublished opinions are more often memorandum opinions.

Court rules, state statutes, or state constitutional provisions in most jurisdictions require courts of last resort to publish their opinions. But the majority of intermediate appellate courts of appeals' opinions are not published.[13] A state's constitution or statutes or a court's rules or internal operating procedures set out standards governing which opinions should be published. The standards encourage limiting publication in order to conserve money, save judges' time for researching and writing opinions that will have precedential value, and reduce the proliferation of published reports.

While the judges on the panel deciding the case generally decide whether an opinion should be published, you may be called upon to recommend whether the opinion in a case you are working on should be published because of your knowledge of the particular case and the relevant law. If you recommend publication, you should support that recommendation with specific reasons.

As discussed in earlier chapters, despite their designation, many unpublished opinions are easily accessible to the public. Some are

13. In the federal court system, over eighty percent of appellate decisions are not published. *See id.* In the state appellate courts, the statistics are similar. For example, in the year ending March 31, 2008, approximately ninety percent of the California Courts of Appeal's opinions were unpublished. *See* Mike McKee, *Appeal Courts Publishing More, Barely*, The Recorder, June 27, 2008, *available at* http://www.nonpublication.com/mckee.htm. The Minnesota Court of Appeals in recent years has designated as unpublished between seventy-six and eighty-three percent of its decisions. *See* Michelle Lore, *Debate Exists on Use of 'Unpublished' Designation on Cases*, Minn. Law., Nov. 24, 2008, at 14, *available at* http://www.minnlawyer.com/article.cfm?recid=79723 (reporting on an interview with Chief Judge Edward Toussaint). Approximately ninety-two percent of opinions of the Pennsylvania Superior Court, the state's intermediate appellate court, were designated unpublished in 2007. *See* Mary Jane Bowes & Megan Bode, *Private Justice or Public Right? A Call to Reconsider the Pennsylvania Superior Court's Policy Against Reliance on Unpublished Decisions*, Pa. Law., Nov.–Dec. 2008, at 49–50.

actually published in books—many unpublished federal appellate court opinions are published in West's *Federal Appendix*; are annotated with headnotes, topics, and key numbers; and are fully searchable on Westlaw and in the *Federal Practice Digest*. Unpublished opinions are also available on web sites including Westlaw, LexisNexis, and court web sites.[14] Finally, a court's unpublished opinions are also available from the clerk of court. Thus, even if you are drafting an opinion that will be unpublished, you should not abandon a standard of excellence. The reputation of the judge and your court will depend on the quality of these opinions as well as on the quality of full published opinions.[15]

9.2 Appellate Opinion Preliminaries

If you wrote a bench memo for the case, you have already done much of the work to prepare for drafting an opinion. For example, you probably will not need to examine the record or do much legal research other than updating the authorities in the bench memo. One additional task you must undertake, though, is attending the oral argument for the case. Listen carefully and take notes during the argument; the judges' questions often indicate their concerns, and may guide your analysis or the manner in which you express the reasoning. You may discover, for example, that the judges be-

---

14. The E-Government Act of 2002, which took effect in 2004, requires that all opinions of federal courts, published and unpublished, be posted on the courts' websites. E-Government Act of 2002, Pub. L. No. 107-347, § 205(a)(5), 116 Stat. 2899, 2913 (codified at 44 U.S.C. §§ 3501–3521 (2006)). The courts' requirements are listed in 44 U.S.C. § 3501, sec. 205.

15. In addition, the trend in both federal and state courts is to allow citation of unpublished opinions. For example, Federal Rule of Appellate Procedure 32.1, which took effect on December 1, 2006, requires federal appellate courts to permit citation of cases that have been "designated as 'unpublished,' 'not for publication,' 'non-precedential,' 'not precedent,' or the like," that were issued beginning on January 1, 2007. Fed. R. App. P. 32.1(a)(i).

lieve a particular issue that you addressed in detail in your bench memo deserves little analysis or one that seemed insignificant is actually more important than you first thought. If you are unable to observe an oral argument, listen to or watch the recorded argument or read the argument transcript.

In addition, you should consider the purpose of the opinion and its potential audience, because these differ from the purpose of and audience for the bench memo. While the bench memo was written to educate the judges on the panel about the case and help them get past the advocacy of the parties, an appellate opinion has a broader audience and a more complicated purpose.

Purposes of an Appellate Opinion

In a broad sense, written appellate court opinions are intended to maintain the credibility of the court and create consistency in the law.[16] Judges are mostly appointed, not elected, and as one judge pointed out: "[o]ne of the few ways we have to justify our power to decide matters important to our fellow citizens is to explain why we decide as we do."[17] In addition, written opinions help maintain consistency in the law because they create precedent that guides future courts' application of the law.

In a narrower sense, one purpose of an opinion is to inform: to announce and explain the decision of the court in a particular case to the parties and the broader audiences of the decision. Another purpose of an opinion is to persuade. An appellate opinion should persuade readers that the court's reasoning and ultimate decision are correct. In addition, an appellate opinion, at least in early drafts, may be written to persuade other judges on the panel to join the opinion.

Concurring and dissenting opinions have additional purposes. Besides expressing disagreement with the reasoning or the result,

---

16. *See* Patricia M. Wald, *The Rhetoric of Results and the Results of Rhetoric: Judicial Writings*, 62 U. Chi. L. Rev. 1371, 1372–73 (1995).

17. *Id.* at 1372.

a judge writing a concurrence or dissent may intend to clarify or supplement the majority opinion, define issues for further review,
guide future change in the courts or legislature, or narrow the scope
of the majority opinion.

The writing process itself also serves a purpose. Writing an opinion — as opposed to simply announcing a decision orally — forces
the author to clarify the reasoning and assess the strength and suf-
ficiency of the authority relied upon to support the reasoning. Writing improves judicial decision making by exposing "fuzzy thinking"[18]
that the writer can then tighten and clarify.

Audiences for an Appellate Opinion

An appellate opinion has a number of audiences. You have been
a member of at least one of these audiences in your role as a member of the public. Perhaps you have been a member of another audience as well, such as a party to a law suit or an attorney (or
summer clerk in a law firm).

The immediate or primary audiences for an opinion are those
interested in the resolution of the case: the parties, the parties' attorneys, the trial court judge who may preside over further proceedings, and the other judges on the panel. Secondary audiences
include the higher court to which the case may be appealed and
members of the public whose conduct may be directly affected by
the opinion and their attorneys. Finally, a large group of audiences
may use the opinion to learn and understand the law, including
law students, legal scholars, the press, and the general public.

Unpublished memorandum opinions have more limited audiences than full opinions. Because a memorandum opinion is intended to announce the court's decision but not create precedent,
the intended audience is usually only the parties and their attorneys.

---

18. *See* George, *supra* note 9, at 553.

9.3 Appellate Opinion Structure

Most appellate opinions use a similar structure that includes these sections: (1) caption; (2) opening paragraph; (3) statement of the issues; (4) statement of facts; (5) analysis; and (6) disposition. The court or judge you work for probably prefers or requires a particular structure for opinions; check past opinions or ask a co-clerk or the judge which structure you should use. The titles of the parts and the organization may vary slightly from the structure described below, but the major components will be the same. You may choose to vary this structure to meet the needs of a particular case; parts may be combined in a short opinion, for example. The key, as with any legal writing, is to make the opinion accessible to readers.

One way to make an opinion more accessible to readers is to use visual rhetoric effectively, for example by identifying parts of the opinion with headings or Roman numerals. Headings and subheadings help orient readers and make it easier for them to find a particular spot in the opinion. You can label the major sections, like you would in an office memorandum: "Facts," "Analysis," and "Disposition." You can also label the issues within the analysis section. Using Roman numerals to identify the issues allows a judge to easily identify the part of an opinion the judge is dissenting from or concurring with. Using either headings or Roman numerals in an opinion may allow you to eliminate introduction or transition sentences.

The order in which you draft the sections of an opinion doesn't really matter (although we do suggest drafting the opening paragraph first). If you're having trouble beginning, just begin with the easiest part, because writing anything is more productive than staring at the computer screen. Then write without stopping to evaluate what you've written. As discussed in Chapter Five, give yourself the freedom to write a poor quality first draft, knowing that you will revise it many times before you give it to the judge.

Caption

The caption of an opinion identifies the court, the parties, and the case. Follow the court's standard format, which will include most, or perhaps all, of this information: the court name; the case name (the names and procedural designations of the parties); the opinion date; the case identification number (which may include a docket or file number); the opinion title; the attorneys' names; and the judges' names (including names of the panel members, the author of the majority opinion, and the authors of concurring or dissenting opinions) or, if the opinion is unsigned, the phrase "per curiam" or "by the court." Make sure that the party names are correct; parties may have been added or removed since the case began. In addition, party names may have changed, for example a party named in an official capacity (such as a revenue commissioner) may have been replaced.

Opening Paragraph(s)

The opening paragraph (or paragraphs) orients readers and aids their understanding of the rest of the opinion. Begin the opening paragraph by briefly describing the nature of the case—whether the case is about a breach of contract or a burglary, for example. Identify the parties and the roles they played in each step of the proceedings. After identifying the parties and their procedural designations, refer to them by their names or functional designations, such as "lender" or "homeowner." Develop shortened names for the parties if doing so will improve readability. Briefly state the procedural history of the case: identify the courts or administrative bodies that have considered the case and their decisions.

The opening paragraph should also summarize the issues addressed by the court and the court's holding on each issue. Not all opinion writers agree that the holding should be stated early in the opinion. But "opinions are not mystery stories,"[19] and readers can

---

19. Fajans et al., *supra* note 4, at 345.

better understand the relevance of the facts and analysis if they
know the outcome of the case.

Include a statement describing the basis of the court's jurisdiction if necessary. Courts of appeals have jurisdiction to hear appeals of final orders, some interlocutory orders, and questions
certified for appeal by the lower court.[20] Federal courts are courts
of limited jurisdiction, so if you are drafting an opinion for a federal appellate court, you generally should state the basis for the trial
court's original jurisdiction.[21]

It is a good idea to draft the opening paragraph first and revise
it last. Drafting it first can help you organize your thoughts and will
give you a roadmap to follow while you draft the rest of the opinion. If the opening paragraph is the last thing you revise, you can
ensure that it truly reflects the substance of the rest of the opinion.

Statement of the Issues

Next, identify the issues that are before the appellate court. While
the opening paragraph stated the issues in summary fashion, they
should be stated more completely here (unless they are simple issues that were stated adequately in the opening paragraph). State
the issues clearly, concisely, and specifically. Within each issue, the
most effective organization places the legal question first, followed
by the facts; this order aids readers' understanding because the legal
question provides context for the facts.

---

20. *See, e.g.*, 28 U.S.C. § 1291 (courts of appeals have jurisdiction over
appeals from final decisions of the district courts); 28 U.S.C. § 1292(a)
(courts of appeals have jurisdiction over appeals from certain interlocutory decrees); 28 U.S.C. § 1292(b) (a court of appeals may permit an appeal to be taken from an order that a district court identifies as involving
"controlling questions of law as to which there is substantial ground for
difference of opinion").

21. *See* 28 U.S.C. § 1331 (federal question jurisdiction); 28 U.S.C.
§ 1332 (diversity jurisdiction).

You may be able to use the issue statements from the bench memo, although after the oral arguments and the judges' conference about the case, the issues may have been slightly altered. Nevertheless, the issues must be stated fairly and objectively, without bias to the winning side, and without suggesting the answer. The public will more readily accept the opinion as a legitimate and impartial application of the law if the court states the issues objectively.

Some judges prefer to state the issues after the facts, so that the issue statements immediately precede the issue discussion. Even if you usually state the issues first, you may decide to place the issues after the facts in some opinions, for example, in a complex case in which readers may not be able to understand the issues unless they are familiar with the facts.

Statement of Facts

Next, set out the facts of the case. You might be able to copy the facts directly from your bench memo. On the other hand, it's possible that the oral argument, the judges' thinking, or your own reconsideration may change your original idea of how the facts should be organized or which facts should be emphasized. Thus, you should think about the facts before you import them wholesale from the bench memo. Like the issues, the facts should be stated objectively, without bias towards the winning party. Facts significant to the losing party should not be omitted.

Include only the essential facts: the legally relevant facts (those on which the court's decision turns) and the necessary background facts (those readers need in order to understand the context). Omit nonessential facts, even if they are interesting, including nonessential names and dates. In particular, take care to omit identifying information that could embarrass or humiliate nonparties to the case if their identities are not essential. Avoid long quotations of testimony or depositions, unless the information is necessary, for example the operative language of a contract or the critical testimony of a witness.

Remember that an appellate court is not a fact-finding court— neither you nor the judge is "the author of the facts," you "merely record[] them."[22] Likewise, you must take the facts from the record, not from the briefs of the parties, because good appellate brief writers frame the facts to benefit their clients. The facts should not express legal conclusions. "Smith was driving eighty-five miles an hour," is a fact; "Smith was driving recklessly," is a legal conclusion. It may be necessary, however, to make logical inferences from the known facts.

Sometimes the facts are not easily determined. If the trial court judge made findings of fact or the parties stipulated to the facts, the facts should be clear. But if the case was tried to a jury, you may not know exactly which facts the jurors relied upon in reaching their decision. In this situation, all you can do is assume that the jury relied upon the facts that were supported by the evidence, favorable to the winning party, and consistent with the jury instructions.[23]

State the facts completely. If the opening paragraph did not contain all the necessary procedural details, include them in the facts statement. Include all the facts used in the analysis section and clearly identify which facts are essential to the court's holding. In a full opinion, readers should be able to learn all the essential facts from the opinion, without reading the opinion of the court below. On the other hand, in an unpublished memorandum opinion whose only intended audience is the parties, you can omit background facts because the parties are familiar with them. Likewise, in a memorandum opinion, you can state that the court adopts the facts as stated by the trial court.

Facts are usually presented in chronological order, although you may wish to organize complex facts by topic or issue. Insert a roadmap at the beginning and subheadings within the facts statement to help readers navigate long or complex facts statements. State the facts in the past tense. When describing the trial court's actions, state that the court "found" the pertinent facts and "held" the conclusions of law.

---

22. George, *supra* note 9, at 293–94.
23. *See* John Leubsdorf, *The Structure of Judicial Opinions*, 86 Minn. L. Rev. 447, 459–60 (2001).

Analysis

The analysis is the most important part of an opinion because it explains and justifies the decision. Again, you can probably use your bench memo as a starting point. But the analysis section of an opinion will not lay out both parties' arguments in as much detail as the analysis section of the bench memo, because the opinion will be explaining and supporting the winning arguments. In addition, if the judges want to rule differently than you recommended in your bench memo, you will need to change your analysis to support their decision.

The opinion must state the standard of review that the court will employ for each issue, and the beginning of the analysis section is the most common place for the standard or standards of review to appear. (Another placement option is at the beginning of the facts section, which can help readers understand how to view the facts.) The attorneys should have included the standard of review in their briefs, but you should independently verify the standard for each issue. See Chapter Seven for more information about specific standards of review. Unless the parties dispute which standard of review applies, don't cite to more than one recent case from the jurisdiction to support the statement of a standard of review. If more than one standard of review will be applied in the case, you may place all of them together in one paragraph or state the standard for each issue at the beginning of the analysis of that issue.

As noted above, you may choose to include headings or Roman numerals to guide readers through the analysis, and you may also want to add a roadmap at the beginning of the section that summarizes what follows. Roadmaps orient readers and are particularly helpful in long opinions and opinions that cover several issues.

Organize the issues and subissues logically and in a manner that aids readers. For example, address threshold or dispositive issues first and analyze factors or elements in the traditional order. Remember that you need not follow the organization used by either of the parties in their briefs; use the organization that makes sense for the purposes and reasoning of the opinion. Within each issue, your default organization should be the traditional IRAC organization as discussed in Chapter Five. Following are some pointers specific to opinions.

Begin by stating the issue objectively, concisely, clearly, and specifically, as you did in the statement of the issues. (The "I" part of the IRAC.) Next state and explain the rule of law. (The "R" part of the IRAC.) Only the rule applicable to the essential facts should be stated and explained. The amount of detail to include in this part will depend on how difficult or contentious the issue is. A simple, non-controversial rule will require little explanation and perhaps citation to just one case, while a more difficult or controversial rule may require much more explanation and citation to numerous authorities. Remember that you are not writing a law review article or a treatise; the primary readers of the opinion will be busy attorneys and law students who want to learn the law that applies to the facts of this case. So even though you may be very good at following every potential rabbit down its hole, an appellate opinion is not the place to demonstrate your hunting prowess. You can discuss the rabbits and rabbit holes with the judge or fellow clerks, but don't burden opinion readers with them. Don't cite all the authorities you consulted merely to show that you did the research. See Chapter Six for more citation pointers.

You should generally rely on the law stated by the court of last resort in the appropriate jurisdiction, and should not trace the development of the law. Some exceptions exist, of course; you may need to discuss other jurisdictions' law or the historical progression of the law if the issue is one of first impression or if the court is clarifying or extending the law. Use past tense when discussing law that is no longer in force; use present tense when discussing law currently in force.

Next, apply the law to the facts of the case. (The "A" part of the IRAC.) The depth of your analysis will depend on the difficulty of the issue and the merit of the claim. Your draft should address all of the serious contentions of the parties. Minor or meritless claims need not be addressed in depth, though, and can sometimes be disposed of together in one or two sentences (perhaps in the disposition, described below). In fairness to the losing party, discuss the cases the losing party cited, explain why the cases are not controlling or how they are distinguishable, and explain why ultimately the winning party's arguments are more persuasive. The winning party's arguments probably will not be laid out in as much detail as in the bench memo, because they will be subsumed in your analysis. Thus, this part of the analysis will probably vary the most from the analysis in the bench memo.

In this section the analysis should focus narrowly on the law that governs the particular factual situation and on applying that law to the situation. Opinions typically should not contain dicta. However, occasionally dictum will promote judicial economy, for example if the judge expresses an opinion on an issue that is not essential to the decision, but that may arise on retrial.

If you disagree with the judge's reasoning or the outcome the judge wants you to support, you may find it difficult to draft the analysis section. The key is to understand every step of the judge's reasoning. Remember that you probably faced a similar problem when you disagreed with the position of the party you were assigned to represent in your appellate brief assignment, a moot court competition, or a matter your law firm was working on. In those situations you were able to successfully advocate for your real or imaginary client. In this situation you may simply need to spend extra time discussing the case with the judge and then you should be able to successfully convey the judge's decision.

Whether you agree with the judge or not, you may discover that when you attempt to draft the opinion in the manner the judge wants, the opinion "won't write." In other words, the reasoning for the decision made sense when the case was being discussed (by the panel of judges, the judge, or you), but when you attempt to write the reasoning, there is a flaw in the logic. This is a serious problem that you should not ignore.[24] It may be that you simply do not un-

---

24. Some commentators view this as a danger of clerks drafting opinions. If a clerk drafts an opinion for a judge, the judge doesn't have the opportunity to learn by writing. *See* Richard A. Posner, *Judges' Writing Styles (And Do They Matter?)*, 62 U. Chi. L. Rev. 1421, 1448 (1995).

derstand the judge's reasoning, in which case you should discuss the reasoning again with the judge and perhaps also with your fellow clerks. But it may be that you are correct, and the reasoning truly doesn't work. In this case you should attempt to persuade the judge to change the reasoning or the result. In the end, though, you are merely a clerk, so you must draft an opinion that conveys the judge's reasoning and supports the judge's conclusion.

At the end of the analysis of an issue, conclude with a statement of how the court holds on that issue—a mini conclusion. (The "C" part of the IRAC.)

Disposition

The final part of an opinion is the court's disposition: a statement of the decision reached by the court and the relief to be granted. State the precise effect the opinion has on the lower court's decision (to affirm, reverse, vacate, remand, modify, or dismiss) so the parties and other readers will understand the scope of the court's action.

If the case is being remanded to the trial court, give clear directions to that court. A command to "enter judgment consistent with this opinion" may not be clear enough, unless the analysis section explicitly lays out the directions. More detailed directions are more useful, such as: "We remand for resentencing and instruct the trial court to impose a sentence of no longer than life plus twelve months for Novak's first-degree murder conviction."

Include the dispositions of all issues raised by the parties in the appeal, even if the issues were not fully analyzed. The disposition may include a statement like this: "The Court has considered Samuelson's other assignments of error and concludes that they are without merit. The judgment of the trial court is affirmed in all respects." In a criminal case, however, you should specifically dispose of each issue even if the issue is not discussed in the opinion. For example: "Samuelson's assignment of error based on violation of the Fourth Amendment is without merit. Likewise, Samuelson's assignment of error based on the trial court's failure to bifurcate his trial is without merit." Stating a ruling on every issue will satisfy the parties, the attorneys, and other readers that the court has addressed all of the parties' contentions, and will alert courts in any later proceedings that every issue was ruled upon.

Structure of Opinions Other Than Full Opinions

Per curiam and memorandum decisions are often structured like full opinions, but are shorter and less detailed. For example, an unpublished memorandum opinion intended only for the parties need not include historical or background facts, because the parties are familiar with them. Drafting a per curiam or memorandum opinion is therefore generally less time-consuming than drafting a full opinion. An exception may be drafting a per curiam opinion that the court is issuing to make a strong point on a significant matter. In that instance, the judges may wish to take extra care with the language of the opinion, so their collaboration may require more drafts and more time to produce an opinion that all of them agree with.

A concurring or dissenting opinion can also contain less background detail than a full opinion. The introductory information can be minimal. Many dissents begin simply with "I respectfully dissent," and then immediately move to the judge's reasons for dissenting. The opinion's format will depend on the points the judge wants to make. If the judge disagrees with the majority's statement of the issues, then you will need to clearly restate the issues. If the judge believes the majority misstated the facts, then the dissent will need to include a facts section that lays out the correct facts. A concurrence or dissent should clearly state the points of disagreement with the majority opinion, which will help readers understand the scope of the majority opinion and can guide future evolution of the law.

If you are assigned to draft a concurrence or dissent and did not write the bench memo for the case, you may need to read the bench memo, briefs, and authorities to bring yourself up to speed. However, because other judges usually need not be consulted about a concurring or dissenting opinion, the process of producing one can take less time than the process of producing a full opinion.

9.4 Revising, Editing, and Proofreading

After you have completed a draft of the opinion, you will need to revise, edit, and proofread the draft before giving it to the judge. In particular, you should ensure that you are writing in the judge's voice, ensure the tone is appropriate, evaluate the draft's length, and limit the use of quotations and footnotes. See Chapter Five for additional revising, editing, and proofreading tasks.

One challenge of drafting an opinion is writing in the judge's voice. When you begin your job as a clerk (or even before you begin your job if you have the time), read opinions by the judge to become familiar with the judge's voice. Other members of the judge's staff can also give you tips. Then work to emulate the judge's voice and style in your opinion draft. Your goal is to draft an opinion that is consistent with earlier opinions authored by the judge. Readers should not be able to tell that different clerks have drafted the judge's opinions over the years.

Check the tone of the writing during the editing process. Appellate opinions traditionally employ a formal tone. When drafting a majority opinion, you should use the third person (although using an occasional "we believe" is acceptable). Formal does not mean stuffy, though. Use plain English and simple words. For more tips about writing in an accessible manner, see Chapter Five.

The tone of an opinion should also be respectful. The parties to a lawsuit take their case seriously, and an opinion should reflect that the court also takes the case seriously. First, the opinion should show respect for the readers. Assume readers are intelligent — explain, but don't patronize or condescend to them. Second, show respect for the parties, their attorneys, and their arguments. If an attorney makes an argument that you consider meritless, you can respond by dismissing it as "meritless" or by refuting the argument, but you should not ridicule the argument or chastise the attorney.

Third, show respect for other judges on the court who have written other opinions in the same case. Whether you draft the majority opinion, a concurrence, or a dissent, your tone should not be dismissive or condescending of the authors of other opinions. You have certainly read dissents that were scathing indictments of the majority's reasoning. But attacks on the majority opinion can damage relationships between the judges and create an impression of disharmony that can weaken the court's authority. Remember that even though you will work for the court for only a year or two, many of the judges will continue to work together for years. Do not make personal attacks, use offensive language, or employ a condescending tone regarding other opinions. The tone should exhibit "appropriate restraint;" thus, it should "assail[] the erroneous nature of the reasoning without personally attacking colleagues."[25]

Finally, show respect for the authors of previous opinions that you rely upon. If you (or the judge) disagree with a doctrine, you can explain your disagreement but should not show lack of respect for the authors of the opinions in which those doctrines appear.

The tone of a dissent or concurrence can differ from that of a majority opinion. These opinions are often less formal than majority opinions. First-person references are acceptable in dissents and concurrences; as previously discussed, dissents often begin with "I respectfully dissent."[26]

---

25. George, *supra* note 9, at 328.

26. If the judge chooses to write in a disrespectful manner, that's the judge's call, not the clerk's call. Likewise, if the judge chooses to insert humor in the opinion, the judge may do so. For the dangers of attempting to include humor in judicial writing, see Nancy A. Wanderer, *Writing Better Opinions: Communicating with Candor, Clarity, and Style,* 54 Me. L. Rev. 47, 68–69 (2002); Jennifer Sheppard, *The "Write" Way: A Judicial Clerk's Guide to Writing for the Court,* 38 U. Balt. L. Rev. 73, 109–10 (2008) (advising against using humor in judicial writing).

You should also evaluate the length of the opinion draft. Appellate opinions are often criticized for their length, and some commentators believe they can tell when an opinion was drafted by a clerk because the opinion is too long.[27] Look at the substance of the opinion for ways to shorten it: state the issues concisely, cut out unnecessary detail such as irrelevant facts and excessively detailed descriptions of cases, and avoid writing dicta. Make sure the opinion does not repeat or over-explain information. Readers will appreciate your efforts to produce a tightly written and concise opinion.

Use quotations sparingly. In stating or explaining the law, do not simply string together quotations from the relevant authorities. Instead, add analysis to help readers understand the significance of the information and the connections between the authorities. The relevant text of statutes and rules should be quoted, but long block quotes should be avoided if possible because readers tend to skip over them.

Resist the urge to include footnotes in your draft. In most instances, if the point is important enough to be made, it should be made in the main text rather than in a footnote. Footnotes can distract readers and leave them wondering whether the information in the footnotes is a critical part of the court's reasoning. Note, though, that some judges prefer to place citations in footnotes rather than in the text.

Even though the opinion is not yet in final form, you should strive to produce an excellent product, because doing so will make the judge's job of revising the opinion that much easier.

9.5 Finalizing the Opinion

After you have revised, edited, and proofread the opinion draft, you should give the draft to the judge. The judge may do one of a num-

---

27. *See* J. Daniel Mahoney, *Law Clerks: For Better or For Worse?* 54 Brooklyn L. Rev. 321, 339 (1988).

ber of things: simply pass your draft along to the other judges on the panel with no alterations, make a few changes to it, or ask you to begin again and write a new draft. When the other panel judges get the draft, they (and possibly their clerks) will review and comment on the draft. They may be satisfied with the draft and send it back to be finalized. Or your judge and the other judges on the panel may negotiate over the language or the reasoning as they work to agree on a unanimous (or at least a majority) opinion. If a judge drafts a concurrence or dissent, that opinion will also be read by the other panel judges, who may respond in the majority opinion.

The process may continue through many drafts, until all of the judges are satisfied with the opinion. The judge may ask for your assistance during the process of hammering out the final opinion. You may be asked to draft or redraft portions of the opinion, incorporate the language or ideas of other judges into the draft, conduct additional research, or simply act as a sounding board for the judge. The judge could also ask you to convert one kind of opinion into another kind. For example, judges sometimes change their views after reading a dissent, which may cause the dissent to become the majority view. The converse could also happen: what started out as the majority opinion could become a concurrence or a dissent. Thus, you may need to change the depth of the analysis or the format to be consistent with the opinion's new purpose. Finally, the judges on the rest of the court will probably be given the opportunity to read the majority and any minority opinions as well.

After the other judges have had their say, you and the judge will finalize the substance of the opinion. Then you should do a final proofread to catch any remaining spelling or punctuation errors, and check citations a final time for form and to make sure they are up to date. Another clerk may also proofread and cite check the opinion. All of these steps are aimed at producing an excellent final product.

9.6 Final Words about Drafting Appellate Opinions

If you are concerned about any aspect of drafting an opinion—that you are not writing in the judge's voice, that your reasoning is not sound, that the judge is giving you too much responsibility—remember that others will work on your draft as well. The judge will tinker with and perhaps rewrite your draft. Then the other judges on the panel may suggest additional changes. While you should put forth your best effort when writing the draft, it's unlikely that your draft will become the final version of the opinion.

Remember to remain flexible, good humored, and diplomatic during the process of drafting an opinion. Don't be offended if your judge or the other judges on the panel suggest major changes to your draft. The judges are attempting to solve a legal problem, not attack your writing or you personally. And don't become too attached to the particular words or reasoning you use, because they will likely be changed. Remember that you are part of a team that is collaborating to reach a just result and to explain that result in the clearest and best-reasoned opinion possible.

9.7 Opinion Drafting Checklist

Caption

- Follows the standard format?
- Includes all parts?

Opening Paragraph(s)

- Begins with a brief description of the nature of the case?
- Identifies the parties and their procedural designations?
- Briefly states the procedural history?
- Summarizes the issues?

- States a holding for each issue?
- Addresses jurisdiction if necessary?

Statement of the Issues

- Stated clearly, concisely, and specifically?
- Organized in the same order that the issues are addressed in the analysis?
- Stated fairly and objectively?

Statement of Facts

- Stated objectively?
- Includes only essential facts?
- Clearly indicates which facts are essential to the holding?
- Accurate?
- Complete?
- Organized logically?

Analysis

- Begins with a roadmap?
- Includes standard(s) of review?
- Uses IRAC organization for each issue?
- States issues objectively, concisely, clearly, and specifically?
- States rules clearly and fairly?
- Explains rules in sufficient but not too much detail?
- Relies on mandatory authority unless the issue is one of first impression or the court is clarifying or extending the law?
- Analyzes issues in appropriate depth for their complexity?
- Addresses the losing party's arguments in appropriate detail?
- Includes no dicta, few footnotes, and minimal quoting?

Disposition

- States precise effect the decision will have on the lower court's decision?
- Is precise and clear?

- Gives clear direction to the trial court if the case is remanded?
- Disposes of all issues raised by the parties?

Writing, Revising, Editing, Proofing, Citation

- Uses topic sentences throughout to help guide readers through the analysis?
- Checked for grammar, usage, and style to make the document as clear and concise as possible?
- Proofread for spelling and other typographical errors?
- Checked for proper citation form, content, and placement?

9.8 Additional Resources

Ruggero J. Aldisert, *Opinion Writing* (1990)

Ruggero J. Aldisert, Meehan Rasch, & Matthew P. Bartlett, *Opinion Writing and Opinion Readers*, 31 Cardozo L. Rev. 1 (2009)

Appellate Judges Conference, A.B.A., *Judicial Opinion Writing Manual* (1991)

Federal Judicial Center, *Judicial Writing Manual* (Sylvan A. Sobel ed., 1991), *available at* http://www.fjc.gov/public/pdf.nsf/lookup/ JudicialWritingManual.pdf/$file/JudicialWritingManual.pdf

Joyce J. George, *Judicial Opinion Writing Handbook* (5th ed. 2007)

Jennifer Sheppard, *The "Write" Way: A Judicial Clerk's Guide to Writing for the Court*, 38 U. Balt. L. Rev. 73 (2008)

Nancy A. Wanderer, *Writing Better Opinions: Communicating With Candor, Clarity, and Style*, 54 Me. L. Rev. 47 (2002)

9.9 Sample Full Opinion with Dissent

STATE OF SOUTH DAKOTA   IN COURT OF APPEALS
May 22, 2008   DISTRICT III
Appeal No. S-07-0178   Dist. Ct. No. 2007CV18

Michael Baldry, as Personal Representative for
   Kimberly Baldry and Marisa Baldry, Minors,
   Appellant,
   v.
DSG, Inc.,
   Appellee.

APPEAL from a judgment of the Jefferson County District Court: ERICA R. NELSON, Judge. *Affirmed in part, reversed in part, and remanded.*

Representing Appellant: Kenneth Cole of Dakota Legal Group, LLC, Stockton, South Dakota.

Representing Appellee: Melinda Horst of Horst, Whitehorse & Martin, Stockton, South Dakota.

Before HUNTER, Chief Judge, and VOGEL and COBIN, Judges.

VOGEL, Judge, filed a dissenting opinion.

HUNTER, Chief Judge.

This case involves claims for damages resulting from personal injury caused by a fall down the stairs of an apartment building. Appellant Michael Baldry, on behalf of his daughters, Kimberly and Marisa Baldry, appeals the order granting summary judgment in favor of Appellee DSG, Inc. DSG is the owner of the apartment building where Nora Baldry, the mother of Kimberly and stepmother of Marisa, was injured when she fell down the stairs. At issue is whether the district court properly granted summary judgment on Kimberly's negligent infliction of emotional distress claim and on Marisa's loss of consortium claim.

We reverse in part and affirm in part. We reverse on the negligent infliction of emotional distress issue and remand for trial because we disagree with the district court that the immediacy requirement was not met as a matter of law. We affirm on the loss of consortium issue because, under current South Dakota law, a stepchild is not entitled to recover for loss of a stepparent's consortium.

Facts

Pursuant to our standard of review for summary judgment, this recitation of facts is from the vantage point most favorable to Michael Baldry, as the party opposing the motion, awarding him all favorable inferences that may be drawn from the facts. *See H & G Investors, LLC v. Walls,* 194 N.W.2d 41, 43 (S.D. 2000).

On June 26, 2007, Nora Baldry dropped off her six-year-old daughter, Kimberly, at the apartment of a friend in Stockton, South Dakota. The apartment was on the third floor of the building. As Nora was leaving the building she slipped on the stairs and fell down the last flight of stairs from the second floor to the building entrance. Kimberly, her friend, and the friend's mother heard "something banging on the stairs," but did not discover it was Nora until approximately ten minutes later when they heard an ambulance siren in the street. When they went down to investigate they discovered Nora being attended to by paramedics. The paramedics had stabilized Nora's neck and back, placed her on a stretcher, and covered her with a blanket, and were in the process of loading the stretcher into the ambulance. Nora was unconscious but was breathing. Although she had substantial internal injuries and her right shoulder and arm were broken, these injuries were not visible to Kimberly.

Nora was seriously injured in the accident and spent a number of days in the intensive care unit of the hospital. She spent a total of two weeks in the hospital and then another two months in a rehabilitation center. She continues to receive physical therapy services and will never regain the full use of her right arm, according to her doctors.

Nine-year-old Marisa Baldry, Nora's stepdaughter, learned of the accident later in the day. She did not see Nora until Nora was out of the intensive care unit.

Kimberly Baldry is the natural child of Nora Baldry and her husband Michael Baldry. Marisa Baldry is the natural child of Michael Baldry and his previous wife, who is deceased. Michael married Nora when Marisa was eleven months old. Nora has not adopted Marisa.

Michael Baldry brought this action on behalf of Kimberly and Marisa against DSG Inc., the apartment building owner, alleging that DSG negligently maintained the stairway, which was the cause of Nora's injuries. The complaint alleges, in part, that DSG is liable to Kimberly for negligent infliction of emotional distress damages and to Marisa for loss of consortium damages.

DSG filed a summary judgment motion regarding both issues, which was granted by the Jefferson County District Court. First, the court held that because Nora's condition and location had been materially changed before Kimberly observed her, as a matter of law, Kimberly could not recover for negligent infliction of emotional distress. Second, the court held that because a stepchild does not have a cause of action for loss of a stepparent's consortium, Marisa's claim must fail.

Issues

This case raises two issues. The first issue is whether, as a matter of law, a bystander should be denied recovery for negligent infliction of emotional distress when the bystander comes upon an accident soon after its occurrence and after the victim has been moved a short distance and is being assisted by medical personnel. The second issue is whether South Dakota should recognize a cause of action for a stepchild to recover for the loss of a stepparent's consortium.

Analysis

I. Standard of Review

Summary judgment is appropriate when no genuine issue of material fact exists and the prevailing party is entitled to judgment as a matter of law. *Tribal Resource Ctr. v. Bison County Bd. of Supervisors*, 25 N.W.3d 90, 92 (S.D. 2008). A genuine issue of material fact exists when a disputed fact, if it were proven, would establish or refute an essential element of a cause of action or a defense that the parties have asserted. *Id.* We review a grant of summary judgment deciding a question of law de novo and affirm the district court's decision "on the basis of any proper legal theory appearing in the record." *Id.* at 93. However, because we do not favor granting summary judgment in negligence actions, we review the district court's decision with "exacting scrutiny." *See Dahle v. Jackrabbit Twp.*, 903 N.W.2d 148, 151 (S.D. Ct. App. 1995).

II. *Negligent Infliction of Emotional Distress*

The first issue is whether a close family member of an accident victim can recover for negligent infliction of emotional distress when she comes upon the accident scene before the victim has been removed. We reverse the district court's summary judgment and hold that Kimberly Baldry may pursue damages for negligent infliction of emotional distress.

A bystander who witnesses the injury of another must prove three elements to recover for negligent infliction of emotional distress: (1) the witness must have a close family relationship with the victim; (2) the victim must have been seriously injured or killed in the accident; and (3) the witness must see the accident or arrive at the scene before there is a material change in the condition and location of the victim. *Growe v. Richards*, 808 N.W.2d 193, 199 (S.D. 1986). By placing a limitation on who may recover for negligent infliction of emotional distress, the South Dakota Supreme Court has recognized that "part of living involves some unhappy and disagreeable emotions with which we must cope without recovery of damages." *Id.* at 200. The limits exist, in part, to prevent fraudulent claims and to avoid the potential economic burden on defendants of recovery by an unlimited class of plaintiffs. *See id.*

The parties stipulated that Kimberly has a close family relationship with Nora and that Nora was seriously injured in the accident. Thus, the only issue is whether Kimberly, who did not witness the accident, met the immediacy requirement, i.e., whether she "observed the serious bodily harm ... shortly after its occurrence but without material change in the condition and location of [Nora]." *See id.* at 199.

A plaintiff need not be present at the time of the accident in order to recover for negligent infliction of emotional distress; he or she must simply show his or her "sensory and contemporaneous observance" of the defendant's acts. *Ramirez v. Krane Enters.*, 713 N.W.2d 431, 433 (S.D. Ct. App. 1996). Consequently, the plaintiff is not required to have seen the injury-causing event to recover, if he or she gained "personal and contemporaneous knowledge" of the event through the use of other senses. *Id.* at 434. Thus, the fact that Kimberly did not observe her mother falling down the stairs does not prevent her from recovering, as claimed by DSG. Kimberly heard the sound of her mother falling down the stairs, and even if she did not realize the nature of the sound at the time, as soon as she saw her mother, she was aware of its nature.

However, to recover, Kimberly must show that the condition and location of her mother had not materially changed by the time she got there. *See Growe*, 808 N.W.2d at 199. A plaintiff meets the immediacy requirement if he or she arrives at the scene of the accident shortly after its occurrence, before the victim has been moved and before the victim's condition has changed. *Id.* at 200. Viewing the immediate aftermath of the accident may be "more shocking" than viewing the accident itself, according to the *Growe* court. *Id.* In *Growe*, the victim's mother and brother arrived at the accident scene moments after the accident and observed the victim's severe injuries. *Id.* at 195. The impact of the car hitting the victim's bicycle had carried the victim over fifty feet, and she was still on the pavement when her family arrived. *Id.* The South Dakota Supreme Court held that both the mother and brother met the immediacy requirement. *Id.* at 201.

On the other hand, the immediacy requirement is not met if the victim has been moved from the scene of the accident and has been treated by medical personnel. *Ramirez*, 713 N.W.2d at 433. We have held that if the victim was transported to the hospital before being seen by family members, the family members cannot recover for negligent infliction of emotional distress. *See id.* Even if the victim has not been taken to a hospital, but has merely been moved a significant distance, the plaintiff cannot recover. For example, in

Makovich v. School District Number 155, 61 N.W.2d 589, 591 (S.D. 1992), the victim was injured while playing on the school playground. His mother did not see him until he had been moved to the school nurse's office, which was approximately 200 feet from the injury site. *Id.* The mother did not meet the immediacy requirement. *Id.* at 593.

The district court accepted DSG's argument that Kimberly did not meet the immediacy requirement because, as a matter of law, Nora's condition and location had been materially changed by the time Kimberly saw her. We disagree. Nora was still at the scene of the accident when Kimberly saw her. She had been moved only a short distance: onto a stretcher that the paramedics were in the process of moving into the ambulance. In addition, although the paramedics had stabilized her back and neck, she was still unconscious, her broken bones had not been set, and the extent of her injuries had not been diagnosed. She had not yet been hospitalized or treated in the hospital.

The effect on Kimberly of seeing her mother in that condition may have been more shocking than seeing the actual accident, *see Growe*, 808 N.W.2d at 199, and the effect on Kimberly was certainly more emotionally disturbing than if Nora had already been treated in the hospital. Thus, a reasonable jury could find that Nora's condition and location had not been materially changed, and DSG is therefore not entitled to judgment as a matter of law. The district court's decision is reversed and the case is remanded for trial on the issue of whether Kimberly met the immediacy requirement, and if so, whether she is entitled to damages for negligent infliction of emotional distress.

III. Loss of Consortium

The second issue is one of first impression in South Dakota: whether a stepchild can recover for loss of her stepmother's consortium. We agree with the district court that a stepchild does not have a cause of action for loss of consortium of a stepparent under South Dakota law and that if the policy is to be changed, the legislature should initiate the change.

The South Dakota Supreme Court held in 1990 that a child could recover for loss of a parent's consortium. *Norton v. River Hills Hosp.*, 597 N.W.2d 1171, 1177 (S.D. 1990). The *Norton* court recognized that under South Dakota statute, a child may recover for wrongful death of a parent, and that the policy reasons for allowing a child to recover for loss of a parent's consortium are the same. *Id.* at 1175. In addition, the court stressed the South Dakota policy of compensating victims for substantial injury caused by third persons. *Id.* The *Norton* court was willing to change the common law because the common law "was no longer compatible with current social policy." *Id.* at 1176.

Marisa argues that the time has come for South Dakota to extend loss of consortium recovery to stepchildren, because such recovery is compatible with current social policy. She argues that the reasons for allowing stepchildren to recover are the same as the reasons for allowing children to recover. In particular, she argues that the loss of companionship and support suffered by a stepchild when a stepparent is injured or killed can be just as great as the loss to a natural child when a natural parent is injured or killed. In addition, she asserts that the calculation of damages would be no more difficult than in the case of a natural child.

We disagree. Despite the fact that stepchildren are increasingly common in our society, the South Dakota legislature continues to treat them differently than it treats natural children. In *Norton*, the court held that the class of plaintiffs who may bring an action for loss of consortium consists of those who are permitted to bring wrongful death actions. *Id.* at 1177. When *Norton* was decided, those who could recover for wrongful death of another under South Dakota Codified Laws § 45-15-01 (1996) (amended 1998) were the "husband, wife, child, father or mother" of the deceased.

The class of persons who can recover for wrongful death of another has been expanded, but the class continues to be consistent with the traditional understanding of beneficiary dependence. In 1998 the legislature amended the statute to include grandparents, uncles, aunts, and cousins. *See* S.D. Codified Laws § 45-15-01 (2008). The legislature reasoned that the list should be compatible with the South Dakota intestate succession statute because "extending to those related persons the opportunity to participate in a wrongful death action does not unduly extend the class of persons for whose benefit such actions may be brought to the point that it would be unmanageable." *See Basel County v. Ringsted*, 775 N.W.2d 698, 700 (S.D. 2000). Stepchildren are not included in the statutory list; thus, they cannot recover for the wrongful death of a stepparent.

Other jurisdictions also treat stepchildren differently in wrongful death actions. Most jurisdictions that have considered the issue do not allow stepchildren to recover for the wrongful death of a stepparent. *See, e.g., Lenz v. Thunder Hawk*, 651 P.2d 522 (Alaska 1979); *Nichols v. Conway Trucking, Inc.*, 745 P.2d 29 (Cal. 1974); *Finch Bros. v. State*, 15 So. 3d 115 (La. Ct. App. 2007); *Lang v. Lang*, 277 A.2d 553 (Md. Ct. App. 1971); *In re Johnson*, 155 N.W.2d 47 (Minn. Ct. App. 2003); *Patrin v. Garbe*, 438 P.2d 34 (Or. 1974); *Lomeli v. Olympic Stores, Inc.*, 605 P.2d 330 (Wash. 1980). *But see, e.g., Jonah v. City of Elizabeth*, 338 S.W.2d 19 (Ark. 1968) (stepchildren can recover for wrongful death of stepparent under Arkansas statute).

Likewise, recovery for loss of consortium is limited in other jurisdictions. In fact, in most jurisdictions, even natural children cannot recover for the loss of their parents' consortium. *See* Linda Jong-Lee, *Whither the Children? Children's Right to Recover Damages in Tort Actions*, 3 Hamline J. Fam. & Child. L. 1, 9 (2007) (explaining that only twelve states allow children to recover for loss of parental consortium). The courts in those jurisdictions list various reasons to deny children a cause of action for loss of parental consortium, including "(1) the uncertainty and remoteness of the damages involved, (2) the possible overlap with the parent's recovery, (3) the multiplication of litigation, (4) the possibility of upsetting settlements made with parents, (5) the danger of fabricated actions, and (6) the increase in insurance costs." *Lewis v. Sandeen*, 149 N.W.2d 636, 640 (Iowa 1976). These reasons carry even more weight in the case of stepchildren, particularly unadopted stepchildren.

Because the South Dakota Supreme Court has tied recovery for loss of consortium to the wrongful death statute, and because the South Dakota legislature has not seen fit to allow a cause of action in wrongful death for stepchildren, we decline to extend the law. The legislature is in the best position to weigh the factors listed above and to make the appropriate decision regarding whether a stepchild should be able to maintain a cause of action for the wrongful death of a stepparent. Only after the legislature makes that decision should the courts likewise extend loss of consortium recovery to stepchildren.

Thus, we affirm the district court and hold that a stepchild does not have a cause of action for loss of a stepparent's consortium. Accordingly, Marisa's action is dismissed.

The summary judgment in favor of DSG on Kimberly's negligent infliction of emotional distress claim is reversed. The case is remanded for trial on the issue of whether Kimberly met the immediacy requirement, and if so, whether she is entitled to damages for negligent infliction of emotional distress. The summary judgment in favor of DSG on Marisa's loss of consortium claim is affirmed.

Affirmed in part, reversed in part, and remanded.

VOGEL, Judge, dissenting.

I dissent from the court's decision in Section III of the Analysis, regarding loss of stepparent consortium. The policy reasons for allowing stepchildren to recover are the same as the policy reasons for allowing biological children to recover, and the burden on the court system would be no greater. Thus, in the interest of justice, the court should hold that stepchildren have a cause of action for loss of a stepparent's consortium.

According to Michael Baldry's affidavit, Marisa's mother died giving birth to her. Michael and Nora married when Marisa was eleven months old; thus, Nora is the only mother Marisa has ever known. Further, the evidence presented to the district court indicates that the support and companionship Nora gives to Marisa is equal to that she gives to her biological daughter, Kimberly. For example, according to Nora's affidavit, before she was injured, she took both girls to school every day and was involved in the activities of both girls to an equal extent. The emotional impact on Marisa has also been severe, just as it would have been if Nora was her biological mother. After Nora was injured, Marisa was "inconsolable" according to the affidavit of her grandmother. She has been seeing a counselor on a regular basis since the accident.

The loss Marisa has suffered will likely have a lasting effect on her life because of the changes to her relationship with Nora. When a young child loses the companionship of a parent, the child not only suffers the absence of enjoyment, care, guidance, and protection from the parent, but also loses a role model. Mary T. Barnard, *Loss of Parental Consortium and Children's Needs*, 19 U. Mass. L. & Pol'y J. 1321, 1359 (1992). In addition, the child may no longer enjoy shared experiences with the parent. *Id.* "Those intangibles are of unquestionable significance to the parent-child relationship." *Id.* The fact that Marisa is not Nora's biological daughter, and through no fault of her own is also not Nora's legally adopted daughter, does not change the type or amount of loss she will suffer.

This case is an example of why the law should recognize a stepchild's loss of consortium claim. There often is no difference in the manner in which children and stepchildren are treated or in how they suffer when the parent or stepparent is injured. While the legislature has spoken about wrongful death actions, this is not a statutorily created wrongful death action. Loss of consortium is a common law theory of recovery, and the South Dakota courts have not been averse to changing the common law to reflect changes in society. *See Norton*, 597 N.W.2d at 1176. *Norton*, which first allowed children to recover for loss of a parent's consortium, was decided eighteen years ago, and the prevalence of stepchildren has only increased since then. The court should take this opportunity to equalize the status of children and stepchildren in this area.

The policy reasons for allowing stepchildren to recover are numerous. First, as mentioned above, stepchildren can suffer as much as children when parents are injured or killed. Second, arguments that allowing stepchildren to recover for loss of stepparents' consortium will overburden the court system with a multiplicity of complex suits are not convincing. Assessing damages in cases of stepchild recovery will not be any more difficult than assessing damages in cases involving biological children. Barnard, 19 U. Mass. L. & Pol'y J. at 1330. The danger of double recovery because of the possible overlap with the recovery of the other parent can be prevented by proper jury instructions. South Dakota trial courts are fully capable of instructing juries and calculating damages to guard against double recovery or fraudulent actions; indeed, they do so every day. Third, the potential for increased insurance costs was rejected by the *Norton* court as a valid basis for rejecting recovery by a biological child, and should be by this court as well. *See* 397 N.W.2d at 1173. "Insurance is a loss-spreading device by design." *Id.* It is better to distribute the loss to the tortfeasor and the insurer, rather than allow the innocent victim to bear the entire loss. *See id.* at 1174.

While it is true that courts should "proceed with caution in laying down a new rule in the light of conditions affected or to be affected by it," *see Miller v. S.D. Dep't of Health*, 718 N.W.2d 221, 230 (S.D. 2007), the time has come to expand the eminently fair rule of allowing children to recover for loss of consortium to cover stepchildren.

I would reverse the district court and allow the case to proceed to trial on the issue of Marisa Baldry's loss of consortium claim.

9.10 Sample Memorandum Opinion

STATE OF MAINE
COURT OF APPEALS
A08-2046

Andrew Doyle,
Appellant,

v.

Rochester Excavating, Inc.
Respondent.

Appeal from a Judgment of the Orne County District Court, Raymond Meyer, Judge

File No. 73-CV-07-627

Frank J. Rhinehart, Rhinehart Huag Ltd., 11 Seventh Avenue North, P.O. Box 1433, Cape Rome, ME 04972 (for Appellant)

Anne McCloskey, Siddon & Suarez P.A., 400 Fir Street South, Orne, ME 04975 (for Respondent)

Considered and decided by Stowe, Presiding Judge; Brown, Judge; and Chute, Judge.

MEMORANDUM*

This opinion will be unpublished and may not be cited except as provided by Me. Rev. Stat. §470A.08, subd. 3 (2008).

Appellant Andrew Doyle appeals the district court's grant of summary judgment in favor of Respondent Rochester Excavating, Inc. The district court granted summary judgment on the basis that Doyle's injuries were caused by an act of God, and that no negligence by Rochester contributed to Doyle's injuries.

Reversed and remanded.

FACTS

The following facts are not in dispute. On the evening of July 16, 2006, Andrew Doyle was injured when the car he was driving slid into a hole on Pine Street in Orne. Rochester had excavated along the side of the street for a sewer project earlier in the day. Shortly before Doyle was injured, and after Rochester had stopped work for the day, a storm hit the area during which one inch of rain fell in an hour's time.

After Doyle filed a negligence action, Rochester moved for summary judgment, arguing that the rainstorm was an act of God, and that its actions did not contribute to Doyle's injuries.

DECISION

When we review a grant of a summary judgment, we view the evidence in the light most favorable to the party against whom the judgment has been granted and independently determine whether the record supports the conclusion that there is no genuine issue of material fact and that the prevailing party is entitled to judgment as a matter of law. *Lander, Inc. v. Lincoln*, 685 A.2d 51, 52 (Me. 1997). A material fact is one that could potentially affect the outcome of the suit. *Rudquist v. Scott*, 805 A.2d 273, 275 (Me. Ct. App. 2000). A genuine issue of material fact exists when the evidence requires a fact-finder to choose between competing versions of the truth. *Id.*

A defendant can avoid liability for negligence if the plaintiff's injury is the result of an act of God, and if the defendant's own acts or omissions did not contribute in any way to the injury. *Prasha Enters. v. State*, 296 A.2d 653, 654 (Me. 1984). An act of God is "an unusual, extraordinary and unprecedented event," caused by natural forces. *Id.* However, if the evidence indicates that the injury was produced by the defendant's negligence combined with some natural force, the issue of proximate causation is one for the jury to consider. *Joseph Reis Co. v. Yusann*, 441 A.2d 134, 136 (Me. Ct. App. 1993).

After reviewing the affidavits presented by the parties, we determine that substantial evidence exists that would allow a reasonable fact-finder to conclude that Rochester was negligent in maintaining the excavation site, and that Rochester's negligence combined with the rainfall to cause Doyle's injuries. Therefore, genuine issues of material fact remain for trial with respect to whether Rochester was negligent in maintaining the site and with respect to whether Rochester's negligence, if any, was the proximate cause of Doyle's injuries.

REVERSED AND REMANDED.

Cara R. Chute, Judge

Dated: July 10, 2008

Chapter 10

Drafting Correspondence and Other Documents

A judicial clerk's job assignments are often varied and, although some tasks may be enumerated in your contract, many of them might fall under the category "and other duties as assigned." You must be prepared for anything in this job. This chapter provides a sampling of some common writing projects you could be given in addition to drafting the documents described in previous chapters. Remember, however, that the kinds of documents you may be asked to write are only limited by the judge's imagination.

10.1 Letters

Like most professionals, judges and their staff members write letters to take care of both important and mundane tasks. Even though the purpose and tone of these letters will change depending on the content and the recipient, all official letters from chambers should look the same and should be printed on the judge's letterhead stationary. You will likely have many examples in the judge's files that you can follow for format.

Format of Judges' Letters

We assume that readers are familiar with the basic format of business letters. All judges' letters contain the parts that most business letters contain: a date; an inside address (the names and ad-

258 DRAFTING CORRESPONDENCE AND OTHER DOCUMENTS

dresses of the recipients); a "regarding line" that includes the subject matter of the letter, the case name and number if the letter is about a specific case, and additional information about the contents of the letter, if appropriate; a salutation; the body of the letter; a closing; and a signature. You should use "Dear [Recipient]:" as the salutation, and the salutation should always be followed by a colon, never a comma.[1]

The body of the letter should be organized in a way that is helpful to the reader — you may use subheadings and bold, italicized, or underlined type to help guide the reader through the letter. No matter what the subject matter of the letter, get to the point right away. Do not make the reader guess what the letter is about. Multipage letters should have page numbers for easy reference.

Types of Judges' Letters

Although a letter can be written for any reason, the following list describes some of the most common reasons that judges write letters.

Scheduling. If you are a clerk in a chambers where the judge does not have a judicial assistant or a calendar clerk, you may be writing letters to attorneys confirming or assigning hearing dates or communicating due dates for trial documents. Most judges have form letters they send to communicate this type of information and guidelines they use for establishing various due dates. If you need to draft this type of letter, ask if there is a template or a form that you can use. Some judges sign these letters, and some judges have their judicial clerks sign them. It is common for someone other than the judge to write this type of letter, so it is not necessary to explain why you are writing instead of the judge. Letters that set trial schedules are sometimes called "trial notices," and although clerks often sign these letters, they have the practical force of orders

---

1. Bryan A. Garner, *The Redbook: A Manual on Legal Style* § 1.24 (2d ed. 2002).

over the parties. Absent good cause, parties must meet trial deadlines.

Since scheduling letters are written to attorneys, they should have a professional tone and may include legal terms that lay readers might not understand. These letters should not be a challenge to write, and if you are required to write them, they will likely become a routine part of your job.

Other communication related to a case. In addition to communicating about scheduling matters in letters, judges may communicate with parties about other matters in letters. As a general rule, in our legal system, communicating with "parties" means communicating with attorneys. As discussed in Chapter Eight, some of these letters are actually orders that settle disputes before the court. A letter that disposes of a motion or explains a decision that has an effect on a case must be signed by the judge, even if it is originally drafted by a clerk. A letter that affects the disposition of a case should have the same formal, serious tone as an order or opinion and should be filed in the docket like a regular order or opinion.

If the judge assigns you to write a letter to the parties for a purpose other than routine scheduling, you should explain to the parties why you are writing instead of the judge. You should be direct: "Judge Jones asked me to write to you regarding the status of deposition progress in *Hilltop Services, Inc. v. Michaels*, No. 07-CV-44, the companion case to your case."

Pro se litigant communications. Judges sometimes receive letters from pro se litigants that ask for ex parte relief or contain ex parte communications.[2] If a judge receives such a letter, someone in chambers must inform the litigant that ex parte communications are not allowed in our legal system. Judges sometimes ask judicial clerks to draft letters to pro se parties explaining these rules

---

2. Ex parte communications are communications "[d]one or made at the insistence and for the benefit of one party only, and without notice to, or argument by, any person adversely interested." *Black's Law Dictionary* 657 (9th ed. 2009).

and telling the litigants where they can get more information on filing motions and giving proper notice to opposing counsel.

Since these letters are written for non-attorneys, the language used can be less formal than in letters written for attorneys. You might also need to define legal terms that you cannot avoid using in the letter. However, even if the tone is less formal, the structure of the letter and the overall appearance of the letter must still be professional. Judges may sign these letters themselves, or they may assign these communications to clerks. So, again, drafting these letters may become a routine part of your job.

RSVPs. Judges receive many invitations to attend or speak at programs, bar events, CLEs, and law school classes; and, as you know, judges often accept these invitations. Judges should respond to all legitimate invitations, either to accept or decline, and may assign clerks to take care of these responses. In general, this type of correspondence should not pose much of a challenge. Unless the judge gives you different standing instructions, always make sure you ask the judge how to respond before sending a particular letter.

Tone and Professionalism in Judges' Letters

Judges will, of course, read and make necessary changes to the tone and content of letters they will sign. Although letters should typically be written in a professional tone, if the letter is to the judge's friend or acquaintance, the judge might want you to adopt a more casual collegial tone. However, that is the judge's decision, not yours. Make sure you understand the judge's preferences when you first begin drafting letters for the judge's signature.

On the other hand, if the judge assigns you the task of writing routine correspondence, such as scheduling letters and pro se litigant letters, you will be your own proofreader. Just as every order or opinion that comes out of chambers must be as perfect as possible, every letter that comes out of chambers must be as perfect as possible. Double-check all your letters to ensure that they are grammatically and substantively correct before you mail them. Letters that you sign should have a tone of neutral professionalism.

Even if you sign the letter, the letter still represents the judge and must satisfy the standards the judge sets for all writing projects. A typographical error could not only cause a disruption in the court's schedule if, for example, two motions were inadvertently scheduled for oral argument at the same time, but also could cause the judge unnecessary embarrassment and lead the public to question the integrity of the judiciary as a whole.

10.2 Email Correspondence

Like most other professionals, legal professionals increasingly rely on email as a primary means of communication. You will likely use email to communicate with other court employees. However, using email to communicate with attorneys and parties is not widespread.

As a rule, proprietary and confidential information should not be sent via email. Nonetheless, there may be situations in which you will be called upon to send confidential information in an email, such as when you and the judge cannot be in the same building for some reason.[3] If you must conduct official business via email, make sure your correspondence contains a confidentiality disclaimer that has been approved by the judge.

As with all communications that come from chambers, emails must be professional and accurate. You cannot lower your standards simply because the medium is more immediate and, arguably, more casual than a formal letter. Always include a proper subject line and salutation in your emails; do not forsake proper paragraph structure, sentence structure, spelling, and grammar. Remember that

---

3. *See* Massey Mayo Case & Jill E. Tompkins, *A Guide for Tribal Court Law Clerks and Judges* 22, 30, 34 (2007), http://www.colorado.edu/iece/docs/Thompson/Final_version_Guide.pdf (explaining that sometimes "remote" clerks who do most of their work from home and never see the courthouse or the judge may conduct most of their communications with the judge via phone and email and may need to establish procedures to promote email confidentiality and security).

not all email programs contain a spell check function. A good way to achieve error-free emails is to first type the text into a word processing document so you can run a spell check and grammar check on the text before you copy and paste it into the body of your email.

And, of course, make sure that you do not hit "send" prematurely. Double-check the recipient list, and proofread the content not only on the screen, but also in hard copy before you send an email. The rules regarding ex parte communications are not relaxed for email communications. Unless the judge has a specific reason to communicate with only one party to a case, all parties should receive judicial email communications.

10.3 Speeches and Talking Points

Judges are respected citizens of not only their legal communities, but also of their broader communities, and, as mentioned above, are frequently invited to speak at CLEs, conventions, classes, and other gatherings. Judges often have their clerks research and draft the remarks they give at these events. Drafting speeches can be a welcome diversion from the usual tasks that judicial clerks perform. Judicial clerks who usually spend the day researching strictly legal topics might be called upon to research very different topics: the history of trademark protection in another country or the life of a famous or not-so-famous state citizen, for example. At times like this, a good understanding of the breadth of your law library's collection, the electronic resources you can access, local news media, and the local public library will be helpful.

When you are called upon to do non-traditional research, the courthouse law librarians can still be valuable resources because they are experts in both legal and non-legal resources. Even if the courthouse library does not contain the resources you need, courthouse librarians are connected to the broader library community in your area and can direct you to helpful people and resources. You should also explore the previously-not-traveled parts of the law library and the non-legal, news, and international law databases that may be part of the court's Westlaw or LexisNexis subscriptions.[4]

We have mentioned writing in the judge's "voice" in several chapters of this book. Those were metaphorical references. When you are writing a speech, there is no metaphor. You are writing something that the judge will actually say in public. Thus, the judge may take a very active role when you are drafting a speech.

Once you have done your research, you should report what you found to the judge and discuss what, exactly, the judge wants for a finished product. If the judge is part of a panel at a bar event or a CLE seminar, note cards and "talking points" might suffice. If the judge is the keynote speaker at a prestigious symposium, you may need to draft a complete speech that will be published at a later date in a law review or journal. But in some situations, the judge might prefer an outline or a copy of the speech that contains visual cues such as color coding or unusual indents to help the judge stay on track. The judge might even want you to punch up the speech by creating a visual presentation of some kind.

When drafting a speech, remember that public speaking is not legal writing. Although the judge might need to demonstrate knowledge of the law and an understanding of legal analysis in a speech, the judge probably will not appreciate reading a first draft that sounds like a judicial opinion or an argument from an appellate brief. Writing for the listener is different from writing for the reader. You and the judge will need to learn together what process works best for you — it may be much different from the process you use together to draft orders or opinions. Be flexible.

10.4 Updates and Abstracts

Judges sometimes ask clerks to keep them keep abreast of current changes in the law by abstracting new cases or summarizing new

---

4. Chapter Four contains more detailed lists of research sources.

legislation. Although a document like this will likely not be seen by anyone outside of chambers, you must not relax your writing standards when creating abstracts and updates for the judge. Abstracts and updates are probably the most helpful for specialty areas of the law or when the law on a certain subject is in flux.[5]

10.5 Additional Resources

K.K. DuVivier, *E-Etiquette: Thoughtful E-mail Correspondence*, Colo. Law., Mar. 2007, at 79

Federal Judicial Center, *Law Clerk Handbook: A Handbook for Law Clerks to Federal Judges* 98–99 (2007), *available at* http://www.fjc.gov/ public/pdf.nsf/lookup/lawclhbk.pdf/$file/lawclhbk.pdf (discussing judicial correspondence)

Gerald Lebovits, *E-mail Netiquette for Lawyers*, N.Y. St. B. J., Nov./Dec. 2009, at 64

Wayne Schiess, *Writing for the Legal Audience* (2003) (Chapter Four explains how to properly write email in a legal setting.)

---

5. *See* Case & Tompkins, *supra* note 3, at 28 (explaining that tribal court clerks may be asked to summarize "relevant cases or enactments expected to affect Indian country").

10.6 Sample Scheduling Letter

The Honorable Christine D. Huotari
Sandburg County District Court
Sandburg County Courthouse
298 Willow Avenue
Smithville, Minnesota 99999
(999)-555-1111

June 24, 2009

LaChelle Singh, Esq.
Jones, Miller, and Goldman L.L.P.
4440 8th Avenue
Suite 900
Smithville, MN 99999

Emma L. Gonzalez, Esq.
Kane and Associates L.L.P.
786 Marinette Avenue
Suite 5B
Jewel, MN 77777

    Re: Delta Power and Gas Company v. Wilcox
          Civil File No. 08-CV-2231
          Trial Notice

Dear Ms. Singh and Ms. Gonzalez:

Delta Power and Gas Company v. Wilcox, No. 08-CV-2231, is scheduled for a three-day trial beginning at **9:00 a.m. on December 7, 2009 in Courtroom 4** of the Sandburg County Courthouse.

The following pretrial deadlines apply. All submissions must be filed via the Court's electronic filing system, with two courtesy hardcopies to Chambers, and must be served on opposing counsel.

- **Expert witnesses** must be identified by **5:00 p.m. on October 5, 2009.**
- **Opposition to expert witnesses** and supporting memoranda are due by **5:00 p.m. on October 26, 2009.**

- **Replies** to opposition to expert witnesses are due by **5:00 p.m. on November 2, 2009.**
- **Witness lists** are due by **5:00 p.m. on November 9, 2009.**
- **Exhibit lists** are due by **5:00 p.m. on November 9, 2009.**
- **Motions in limine** are due by **5:00 p.m. on November 9, 2009.**
- **Proposed voir dire questions** are due by **5:00 p.m. on November 9, 2009.**
- **Opposition to motions in limine** and supporting memoranda are due by **5:00 p.m. on November 16, 2009.**
- **Joint jury instructions and verdict form** are due by **5:00 p.m. on November 23, 2009.** Each instruction must be submitted on a separate page and must include citations to the source of the instruction.
- **Disputed jury instructions** are due by **5:00 p.m. on November 23, 2009**, along with a short memorandum of law or a citation to the source of the proffered instruction.

If necessary, oral argument will be heard on disputed motions in limine and opposition to expert witnesses at **2:30 p.m. on November 30, 2009,** in **Courtroom 4.** The Court will notify counsel via telephone by **November 23, 2009,** if this hearing is necessary for the Court to resolve outstanding evidentiary issues.

Pretrial conference will begin at **9:00 a.m. on December 7, 2009,** in **Courtroom 4,** and jury selection will commence at 10:30 a.m.

Sincerely,

John N. Chang
Law Clerk to Judge Christine D. Huotari

10.7 Sample Letter to a Pro Se Litigant

The Honorable Christine D. Huotari
Sandburg County District Court
Sandburg County Courthouse
298 Willow Avenue
Smithville, Minnesota 99999
(999)-555-1111

June 24, 2009

Mr. Michael M. Wilcox
444 Greenway Avenue
Smithville, MN 99999

    Re: Delta Power and Gas Company v. Wilcox
        Civil File No.: 08-CV-2231

Dear Mr. Wilcox:

The Judge received your letter explaining why you feel you should not be bound by the terms of the noncompete agreement you signed when you started working for Delta Power and Gas Company. In that letter, you asked the Judge to let you start your new job with Minnesota Electric while your case is progressing through the judicial system. Judge Huotari asked me to write to tell you that she cannot consider your request at this time.

The Judge cannot accept letters from one party to a case if the other parties to the case have not also received copies of the letter. In our legal system, parties are not allowed to have private communications with judges.

If you want the Judge to grant you any relief, such as allowing you to work at your new job before this case is over, you must file a motion in the Office of the Clerk of Court. A motion is a way to ask the Judge to do something. Motions must be in writing. Along with that motion, you can file a memorandum explaining all the reasons you think the Judge should grant your motion. You must send a copy of these papers to Delta Power and Gas's attorneys. Along with the motion and memorandum, you must submit a signed affidavit stating that you mailed the papers to Delta's attorneys.

Delta will then have 30 days to file a written response to your motion, and will send you a copy of that response. Normally, the Judge will read both parties' papers and make a decision, which she will send to both parties. If, after reading both parties' papers, the Judge thinks she would benefit from hearing oral argument on the motion, she will schedule an oral argument at the courthouse where you and attorneys for Delta Power and Gas will have the opportunity to tell the Judge why the motion should be granted or denied.

More information about court procedure and filing motions can be found in any county law library or by following the links on the Minnesota Judicial Branch web site: http://www.mncourts.gov/Default.aspx?page=511. The Minnesota Rules of General Practice for the District Court are available in county law libraries or online at http://www.mncourts.gov/rules/general/GRtitleIV.htm.

Sincerely,

John N. Chang,
Law Clerk to Judge Christine D. Huotari

Chapter 11

Reviewing Others' Work

Many judicial clerks will spend some time each week reviewing final documents produced by other clerks. Because court documents set precedent and finalize legal rights, they must be accurate and error-free. Formal review of the text and the citations by a fresh set of eyes helps to maintain this standard. While citation checking and proofreading in this context may consume only a small percentage of a clerk's time, they are important tasks that must be undertaken with care.

As a judicial clerk, you shoulder an important responsibility when you review the work of others. But keep in mind that your job at this stage of the writing process is not to critique style, reorganize content, or comment on the argument. Your job is to make sure that the information on the page is presented flawlessly.

Also, as you make corrections, remember that the clerk who drafted this document may be reviewing *your* work next week. Be honest but professional when communicating about errors or any other issues that arise during the review process.

11.1 Citation Checking

Citation checking should accomplish three main goals: (1) ensure that the citations in the document comply with the governing citation system; (2) ensure that the content associated with each citation accurately represents the cited source; and (3) ensure that all cited authorities are current and are still good law. To accomplish these goals, your citation-checking process should include the following steps:

(1) Check the validity and currency of all primary authority cited in the document using KeyCite on Westlaw or Shepard's on Lexis-Nexis. If any issues arise, bring them to the attention of the clerk who drafted the document.

(2) Scan the document to identify any unusual or unfamiliar sources that may not be easily available in the library or online. Check with the clerk who drafted the document for help with locating those sources if necessary.

(3) Gather sources. This may involve working in the library or checking all sources through Westlaw, LexisNexis, or other online resources, such as Hein Online, available either without charge or through your law library's subscription.

(4) Go through the document and compare each statement followed by a citation with the content in the original source. For each cited statement in the document, verify that the cited statement fairly represents the statement in the original source. Make sure the proper signal precedes the citation if a signal is required. If the document quotes the original source, verify word by word that the quote is accurate and that any changes or omissions are properly indicated. Remember that quotations of fifty words or more should be in block format. If you discovered any inaccuracies in the citation itself when you located the source, correct them.

(5) Once you have verified the content related to every citation, review the form of each citation. Correct any errors. Keep a citation manual at hand so you can review the abbreviation tables and the rules for citing unusual sources, and can answer questions as they come up.

You can develop your own system for citation checking. For instance, you may prefer to check form first and content second. As long as your system results in complete, accurate citation, whatever works for you is acceptable.

11.2 Proofreading

Even though the drafting clerk and authoring judge have undoubtedly read through the document numerous times, applying another set of eyes will make certain that the final document released to the public is as error-free as possible. The following paragraph illustrates the value of word-for-word proofreading:

> Aoccdrnig to rscheearch at an Elingsh uinervtisy, it deosn't mttaer in waht oredr the ltteers in a wrod are, the olny ipmoertnt tihng is taht the frist and lsat ltteers are at the rghit pclae. The rset can be a toatl mses and you can sitll raed it wouthit porbelm. Tihs is bcuseae we do not raed ervey lteter by itslef but the word as a wlohe.[1]

As you can see from this example, no matter how many times writers read through their documents, they may miss errors because their brains will compensate for switched letters, missing words, and other problems.

Consequently, as a final proofreader, you are responsible for looking at each word as a unit of type rather than as a unit of meaning. Chapter Five includes a list of suggestions to help you improve the proofreading skills you apply to your own work. The same principles apply when you proofread the work of others. Read the document backwards. Read it aloud. Use a ruler or piece of paper to help you focus on one line at a time. As with citation checking, whatever system works for you is acceptable, as long as it achieves the ultimate goal: an error-free document.

---

1. See Dr. Matt Davis's homepage at the MRC Cognition & Brain Sciences Unit, www.mrc-cbu.cam.ac.uk/people/matt.davis/cmabridge/, for a discussion of the origin of this paragraph, which began circulating on the internet in 2003.

272 · REVIEWING OTHERS' WORK

11.3 Additional Resources

Linda J. Barris, *Understanding and Mastering the Bluebook* (2007)
Debra Hart May, *Proofreading Plain and Simple* (1997)

Chapter 12

Ethics and Professionalism

Judicial clerks are privy to the inner workings of courts and gain insight into the decision-making processes of judges that most attorneys never get. This access, and the knowledge gained through it, is so valuable that many law firms give new associates credit toward partnership for years spent clerking. With this great privilege comes great responsibility. The Federal Judicial Center (FJC) describes clerks' unique position in the following way:

> Law clerks play important roles in the judicial process and must maintain its integrity. Because of the close association between the judge and law clerks, [the clerks'] professional and personal actions reflect on [the] judge and ultimately on the judiciary as a whole. [Judicial clerks] are held to the very highest standards of conduct. Like judges, [judicial clerks] hold a position of public trust and must comply with the demanding requisites of that position.[1]

Judicial clerks must conduct themselves with integrity at all times. This means not only maintaining confidentiality regarding the judge's decisions and being professional and respectful to everyone

---

1. Federal Judicial Center, *Law Clerk Handbook: A Handbook for Law Clerks to Federal Judges* 5 (Sylvan A. Sobel, ed., 2007), *available at* http://www.fjc.gov/public/pdf.nsf/lookup/lawclhbk.pdf/$file/lawclhbk.pdf [hereinafter "*Law Clerk Handbook*"].

in chambers, the courthouse, and the courtroom, but also disclosing any potential conflicts regarding a case, and following strict rules when negotiating with future employers.

All judicial clerks in the federal system, except United States Supreme Court clerks, must comply with the Code of Conduct for Judicial Employees.[2] The Code of Conduct contains five broad canons and is similar to the Code of Conduct for United States Judges that federal law clerks' "bosses" must comply with. In addition, the FJC has published *Maintaining the Public Trust: Ethics for Federal Judicial Law Clerks*[3] and *Law Clerk Handbook: A Handbook for Law Clerks to Federal Judges*[4] to help clerks understand their ethical obligations.

If you are unsure about a particular course of conduct or a potential conflict and you cannot ask your judge or a fellow law clerk what to do, you may find guidance in these publications, all of which are available online. Although they are written for federal judicial clerks, the advice they contain can be helpful to clerks in all courts. *Maintaining the Public Trust* is particularly helpful because it contains answers to hypothetical questions and information about where to find advisory opinions issued by the Committee on Codes of Conduct of the Administrative Office of the United States Courts.[5] Another good default rule to follow is that if the judge you work for would be ethically prohibited from engaging in a certain activity, you

---

2. Code of Conduct for Judicial Employees (1995), http://www.us courts.gov/guide/vol2/ch2a.html [hereinafter "Code of Conduct"]. Supreme Court clerks must comply with standards established by the Justices of the Supreme Court. *Id.* at n.1.

3. Fed. Jud. Ctr., *Maintaining the Public Trust: Ethics for Federal Judicial Law Clerks* (2002), *available at* http://www.fjc.gov/public/pdf.nsf/ lookup/Ethics01.pdf/$file/Ethics01.pdf [hereinafter "*Maintaining the Public Trust*"].

4. *Law Clerk Handbook, supra* note 1.

5. Advisory opinions can be found at http://www.uscourts.gov/guide/ advisoryopinions.htm.

are also prohibited from engaging in that activity.[6] State courts have their own codes and policies, written and unwritten, to which clerks must adhere.[7]

The judge a clerk works for will ultimately determine the limits on the clerk's outside contacts and activities. The guidelines below are a starting point for a discussion between you and the judge.

12.1 Confidentiality and Loyalty

Because a judicial clerk occupies a special position in the court, the clerk has an obligation to maintain confidentiality about the judge's decision-making process and about the progress of cases on the judge's calendar.

---

6. Massey Mayo Case & Jill E. Tompkins, *A Guide for Tribal Court Law Clerks and Judges*, 33 (2007), http://www.colorado.edu/iece/docs/Thompson/Final_version_Guide.pdf.

7. *See e.g.,* N.H. Sup. Ct. R. 46 (Law Clerk Code of Conduct); Code of Conduct for Law Clerks and Staff Attorneys of the Supreme Court of Texas (2002), http://www.supreme.courts.state.tx.us/rules/pdf/clk-conduct-atty.pdf; Judicial Branch of the Navajo Nation Employee Code of Conduct (1991), http://www.navajocourts.org/Policies/EmployeeCode.htm; Charles W. Sorenson, Jr., *Are Law Clerks Fair Game? Invading Judicial Confidentiality*, 43 Val. U. L. Rev. 1, 38 (2008) (explaining that judges employ a variety of rules, both written and unwritten, to control law clerks' ethical behavior); Todd C. Peppers, Micheal W. Giles, & Bridget Tainer-Parkins, *Inside Judicial Chambers: How Federal District Court Judges Select and Use Their Law Clerks*, 71 Alb. L. Rev. 623, 636 (2008) (noting that a survey of 311 federal district court judges revealed that eighty-eight percent of the judges discussed confidentiality rules with their clerks). *See also* Peter N. Thompson, *Confidentiality in Chambers: Is Private Judicial Action the Public's Business?*, Bench & B. of Minn., Feb. 2005, at 14 (discussing *State v. Greer*, 673 N.W.2d 151 (Minn. 2004), in which the Minnesota Supreme Court accepted judicial law clerks' affidavits about their perceptions of a judge's decision-making process as evidence, and offering suggestions for ways to better protect the confidential nature of the judicial clerk-judge relationship in Minnesota).

No one should know how a judge might rule until the judge is ready to announce the ruling. If a clerk tips off the media or an attorney involved in the case, the judge is not then free to change a decision without significant problems and embarrassment. In addition, knowing the timing of a decision might give one party an advantage during litigation. As a clerk, you should keep the following statement in mind:

> Among judicial employees, law clerks are in a unique position since their work may have direct input into a judicial decision. Even if this is not true in all judicial chambers, the legal community perceives that this is the case based upon the confidential and close nature of the relationship between clerk and judge.[8]

Litigation Information

Judicial clerks are privy to sensitive and confidential information about cases: information about parties that is not for public disclosure; information about the judge's decision-making process and how close a judge or panel of judges is to rendering a final decision in a case; the substance of final decisions; and information about the dynamics of the "court family" and the inner workings of a particular courthouse. You must not disclose any of this confidential information.[9]

To this end, clerks need to be aware that not all court filings are public filings. Sometimes you will work on ex parte motions or motions that are filed under seal. The mere existence of these motions cannot be disclosed to anyone outside of chambers. Accordingly, you may not be allowed to share much of what you see and

---

8. *Maintaining the Public Trust, supra* note 3, at 3.
9. Simply stated, confidential information is any information that "you receive in chambers that is not filed in the public docket." *Id.* at 6.

hear during the day with friends and family.[10] This prohibition also applies to the dissemination of confidential information in documents. If you take work home with you, any copies of confidential documents or any "attorney notes" you write on courtesy copies of publicly filed documents should be kept in a location that no one else in your home can access. Never remove original documents from the courthouse.

Sometimes it is difficult for new clerks to know what information is confidential and what information is not confidential. The FJC provides federal clerks with the following guidelines. Although not exhaustive, the guidelines quoted below are instructive and provide a good overview of the types of information that cannot be shared outside of chambers.

[Information that is Confidential]
- Statements, or even hints, about the judge's likely actions in a case
- Disclosure of the timing of a judge's decision or order, or any other judicial action, without the judge's authorization
- The content of case-related discussions with a judge
- Observations about the judge's decision-making process in specific cases
- Documents or other information related to a sealed case
- Information obtained in the course of a law clerk's work that is not available to the general public

[Information that is not Confidential]
- Court rules
- Court procedures

10. *See* Comment, *The Law Clerk's Duty of Confidentiality*, 129 U. Pa. L. Rev. 1230, 1235–36 (1981) (discussing judicial clerks' ability to discuss confidential information with spouses, people outside the court, and people outside chambers, and noting that judges "generally have forged their own [law clerk confidentiality] policies that vary considerably in content, specificity, and formality").

- In general, how the court operates
- Court records, including the case docket available from the clerk's office
- Information disclosed in public court proceedings[11]

The need for confidentiality arises out of the special relationship between clerks and their judges. As discussed in Chapter Two, judicial clerks advise judges about the law, just as attorneys advise clients about the law. This relationship has prompted one federal judge to give his new clerks the following message:

> As my lawyers, you are absolutely forbidden to disclose the intimate details of this lawyer-client relationship, of the decision-making and decision-justifying processes that take place in these chambers. This court is a family, and there will be times that I will make remarks about my family members. They will be uttered sometimes in the heat of passion or despair. They will not be repeated beyond the chambers door. Even if I occasionally blow off steam, remember that these judges are my colleagues and will be my friends long after you are gone from here.[12]

The Judge's Decision-Making Process and Private Life

A judge hires a particular clerk, in part, because the judge thinks the clerk will get along well with the rest of the chambers staff. The judge knows that law clerks are part of a small circle of people who are privy to the inner workings of the judge's mind and decision-

---

11. *Maintaining the Public Trust, supra* note 3, at 6.
12. Ruggero J. Aldisert, book review, 72 Cal. L. Rev. 275, 282 (1984) (reviewing Bernard Schwartz, *Super Chief: Earl Warren and His Supreme Court — A Judicial Biography*); *see also* Sorenson, *supra* note 7, at 39–46 (discussing attorney-client privilege in the context of the judge-clerk relationship).

making process. If a judge is not free to express doubt or openly discuss and evaluate different theories or ideas for fear that the public might find out, the judge's duty to impartially weigh all aspects of a decision could be compromised. Judges should not have to temper the decision-making process in their own chambers. This is one of the few places where a judge is out of the public eye and can speak freely. Strict confidentiality rules ensure an open exchange of ideas and discourse.

As discussed in earlier chapters, chambers are often collegial places where judges, law clerks, and administrative staff know about each other's day-to-day lives. A judge would likely not want anyone to know if a member of the judge's family is having medical tests or if the judge is moving to a new house. Personal information you know by virtue of working with the judge day after day should be guarded with the same zeal as litigation secrets.

Friends, Family, Attorneys, and the Press

Although judicial clerks must not disclose any information that is not already a matter of public record, clerks are not required to be hermits and cut off all communications with friends and family. Thus, you can acknowledge that a big employer in the state is being sued by former employees for discrimination, and that there is a motion for summary judgment scheduled for oral argument next week. However, you cannot tell anyone that the parties have been in private mediation for three days and just reported to the judge that they have reached a tentative settlement in the case that will make the hearing moot. If your friends are planning to drive 200 miles to hear the oral argument, you cannot tip them off that the trip might be for nothing. Once the cancellation is a matter of public record, then you are free to call your friends and tell them not to bother driving to the courthouse.

In addition to not sharing confidential information with friends and acquaintances, clerks cannot share confidential information with attorneys and the press. It is not uncommon for lawyers or reporters to call and ask when a judge will issue a decision. Clerks cannot provide this information. Many judges forbid their clerks from talking at all to attorneys with actions pending before them.[13] Moreover, clerks must never speak to the press about a case unless instructed to do so by the judge.[14]

The prohibition on speaking to attorneys is defined differently in different chambers. As discussed in Chapter Two, a clerk may keep the judge's calendar and then must speak to attorneys to schedule hearings and trials and to request documents. Even in chambers where clerks do not keep the calendars, they usually get the courtroom ready for hearings and trials and, as part of these duties, check in attorneys and parties. At this time, clerks will often exchange small talk with the attorneys. Most judges do not require their clerks to refrain from this type of innocuous conversation. Indeed, one of the requirements of the clerk's job is to be gracious to everyone in the courtroom. But as a clerk, you must make sure that attorneys do not steer any conversation into areas that you are not allowed to discuss, such as other cases pending before your judge or other judges in the court or the judge's reaction to a unique argument contained in the attorney's brief. If the conversation turns this way, you must politely, but firmly, tell the attorney that you cannot discuss current litigation with the attorney.

Other Judicial Clerks

Different judges may impose different rules regarding a clerk's ability to discuss pending cases with other judicial clerks. Most judges encourage discourse between their own clerks, but some might not want their clerks discussing pending cases with clerks from other chambers. On the other hand, some judges consider other judges' clerks part of the same "court family" who can be trusted to maintain confidences, and therefore do not impose any restrictions regarding communication with these co-clerks. Ap-

13. *Law Clerk Handbook, supra* note 1, at 8–9.
14. *Id.* at 7.

pellate court clerks will likely work closely with clerks whose judges are sitting on panels together. Always make sure you know the judge's rules regarding communications with your fellow judicial clerks.

If you are talking with another clerk about a case or another court matter, be aware of your surroundings. Judicial clerks should not discuss confidential matters in public places like restaurants and elevators because other people can overhear the conversations and learn information that is not yet, and indeed may never be, ready for public dissemination.

Litigants

Although court rules and procedures are not confidential, a clerk cannot give legal advice. This prohibition becomes a challenge when someone, oftentimes a pro se litigant, wants to know if filing deadlines have passed or if statutes of limitations have run. You must not engage in counting days or working out the math for a person in this situation. Rather, you should only direct the person to the applicable rules, and let the litigant read the rules himself or herself, or perhaps read the rules to the litigant.[15] In addition, Chapter Ten contains advice on writing letters to pro se litigants. With the judge's permission, it might be appropriate for you to direct a pro se litigant to a legal services agency or volunteer attorney network. If a litigant who is represented by counsel calls chambers, you should refer the litigant back to counsel.

---

15. Although clerks can never give litigants legal advice, some judges allow their clerks to be very directive with pro se litigants. To be safe, ask the judge what you should say if you are tempted to give pro se litigants any information beyond a strict reading of the rules or an explanation of the court's schedule or procedures.

An Ongoing Responsibility

A clerk's ethical obligation of confidentiality continues after the clerk-ship is over. You may never divulge any confidential information learned during the course of your clerkship, even long after you have moved on to new employment.[16] This applies even as your loyalties switch from your former boss (the judge) to your new boss (your next employer). Most attorneys understand these ongoing obligations and will not press you on this point. But if a co-worker wants to know the judge's views on the propriety of filing certain motions or what kind of arguments might "work" for the judge, you must decline to give out that information. You may, however, direct co-workers to published opinions that articulate the judge's views.

Individual judges will define the exact parameters of their clerks' confidentiality duties, and clerks must scrupulously abide by their own judges' wishes. Maintaining this confidentiality is an important part of maintaining an independent judiciary. As one federal judge tells his staff, "What happens in chambers stays in chambers."

12.2 Conflicts of Interest

Judges must recuse themselves from cases that might present conflicts of interest.[17] The same goes for law clerks. Clerks cannot work on cases in which they have a financial or personal interest or about which they know confidential information. In this situation, "a financial interest" means owning as little as one share of stock in a corporation, acting as a director of or advisor to an organization, or being a member of a group that is a party to litigation.[18] Owning

---

16. *Maintaining the Public Trust, supra* note 3, at 6.

17. Code of Conduct for United States Judges, Canon 3C(1) (2009), http://www.uscourts.gov/library/codeOfConduct/Code_Effective_July-01-09.pdf.

18. *Maintaining the Public Trust, supra* note 3, at 11; Code of Conduct, *supra*, note 2, Canon 3F(4).

bonds or mutual funds usually does not constitute a "financial interest."[19]

At a minimum, a conflict of interest exists in the following situations:

- [the clerk has] any financial interest in the subject matter or in a party to the case;
- [the clerk's] spouse or minor child residing in [the clerk's] household has a financial interest in the subject matter or in a party to the case;
- [the clerk], or a lawyer with whom [the clerk] practiced, [serves or served] as a lawyer in the matter;
- [the clerk has] a personal bias or prejudice concerning a party, or personal knowledge of disputed evidentiary facts;
- [the clerk] or a close relative is a party, lawyer, or material witness, or has an interest that could be affected substantially by the outcome.[20]

Some conflicts are predictable, such as when a clerk's spouse represents a party in a case before the judge, a firm at which the clerk will work after the termination of the clerkship represents a party, or the clerk could be called as a material witness. On the other hand, some situations must be examined on a case-by-case basis to see if they present actual conflicts that require the clerk be disqualified from the case, such as when the name of a clerk's neighbor appears on a witness list.[21]

To avoid conflicts, you must be aware of all your stock and other financial holdings, even holdings in a family trust or holdings that

---

19. *See* Code of Conduct, *supra* note 2, Canon 3F(4) (defining "financial interest" and explaining exceptions to the rule).

20. *Maintaining the Public Trust, supra* note 3, at 9 (citing Canon 3F(2) of the Code of Conduct for Judicial Employees).

21. *Id.* at 10 (differentiating "actual" conflicts from "potential" conflicts); *see also* Code of Conduct, *supra* note 2, Canon 3F(5) (explaining that a law clerk "should inform the ... judge of any circumstance or activity of the [law clerk] that might serve as a disqualification of the [law clerk] or the judge, in a matter pending before the judge").

are exclusively for the benefit of your spouse. In addition, you should be educated about any potential conflicts that will be imputed to you via family members, such as your in-laws' ownership of a company that is involved in litigation or your brother's new job at a local law firm. Generally, however, no financial conflict exists if you merely hold shares in a 401K or other mutual fund that you have no control over.[22]

You must disclose to the judge if there is any chance that pending litigation will present a conflict, even if the conflict arises from something you did prior to accepting the clerkship, such as volunteering on a political campaign or working in a certain industry. Although the judge will decide on a case-by-case basis whether a potential conflict presents an *actual* conflict, it is best to err on the side of full disclosure so that the judge is not blind-sided by a conflict disclosed only after you have worked on a case.[23]

Just as a judicial clerk's obligation of confidentiality continues after the clerkship is over, a clerk may also have conflicts of interest that will continue after the end of the clerkship. For example, former judicial clerks cannot work as attorneys on cases they worked on while clerking.[24] This includes not only cases to which you were officially assigned, but also includes cases to which co-clerks were assigned if you were privy to confidential information about those cases during your clerkship. In addition, most judges have rules that prohibit former clerks from appearing before them as attorneys for a period of time.[25]

---

22. Code of Conduct, *supra* note 2, Canon 3F(4)(i).
23. *Id.*, Canon 3F(3).
24. *Maintaining the Public Trust, supra* note 3, at 16.
25. *See id.*

12.3 Outside Activities

Judicial clerks, unlike attorneys in general, must carefully choose the activities they pursue outside of work hours. Judicial clerks are associated with their judges even outside of the courthouse and, therefore, must always be concerned about how outside activities will reflect on the judge.

> A judicial employee's activities outside of official duties should not detract from the dignity of the court, interfere with the performance of official duties, or adversely reflect on the operation and dignity of the court or office the judicial employee serves. Subject to ... the other provisions of this code, a judicial employee may engage in such activities as civic, charitable, religious, professional, educational, cultural, avocational, social, fraternal, and recreational activities, and may speak, write, lecture, and teach. If such outside activities concern the law, the legal system, or the administration of justice, the judicial employee should first consult with the [judge] to determine whether the proposed activities are consistent with the [standards contained in this code]....[26]

Thus, although judicial clerks are encouraged to have full lives outside of work, there are limits on what clerks can do with their private time. In some specialty courts, the limits might be imposed because of the court's jurisdiction or they might be imposed to avoid the appearance of impropriety.[27]

---

26. Code of Conduct, *supra* note 2, Canon 4A.
27. *See* Case & Tompkins, *supra*, note 6, at 34–35 (explaining that clerks in courts that hear Indian gaming cases may be prohibited from gambling at that tribe's facilities and that to avoid the appearance of impropriety, tribal judicial clerks might be prohibited from socializing with the larger tribal community).

Political Activities

Although any limits on a clerk's outside activities will ultimately be determined by the judge for whom the clerk works, most clerks will be limited in their political activities. Federal judicial clerks may not even participate in non-partisan political activities.[28] Since a judicial clerk is closely associated with the judge for whom the clerk works, the clerk's association with a political campaign may lead the public to believe that the judge endorses the candidates and policies favored by the clerk. This can lead to allegations of lack of impartiality.

At the state level, some judges may allow their clerks to volunteer on non-partisan campaigns and even on partisan campaigns if clerks do this work during their own time and do not implicate the judge or the judicial clerk's position in their volunteering.[29] State judges may also allow their clerks to work on the judge's own re-election campaigns on an after-hours basis. However, all these activities must be authorized by the individual judge.

Limitations on political activities and political contributions do not usually apply to a clerk's spouse, as long as the clerk is not associated with the activities and any financial contributions come from an account that does not belong to the clerk.

Soliciting Funds

Judicial clerks are generally not prohibited from soliciting funds for outside organizations such as charities and schools. However, in doing so, you may neither use the prestige of the clerkship position in the solicitation nor solicit funds from persons likely to

---

28. *See Maintaining the Public Trust, supra* note 3, at 20; Code of Conduct, *supra* note 2, Canon 5.

29. Survey of current and former state and federal judicial clerks, conducted fall 2008. On file with the authors.

come before the court. An exception exists for soliciting funds from other attorneys likely to appear before the court when the solicitation is "incident to a general fund-raising activity"[30] such as a law school alumni fund-raising campaign.

Gifts and Honoraria

Judicial clerks should not accept or solicit gifts from anyone seeking action from the court or from anyone who does business before the court. Moreover, clerks obviously cannot trade their influence with the judge in exchange for gifts.[31] The FJC lists the following exceptions to the general prohibition on receiving gifts:

- ordinary social hospitality
- gifts from relatives and friends on special occasions, such as an anniversary or birthday
- gifts arising out of a spouse's separate business or professional activity
- invitations to bar-related functions
- scholarships or fellowships on standard terms[32]

Federal law clerks cannot accept honoraria—"payments for a single appearance, speech or article, or for a series of appearances, speeches or articles related to official duties."[33] However, they may accept expenses such as mileage payments.[34] Make certain you know the rules of your court and the additional rules of the judge before you accept any gifts or honoraria. There may be times when prohibitions on the receipt of gifts or honoraria are in conflict with

---

30. Code of Conduct, *supra* note 2, Canon 4B(3).
31. *Maintaining the Public Trust, supra* note 3, at 18.
32. *Id.* at 18–19 (noting that an exception for "de minimis" gifts that applies to other federal judicial employees does not apply to law clerks).
33. *Id.* at 19.
34. *Id.*

social custom or tradition, but a judicial clerk's loyalty must be to the ethical rules the court and the judge establish, even if the clerk risks offending someone by following those rules.[35]

Law Practice and Other Outside Employment

Although judicial clerks are generally prohibited from practicing law during their clerkships, they are not usually prohibited from being employed in a second job, as long as they comply with the compensation reporting rules of their particular court. In most cases, a clerk's second job cannot be with a law firm, attorneys, or others who are likely to appear before the court. This is true even if the clerk would hold a non-legal position with the employer.[36] Exceptions to these rules might exist for the pro bono practice of law or providing legal assistance to family members, both subject to certain limitations.[37] Always make sure you ask the judge if you may practice law or work outside of the court in any capacity.

Seeking Future Employment

Most judges assume that law clerks will seek future employment while employed as term clerks or will have future employment already lined up before they begin their clerkships.[38] If you already have a job in place when you begin your clerkship, make sure your

---

35. *See* Case & Tompkins, *supra* note 6, at 35 (explaining that sometimes a tribal judicial clerk must forgo cultural traditions and honors if doing so could lead to the appearance of impropriety or favoritism).

36. *See Maintaining the Public Trust, supra* note 3, at 12–13 (providing a check-list for determining if outside activities are appropriate).

37. *See* Code of Conduct, *supra* note 2, Canon 4D; *Maintaining the Public Trust, supra* note 3, at 14–15.

38. *See* Code of Conduct, *supra* note 2, Canon 4C(4) (providing that a law clerk may seek employment to commence at the end of the clerkship as long as the clerk complies with any restrictions the judge imposes).

judge knows this. The judge may want to disqualify you from working on cases involving your future law firm. If you must job hunt during your clerkship, make sure you understand the limits your judge wants you to abide by.

One problem that current and former law clerks face when job hunting is what to use as a writing sample. Clerks who feel they have become better writers during their clerkships are understandably not interested in using law school projects as writing samples. On the other hand, since all writing that comes out of chambers is really the judge's work, the clerk can be in a quandary as to what to use as a writing sample.

Bench memos usually make good writing samples because you write them independently before collaborating with the judge, so they show your writing and analysis skills in the most honest light. However, ask your judge before you use any work that you created during your clerkship for a writing sample. The judge may want you to redact or change the party names, may want you to remove any personal notes you inserted for the judge to read, and may want to have a hand in choosing the memo that you can use.

Once you have a job interview, you must be careful that you do not divulge confidential information or comment on pending litigation during the interview.[39] If the questioning starts going in the direction of confidential information, tell the interviewer that your judge has instructed you not to discuss that topic. At this point in the interview, one of two things will happen. Either the interviewer will understand and move on, or you will leave the interview knowing that you probably don't want to work for that employer.

---

39. For a discussion of a situation in which the losing party in a divisive lawsuit set up a series of fake interviews for a fictitious "dream job" in the hope of obtaining confidential information from a former law clerk about the judge's decision-making process in the case, *see* Sorenson, *supra* note 7, at 1–4.

During your job search, remember you are still employed by the court, and you may not use the prestige of your current office to influence prospective employers. This does not mean that the judge cannot serve as a reference for you. Indeed, having a good relationship with a respected judge is one reason people choose to clerk.

Once you have an offer for future employment, the judge will likely disqualify you from working on cases in which your new firm represents a party. Your judge might also limit any pre-employment compensation you receive from your employer, such as a signing bonus or bar preparation expenses.

12.4 Professionalism

As discussed already in this chapter, a clerk's actions reflect on the judge and the entire judiciary. Thus, it should not be surprising that judicial clerks also have heightened obligations of professional conduct.

> A judicial employee should be patient, dignified, respectful, and courteous to all persons with whom the judicial employee deals in an official capacity, including the general public.... A judicial employee should diligently discharge the responsibilities of the office in a prompt, efficient, nondiscriminatory, fair, and professional manner.[40]

When dealing with the public, a clerk represents the court and can influence the public's perception of the judge, the court, and the judicial process as a whole.[41] Pro se litigants should leave a courtroom feeling like their arguments were listened to as closely as the arguments made by the opposing high-powered attorneys.

---

40. Code of Conduct, *supra* note 2, Canon 3C.
41. *See Law Clerk Handbook, supra* note 1, at 5, 10.

Although you are not required to pretend you do not know attorneys appearing before the judge, you must not be overly familiar or friendly with these attorneys in the courtroom or other areas of the courthouse. To this end, some judges require their clerks to limit their contact as much as practicable with attorney friends while the friends have motions or appeals pending before the judge or are in trial before the judge.

On the other hand, judicial clerks also have ethical obligations to people who they would never consider friends. Clerks must treat dead-beat parents and criminal defendants accused of heinous crimes with the same respect they show prominent attorneys and well-respected public figures. Friendliness is not required, but accusatory glances and hostility cannot be tolerated. No matter what your personal feelings may be toward parties appearing before the judge, you must present a front of neutral politeness toward everyone in the courtroom.[42]

The clerk's professionalism responsibilities are grounded in the need to maintain not only the fairness and accessibility of the courts, but also the dignity of the courts. Basic legal principles such as informed consent and the voluntary waiver of the right to a jury trial are premised on the presumption that a party has a clear mind and a complete understanding of the risks and benefits of a certain course of action. To that end, you must inform the judge if there is a reason that a hearing or trial should not go forward, such as if you suspect that one of the parties or attorneys is under the influence of drugs or alcohol.[43]

In addition to adhering to professional standards in the courtroom, a clerk must also adhere to professional writing standards. Professional writing meets "high ethical standards, ... ensure[s] accuracy and honesty in research, facts, and analysis.... [and] must exhibit the qualities of good moral character: Candor, respect, hon-

---

42. *Id.* at 10.
43. *See* Case & Tompkins, *supra* note 6, at 35.

esty, and professionalism."[44] As discussed in Chapters Eight, Nine, and Ten, judicial clerks often write the first drafts of orders, opinions, and other documents. In doing so, clerks must write in a way that demonstrates a thorough evaluation of all arguments and independent judgment.[45] All litigants must feel that their arguments were fully considered and that the judge did not summarily dismiss their arguments or summarily adopt the views of opposing counsel.

12.5 Ethics Checklist

The following checklist is a synopsis of a list from *Maintaining the Public Trust* and is a guideline for judicial clerks to follow when making decisions about whether certain activities or associations present potential or actual ethical conflicts. *Maintaining the Public Trust* contains a more detailed list that you should consult if you are making a decision about potential conflicts or outside activities you can pursue while clerking.[46] As with all the advice in this chapter, do not take this list at face value—discuss your particular situation with your judge.

---

44. Gerald Lebovits, Alifya V. Curtin, Lisa Solomon, *Ethical Judicial Opinion Writing*, 21 Geo. J. Legal Ethics 237, 238 (2008) (citing Michael R. Smith, *Advanced Legal Writing: Theories and Strategies in Persuasive Writing* 125 (2002)) (discussing judges' ethical obligations).

45. *See* Carol M. Bast & Linda B. Samuels, *Plagiarism and Legal Scholarship in the Age of Information Sharing: The Need for Intellectual Honesty*, 57 Cath. U. L. Rev. 777, 801–02 (2008) (discussing, among other things, *Bright v. Westmoreland County*, 380 F.3d 729, 731–32 (3d Cir. 2004) wherein the Third Circuit reversed a trial court judge for failing to exercise independent judgment when the judge merely adopted the prevailing party's proposed order and opinion almost verbatim).

46. *Maintaining the Public Trust, supra* note 3, at 21–23.

Potential Conflicts

- Do you have any ownership of, interest in, or relationship with a business or other entity that is a party to the case?
- Does your spouse, minor resident child, or other close relative have any ownership of, interest in, or relationship with a business or other entity that is a party to the case?

Actual Conflicts

- Do you have any personal knowledge of the issues involved in the case?
- Do you, your spouse, or another close relative stand to benefit from the outcome of the case?
- Are you, your spouse, or another close relative a potential witness in the case?
- Have you or your previous or future law firm worked on the case?
- Does your spouse or other close relative work for a law firm involved in the case?

Potentially Inappropriate Outside Activities

- Are you a member of, or serve on the board of, a law-related organization or charitable or social organization?
- Are you a member of a political or lobbying organization?
- Do you participate in partisan political activities?
- Do you participate in non-partisan political activities?
- Do you speak, write, or teach about legal subjects?
- Do you speak, write, or teach about non-legal subjects?
- Do you do pro bono legal work?
- Do you have a second law-related job?
- Do you have a second non-law-related job?
- Are you applying for law-related jobs to commence after your clerkship ends?
- Have you received any gifts or honoraria from law firms, individual attorneys, or others with a potential interest in your official position?

12.6 Additional Resources

Carol M. Bast & Linda B. Samuels, *Plagiarism and Legal Scholarship in the Age of Information Sharing: The Need for Intellectual Honesty*, 57 Cath. U. L. Rev. 777 (2008)

Massey Mayo Case & Jill E. Tompkins, *A Guide for Tribal Court Law Clerks and Judges* (2007), http://www.colorado.edu/iece/docs/Thompson/Final_version_Guide.pdf

Code of Conduct for Judicial Employees (1995), http://www.uscourts.gov/guide/vol2/ch2a.html

Code of Conduct for United States Judges (2009), http://www.uscourts.gov/library/codeOfConduct/Code_Effective_July-01-09.pdf

David Crump, *How Judges Use Their Law Clerks*, N.Y. State B. J., May 1986, at 43

Fed. Jud. Ctr., *Law Clerk Handbook: A Handbook for Law Clerks to Federal Judges* (Sylvan Al Sobel, ed., 2007), *available at* http://www.fjc.gov/public/pdf.nsf/lookup/lawclhbk.pdf/$file/lawclhbk.pdf

Fed. Jud. Ctr., *Maintaining the Public Trust: Ethics for Federal Judicial Law Clerks* (2002), *available at* http://www.fjc.gov/public/pdf.nsf/lookup/Ethics01.pdf/$file/Ethics01.pdf

Joyce J. George, *Judicial Opinion Writing Handbook*, 73–139 (5th ed. 2007)

Gerald Lebovits, *Ethical Judicial Writing—Part I*, N.Y. St. B. J., Nov./Dec. 2006, at 64

Gerald Lebovits, *Ethical Judicial Writing—Part II*, N.Y. St. B. J., Jan. 2007, at 64

Gerald Lebovits, *Ethical Judicial Writing—Part III*, N.Y. St. B. J., Feb. 2007, at 64

Comment, *The Law Clerk's Duty of Confidentiality*, 129 U. Pa. L. Rev. 1250 (1981)

Chapter 13

What Comes Next?

Your clerkship will be a great jumping-off point for your future legal career, whether you choose to work for a law firm, government, business, nonprofit, educational, or other employer. And during your entire legal career you will value and draw upon the knowledge, skills, and relationships you have developed during your clerkship. Whether you are nearing the end of your clerkship term or not, you may be thinking about what your next step will be — what comes after your clerkship. A discussion of where you can move on to is beyond the scope of this book, but the following sections address when you should move on and how you can give back both during and after your clerkship.

13.1 When to Move On

Clerking is different from other legal jobs because most clerkships have a set term, and clerks are expected to stay for the full term. Thus, you should commit to stay for the full term. If you don't have a set term, you should not expect to move on to your next job after giving a two-week notice.

There are times when it is inappropriate to move on. Clerking is an honor, and you owe it to the judge to stay for the full term of your clerkship. Leaving before an agreed-upon clerkship term is up violates the unwritten professionalism code of clerking. In addition, every time a judge gets a new clerk, the judge has to train that clerk, and it isn't fair to impose this kind of disruption on the judge. If your clerkship doesn't have a set term, you should plan to stay for at least a year.

If you enjoy your job, you may discuss with the judge the possibility of extending your clerkship. Some judges and courts will allow this. But be aware that extending a clerkship might not be possible because of how the court operates. Also, many judges value the frequent turnover of clerks because it allows them to get fresh thinkers into their chambers every year or two, and it allows them to give more new attorneys valuable experience that will make them productive members of the bar. These judges hire new clerks regularly, no matter how much they like their current clerks. Some judges have the best of both worlds: they hire one long-term clerk and rotate clerks every year or two in the other position. And some judges will allow clerks to work part time or job share while they take on other obligations.

If you want to continue clerking, but cannot stay with your current judge, consider applying for a clerkship with another judge. Clerking for another year or two is a good way to put off making a decision about what you want to do on a more permanent basis. As noted in Chapter Three, it's often easier to land a competitive clerkship if you've already been clerking than if you're just out of law school. Or, if you are interested in even longer-term clerking, look into career clerk or staff attorney positions.

When *is* it time to move on? Obviously, if your clerkship is for a set term, and your term is up, it's time to move on. Your term may be up because of the custom or rule of the court or the judge, or because you have deferred beginning work for a law firm or other employer and need to fulfill your obligation to that employer.

Some clerks get burned out by the work, so need to move on. For example, to some appellate court clerks the work of churning out bench memos and opinions week after week can become routine and repetitive. Other clerks find the job becomes less challenging. There's always more to learn in a clerkship, of course, but once the learning curve begins to flatten, some clerks want to move on.

Judicial clerks also move on for career-advancement and practical reasons. Because clerkships usually only last a year or two, some employers view longer-term clerkships negatively, and some clerks feel that they are putting off their "real" careers by staying in clerkships. You may also need to move out of the area or may be ready to earn more money than you can earn in a clerkship.

While you should avoid leaving before your term is up, a situation may arise that requires you to do so, such as if your family or health circumstances change. If this happens, give the judge as much notice as possible and do what you can to help the judge hire your replacement.

13.2 Giving Back

As a clerk you have been in a privileged position and have had a unique opportunity to learn about the court from the inside. After your clerkship is completed, consider giving back to the individuals and communities that have helped you.

One way to give back is to help the judge find your replacement. Some courts have well-defined procedures for hiring each new crop of clerks, and current clerks do not have any role to play, or their role may be only to screen resumes or interview potential clerks. But other courts have no particular procedure for hiring new clerks, and if you work in one of these courts, you can be especially helpful to the judge. Start by giving the judge as much notice as possible. Many judges hire clerks at least a year in advance of their starting date, so if you can give your judge a year's notice, that will put the judge in the best position to get the most qualified applicants. If it isn't possible to give the judge this much notice, try to time your departure to make it easier for the judge to hire. Most clerkships begin in August or September to coincide with the schedule of new law school graduates. If you can leave at this time the judge may have the best choice of applicants.

Another way to assist both the judge and your law school's alumni is to alert your law school's career office of clerkship openings. The hiring procedure of some judges, particularly state trial court judges, consists of calling the local law schools' career offices to ask for applications, accepting applications for a week, and then interviewing and hiring within another week. Give students at your alma mater a heads up by making sure the career office knows the judge's hiring timetable and preferences. The staff may know of students or alumni who are looking for clerkships and who would be perfect for the job, or they can post the position on the career office web site.

You can also be a resource for your law school and its students and alumni. The career office probably sponsors programs for students featuring alumni describing their judicial clerkships or jobs in general. Make yourself available to be on panels or mingle with students at these events. If possible, make time to speak one-on-one with students and other alumni if they contact you about clerking. If they are following the advice of Chapter Three of this book, they are trying to learn about clerkships and judges, and you are in a perfect position to help them.

Help out your law school in other ways as well. When you do move on, let the alumni and career offices know where you are moving. These offices keep track of alumni and compile employment statistics for their own use and the law school's use. They also report these statistics to accreditation, rating, and law-graduate employment organizations.

Finally, you can give back by being an ethical attorney who displays professionalism and a commitment to excellence in all that you do. You continue to represent the judge and the court after you leave your clerkship, especially in the early years. Your adherence to ethical and professional standards will be a credit to the judge and to the court system in general.

13.3 Additional Resources

Lisa L. Abrams, *The Official Guide to Legal Specialties: An Insider's Guide to Every Major Practice Area* (2000)

Deborah Arron, *What Can You Do With a Law Degree? A Lawyer's Guide to Career Alternatives Inside, Outside and Around the Law* (5th ed. 2004)

Kimm Alayne Walton, *Guerilla Tactics for Getting the Legal Job of Your Dreams* (2d ed. 2008)

Index

Blue pages, 120
Differences from *ALWD Manual*, 115–16, 120
History, 113
International materials rules, 116–17
Neutral citation format rules, 114–15
Non-legal materials rules, 116
Practitioners' rules, 120
Quotation rules, 122
Signals rules, 122
Tribal materials rules, 117
White pages, 120
Briefing cases, 67
Burdens of proof
In bench memoranda, 128
In trial court orders, 157
Calendar clerks, 27
Career clerk positions, 41, 296
Career clerks, 9–10
Career offices, law school, reciprocity agreements between, 42
Case communications letters, 259
Cases, briefing, 67
Central staff clerks, 9–10, 26
Chambers administration, as duty of clerk, 25
Charge, jury, 188, 193, 201
Charge conference. *See* Trial court documents: Jury instructions
Checklists

Appellate opinions, 239–41
Bench memoranda, 137–38
Ethics, 292–93
Findings of fact and conclusions of law, 181–82
Jury instructions and verdict forms, 202–03
Trial court orders and memoranda of law, 165–67
Chicago Manual of Style, The, 116
Chief judges, 25, 44
Citation
In findings of fact, 177–78
Format
Difference between *Bluebook* and *ALWD Manual* formats, 115–16, 120–21
Importance of, 111–12
Goals of, 111–12
International materials, citation of, 116–17
Judges' preferences, 112–13, 157
Local rules, 114
Neutral citation format, 114–15
Non-legal materials, 116
Placement, importance of, 112, 121, 163
Public domain citations. *See* Neutral citation format
Quotations, 122
Signals, 122

Code of Conduct for Judicial Employees, 274
Code of Conduct for United States Judges, 274
Collaborative writing, 83
Committee on Codes of Conduct of the Administrative Office of the United States Courts, 274
Competitiveness of clerkships, 43–44
Conclusions of law, 147, 176–77, 179–81. *See also* Trial court documents: Findings of fact and conclusions of law
Concurring opinions. *See* Opinions, appellate
Sample, 186–87
Confidential information
Defined, 276n9
In email correspondence, 261
Confidentiality. *See* Ethics
Conflicts of interest. *See* Ethics
Congress, authorization for judicial clerkships, 20
Correspondence
Email, 261–62
Letters, 257–61
"Court family," 280
Courthouse staff
Administrative assistants, 26–27
Calendar clerks, 27
Clerk of court, 27

Docket clerks, 153
Librarians, 28
Receptionists, 27
Security personnel, 27
Courtroom observation, as duty of clerk, 24
Courts
Administrative law, 16
Appellate, 12–16
Bankruptcy, 16
District, 12, 14
Error correcting, 12–13
Federal, 14–16
Federal claims, 16
Intermediate appellate, 12–16
International trade, 16
Specialty, 16
State, 12–14
Supreme, 13, 15–16
Tax, 16
Trial, 12, 14
Tribal, 17
Veterans, 16
Cover letters, application component, 48–49
CRAC. *See* IRAC
CREAC. *See* IRAC
Decisions, appellate. *See* Opinions, appellate
Desk references, use of, 104–05
Dispositive motions, 150. *See also* Motions
Dissenting opinions. *See* Opinions, appellate
Sample, 250–52

tion Manual: A Professional System of Citation; Bluebook: A Uniform System of Citation, The
Reading like an attorney, 66
Receptionists, 27
Reciprocity agreements between law school career offices, 42
Recusal. *See* Ethics: Conflicts of interest
Reference books, use of, 104–05
Reports and recommendations, 150n4, 161n19
Research, legal. *See* Legal research
Research plans
  Generally, 64–65
  Sample, 79–81
Resumes, 39, 49
Retired judges, 25–26
Revising, 94–98
Roadmaps
  In appellate opinions, 230
  Generally, 89–90
  In jury instructions, 197
  In trial court orders and memoranda of law, 158
  In verdict forms, 201
RSVP letters, 260
Samples
  Bench memorandum, 139–46
  Dissenting opinion, 250–52

Findings of fact and conclusions of law, 183–87
Full majority opinion, 242–52
Jury instructions, 204–10
Memorandum opinion, 253–55
Pro se litigant letter, 267–68
Research plan, 79–81
Scheduling letter, 265–66
Trial court order and memorandum of law, 168–75
Verdict form, 211
Scalia, Antonin, United States Supreme Court Justice, 94
Scheduling letter
  Generally, 258–59
  Sample, 265–66
Seal
  Confidentiality of information related to cases filed under, 277
  Filing orders under, 164
  Filing statements of reasons for imposing sentence under, 212
  Motions filed under, 276
Second job. *See* Ethics: Outside activities, limitations on
Security personnel, 27
Senior status, judges on, 25–26, 44
Sentence, statements of reasons for imposing, 147, 212–13

Editing, 98–105
Issue formulation, 92
Outlining, 90
Planning of, 90–91
Prewriting as step in, 92–93
Recursive nature of, 90–91
Revising, 94–98

Writing samples
In employment applica-
tions, 39, 49–51
Use of judicial documents
as, 50–51, 289